RECOVERING

RACIST

Peter Boone Schwethelm

TABLE OF CONTENTS

DEDICATION

This book is dedicated to my people, who have contributed greatly to this project by sharing their feelings so openly and honestly while allowing me to do the same.

Alphabetically, I want to thank Herb Baker, Susan Barrett, Malcolm Battle, Darrell Bennett, Alan Branch, Meredith Steele Brewer, Jason Bridges, Craig Brownson, Jennifer Renfro Brownson, David Chisolm, Doug Crandall, Aisha Crumbine, Conti Rice Davis, Joanna Day, Bobby Emmerson, Dain Ervin, Mike Fogo, Michael Ford, Brock Gillespie, Cory Graham, Lynn Graham, Neal Gray, Richard Hayse, Matt Henry, Paul Hewitt, Jimmy Hicks, Torrance Hicks, Charlie Hurd, Shani Jackson-Dowell, Tate Johnson, Windsor Jordan, Casey Kaplan, Richard Law, Caroline Lents, Matthew Lisiewski, Marland Lowe, Mitch Malone, Kyle Martin, Carter Mayfield, Nancy Merriman, Brian Merritt, Jeff Merritt, Barb Minx, Brook Minx, Bryant Moore, Andrea Montgomery, Jamaal Moore, Austine Nwabuisi, Rick Oliver, Willie Outler, Stuart Pradia, Jeff Prendergast, George Raveling, Tommy Rogala, Monica Rojas, Donna Roth, Glenn Russell, Christal Seahorn, Rob Shapiro, Shaka Smart, Bernita Smith, Lisa Smith, Rich Smith, Tyler Smith, Ben Stark, Jen Talley, Roy Taylor, Marty Thompson, Charles Torello, Mohamad Vandi, Terry Waldrop, Frank Weiss, Cyril White, Shelle White, Carlos Wilson, Marcus Wilson, Willis Wilson, Josh Winslow, Charlton Young, Mark Zwald, and the many others I have regretfully failed to mention here.

I also need to send four special chronological shout outs, first to Michelle Cormier, my friend since Kindergarden, and my first black friend, whose friendship most likely played a key subconscious role in building a foundation from which my race-related change of heart could take place. I also need to thank another of my oldest friends, William "Spunkwagon" Scoular, who was, in the 6th grade, the first person ever to call me out for being a racist, which I desperately needed and richly deserved. Next, to Arnold "J.R." Campbell, his parents, and his sisters, for being the first entire black family to think of me as family, and vice-versa. And, finally, to John Herron, as nothing has done more to open my eyes, fix my brain, heal my heart, and save my soul than our thousands of sometimes contentious but always well intentioned Makers-Mark-fueled discussions into the wee hours of the morning. So, to Michelle, Scou, AC, Mr. Campbell, Momma Campbell, Shelle, Ericka, Lori, and Wormy, from the bottom of my heart, I love you, and thank you.

PREFACE I

Before getting started, if you are black or white, conservative or liberal, Northerner or Southerner, urban or rural, parts of this book are going to piss you off. However, this book also makes many points you will agree with, including some that you may not have considered before, so please just keep an open mind as you continue reading and please do not give up on the book after the first couple of times you feel yourself getting pissed off. I have tried as hard as I can to be fair-minded in writing this book, and it is my most sincere hope that you will try as hard as you can to be fair-minded as you read it. All that having been said, the simple fact that you've made it this far means that you care, and that's an awesome start, so thank you so much for giving this book, and the uncomfortable subject matter it covers, a chance.

PREFACE II

I use the word "nigger" in this book. If you are offended by that, I am truly sorry for offending you. I know that, as a rule of thumb, many black people are deeply (and understandably) hurt when white people use this word, and I do not generally run around trying to deliberately hurt people (unless they've hurt me first).

I use this word within specific and limited contexts, mostly because I agree with the late, great George Carlin that to sanitize our language is to sanitize our feelings and our experiences, and I do not want this book to sanitize the ugly race-related feelings of (far too many) American white people or the ugly race-related experiences of (virtually all) American black people.

PREFACE III

In this book, I focus almost entirely on race relations between American white people and American black people, but please don't take that to mean that I am dismissing or diminishing or denying the race-related experiences of any other minority or immigrant group in America. Rather, I am simply "staying in my lane", as my race-related knowledge and understanding beyond the narrow focus of this book is limited at best.

PROLOGUE

MY STORY

As a little boy growing up during the 1970s in Houston, Texas, I knew exactly two black people- my mother's housekeeper Mary, and my grandmother's housekeeper Lee. I do not ever recall thinking of Mary or Lee as being black; rather, they were simply family. I loved them, and they loved me, and that was all I knew or cared about.

When it came time in 1981 to begin Kindergarten at St. John's School, this exclusive Houston private school had exactly one black person in my class, a kind, hilarious, and brilliant young lady named Michelle. I also do not ever recall thinking of Michelle as being black; rather, she was my friend, I loved her, and she loved me, and that was all I knew or cared about.

From the day of my birth in 1975 until 1987, Mary, Lee, and Michelle were just about the only black people I interacted with regularly enough to form multiple and important lasting memories about in my mind.

Yet, perhaps partly due to naively not consciously viewing Mary, Lee, and Michelle as being "black", and despite the fact that the only three black people I had ever known beyond the level of casual acquaintance treated me with nothing but kindness and love, I nevertheless managed to form negative opinions about black people during my early childhood and thought nothing of telling nigger jokes and laughing at nigger jokes when they were told to me, with the jokes growing ever more shameful as I progressed through my primary education.

Q: How do you stop little nigger kids from jumping on the bed?

A: You put Velcro on the ceiling.

Q: What's green, sits on my porch, and does whatever I say?

A: My nigger- I'll paint him any color I want to.

Q: Why are niggers so fast?

A: They spend the first nine months of their lives dodging coat hangers, and the
rest of their lives running from the police.

Beginning in 1987, my life and my world view began to change, as I had fallen in love with the game of basketball. As I suppose it's intuitively understood in America, a person can not truly love basketball without very regularly encountering, observing, and getting to know a fairly wide swath of black people.

My re-education on the topic of American black people began at St. John's Episcopal Church when Rudy, an elderly white man who had served as the lead janitor at St. John's Church for as long as anyone could remember, sort of started his own impromptu after-school program for kids at Lamar High School, the huge public school that was adjacent to St. John's School and across the street from St. John's Church.

My white friends and I had been playing a little ball after school at St. John's Church for years, but it wasn't until 1987 that the church gym became crowded with black kids from Lamar. At first, I was apprehensive, not to mention scared. But within a matter of hours, I had struck up conversations with these older kids, and conversations became relationships. The twins Willie and Billie, their best friend Will, Big James, Taurean, and a whole bunch of other kids whose names I can not remember all these years later. They say that familiarity breeds contempt, but I have always found quite the opposite, as my experiences have been that familiarity is just as likely to breed tolerance, understanding, and friendship.

Unfortunately, but with the benefit of hindsight not surprisingly, the (white) powers that be at St. John's Church soon became aware of and uncomfortable with Rudy's "secret" after-school program, and ordered him to lock the gym. However, by that time, I had discovered that a lot of Lamar kids also played outdoors at "Pumpkin Park" after school, so I started playing there instead, and I was hooked.

Pumpkin Park further opened my eyes to the world outside of my insulated cocoon, as it wasn't just high school kids who played there, but some of the best playground legends Houston had to offer (this was due in large part to the fact that one basket was two inches low with a "break-a-way" rim, thus allowing for easier dunking with less risk of injury to your hands and fingers). At Pumpkin Park, I developed relationships with ET, BO, Big Money, Robert, Harold (who used to hoop shirtless in skin tight black jeans and red snake skin boots and DESTROY people), Mark, Frank, Victor, Kip, Terrance, Cage, Gerald, and a whole other host of additional characters whose names I can not recall.

Through these experiences and many more since then, I've learned a lot about black people:

Some black people are violent, some black people are peaceful.

Some black people are smart, some black people are stupid.

Some black people are lazy, some black people are hard working.

Some black people are kind, some black people are hostile.

Some black people are crooked, some black people are honest.

Some black people are monogamous, some black people are sex addicts.

Some black people are insecure, some black people are confident.

Some black people are rational, some black people are nuts.

I was raised to be a racist, not even necessarily by my parents or even consciously by anyone at all- and yet somehow, as a nine year-old kid, I knew, told, and loved nigger jokes.

However, through basketball, I got to know so many black people personally that I could not help but notice that other than a singular shared experience, American black people are about as monolithic in thought and behavior as American white people, which is to say not at all.

In short, without really even thinking about it, I came to believe that Dr. Martin Luther King, JR was 100% correct when he implored us to judge **each individual** not by the color of their skin, but by the content of their character.

This book details my observations and experiences and research on my journey from being an overt and unapologetic racist to being a recovering racist, along with general ideas to bridge our racial divide. It is not for the most part intended to accuse or condemn but rather to help other people as writing this book has helped me- remember, there's a reason why I say "recovering" rather than "recovered" as the simple truth is that I continue to struggle with being a racist every single day, and I suspect that I always will.

CHAPTER 1

WE HAVE A PROBLEM

The first step to solving any problem is to admit that the problem exists.

Prior to about 1990, I never realized we had a race problem in America, and I didn't recognize the seriousness and the pervasiveness of our problem until the early to mid 2000's.

Throughout this book, we will take a look at what caused me to change my mind on this topic, but for now, please just keep an open mind and open heart to the possibility that at least some of the reasons I changed my mind aren't totally meritless.

P.S. Contrary to popular opinion, "racist" white people aren't the only ones contributing to our massive racial problems, and we're going to talk about that in this book, too.

CHAPTER 2

RECALIBRATE

I think we as a country desperately need to recalibrate the word "racist". For starters, I think virtually all Americans of all races could be described as "racist" in some form or fashion, and as the Prologue hopefully made clear, I am most definitely including myself in this category.

You see, despite how we often use and understand the word, "racist" doesn't mean "evil" and it doesn't mean you want to put on a white hood and lynch black people and it doesn't automatically mean that you're a bad person, nor does it mean that you "hate" anyone. Rather, it simply means that you have at least some opinions about other races as a group, at times causing you to associate the actions of 1 individual member of another race (or a small-ish group of individuals of another race) with that race as a whole.

Too many people think the absence of hate means the absence of racism, but this just isn't true. Sure, the worst forms of racism often involve hatred, but hatred is by no means required for racism to exist. You can have no hatred in your heart whatsoever for other races and still be a racist, and not all racism is even intended to be negative.

"Asians are smart in math."

"Jews are wise with money."

"Once you go black, you never go back."

Now, don't get me wrong, even "positive" stereotypes can be damaging and demeaning, as they tend to make the subject of the "compliment" feel reduced as a human being to nothing but the mentioned "positive" stereotype. Positive stereotypes also often make the members of a group who don't live up to the expectations that accompany a "positive" stereotype feel worthless. However, it clearly can not be seen as hateful to attribute characteristics like being smart, wise, and good in bed to a given racial group. Damaging? I think so. But hateful? Clearly not.

So, if you are a white "ally", unless you are going to use a preface to place the word in context before you use it, please don't shrilly shriek "RACIST!!" to virtually any other white person you encounter. Not only does name calling rarely help a cause, but "woke" white people regularly demonstrate that they too have racist tendencies while almost never being self aware enough to acknowledge their own racism (more on this self-awarded comparative clemency later).

And if you're a black person who likes to hurl the word "RACIST!!" all over town, please keep in mind that most black people are a bunch of racists, too. Now let me be clear, and this book will bear this out, I am not a person who sees black racism as being equivalent to white racism, as the history and the effects of white-on-black racism have been incredibly lopsidedly worse than the history and effects of black-on-white racism. Additionally, I have long been on the record that black-on-white racism is, in my view, not wholly irrational; in fact, considering black people's collective experience, I could almost make a case that it's borderline irrational for black people not to be at least a little bit racist toward white people. However, make no mistake about my feelings here-understandable and justifiable aren't synonyms, and I am not at all "ok" with black-on-white racism.

That having been said, the bottom line here is that being called a "RACIST!!" by a person who is a blissfully or deliberately unaware racist themselves tends to fall on deaf ears, as hypocrisy rarely proves to be an effective element of a successful sales pitch (NOTE: I am not saying black people don't have the right to call racist white people out for being racist, nor am I saying there's no place for that, as I think Martin Luther King, JR and Malcolm X proved that the diplomatic and the non-diplomatic approaches both have their place and can actually work well in conjunction with each other- I'm just saying that Dr. King persuaded a lot more white people than Malcolm X did, and this general rule of thumb most especially applies to interpersonal individual discussions).

Collectively, white allies and black people need to understand that when y'all say "RACIST!!" the person you're talking to hears "HITLER" and "BULL CONNER", which means you've lost your audience immediately, which is 100% not OK, if consistent, broad, and sustained productivity matter. Please realize that when you say "RACIST!!" you offend some people so deeply they will rigidly dislike you too much to listen to anything you say, while others will amusingly/annoyedly tune you out because they have a completely clean conscience regarding Hitler-like thoughts and tendencies. Instead, when you hear or read something that sounds racist to you, please put the word "racist" in context by using a preface, or please consider another approach, such as, "hey, maybe I misunderstood you, but that sounded unfair… have you also considered…" and that sort of thing.

Finally, if you're a white person who finds yourself being accused of racism, take a deep breath. You don't need to feel defensive against impolite people and insulting tones. Ignore the accuser. Rise above the rudeness. But please do consider the accusation, because if you get upset by someone accusing you of being a white racist but you don't generally get upset about white-on-black racism itself, then the accusation is almost certainly true, not necessarily by their definition, or even by your definition, but by mine (and Merriam Webster's).

As you know, I believe that the first step to solving any personal problem is admitting you have one, and it is WAY past time for millions and millions and millions and millions of Americans of all races and all religions and all regions and all political parties to step forward and admit being racist. We desperately need the word "racist" to be a conversation starter, not a conversation ender, because if we can't admit that we're a bunch of *racists, we will never be anything but.

*With this in mind, it would be great if we could somehow collectively decide on substitute words for "racist" to describe a racial moderate or a racial fence-sitter or a racially insensitive person who thinks and feels a certain kind of way about black people but doesn't "hate" them, so I'm going to give it a shot right now, as very few things can help us solve our racial problems quite like maximizing the number of white people who are able to discuss this topic without becoming defensive or upset.

REBA: Racially or Ethnically Biased American

NORA: Non-Overtly Racist American

ARF: American Racial Fencesitter

RDT: Racial Doubting Thomas

P.S. On a semi-related note, I am going to reference "Uncle Ruckus" from the fantastic cartoon Boondocks any time the setting calls for mentioning "Uncle Tom" in this book. Uncle Tom didn't hate himself, or other black people; he was simply trying to play the awful hand life dealt to him as best as he could. People focus way too much on Uncle Tom's day-to-day subservience, and on his refusal to take part in a plot to murder Simon Legree. However, when he believed that Simon Legree had ordered unjust consequences for Lucy, he defied Legree's orders to whip her at great physical peril to himself, and when Simon Legree attempted to torture Uncle Tom into giving up the whereabouts of Cassy and Emmeline, Tom stayed strong to protect the younger ladies who were in the process of attempting to escape, even as Legree slowly and cruelly tortured Tom to death. It's also important to keep in mind that Harriett Beecher Stowe deliberately modeled Uncle Tom after Jesus Christ, and this, not self-loathing, explains his willingness to continuously turn the other cheek. In other words, Uncle Ruckus is an "Uncle Tom", but Uncle Tom was not an "Uncle Tom", and I think it is well past time to change the lingo to better reflect the reality.

CHAPTER 3

SCALE

In life, virtually all human descriptions belong on a relative scale in order to draw comparative distinctions.

For example, I'm a "Houston Rockets fan", but I haven't paid for a ticket in 20+ years and really only pay attention come playoff time. My friend Scotty G is also a "Houston Rockets fan", but he purchases season tickets and watches almost every game. And my friend Money Ball Alex is also a "Houston Rockets fan", but he not only watches every game, he is basically despondent after every loss, and it takes him weeks if not months to recover emotionally after the season ends.

So, on a 1-10 scale of being a Houston Rockets fan, I'd call myself about a 2, and my buddy Scotty G about an 8.5, and my buddy Money Ball a true 10.

Or, I would definitely refer to myself as a "fat guy", as I weigh over 300 pounds. My friend Big "Ron" (not his real name) is also a "fat guy", as he weighs (or has weighed at his peak- I haven't seen him in years) at least 375 pounds. And my old friend Matty Boy is also a "fat guy", because although he appears to be somewhat thin, once he takes his shirt off, he reveals a perfect pair of sloping man tits.

So, on a 1-10 scale of being a fat guy, I'd call myself at least an 8, and my buddy Big Ron is at least an 8.5, and my buddy Matty Boy is about a 3, even though he prefers to think of himself as a 0.

Racism is no different, as there are of course varying degrees. However, when we discuss racism and use the word racist, we often do not account for scale, and neither does our intended audience. As such, without any clarification, the word "racist" sounds like we think the person we are describing is an assumed 10 on the racist scale, when that is in fact only very rarely actually true.

Here are some general parameters to help us better understand racism based on scale, and to help us be more willing to admit that we ourselves can more than likely be accurately described as a "racist", because, again, if we can't bring ourselves to admit it, we can't possibly fix it.

Before getting to the scale, please keep in mind that it is totally non-scientific and represents general parameters based on my own observations and experiences, and basically any thoughtful person may want to add some items, or remove some items, or move some items around, which is totally OK by me. This is more of a sample guide to contemplate the concept that racism, like any human trait, varies widely by degree, person by person, and should therefore be considered as such.

Also, most people will dance around within the scale, so you should measure yourself based on a rough average of all data points.

For example, I dance around on this 1-10 racist scale anywhere from 1-8, and probably average out around a 2.5, and it's critical for me to accept that being a 2.5 on the racist scale makes me a racist. It doesn't matter that I don't hate black people, or that other people are more racist than I am- I still don't get to do the self-issued comparative clemency thing and give myself a pass for being a racist.

1

Active Ally

You are an active ally, attending mass protests, volunteering your time or making career choices based in large part on an intense desire to see real racial justice for American black people, but when you see a black person behaving in a way that you find objectionable, you can not help but make a mental note of his or her race and you probably subconsciously connect the behavior with race, even though, as a legit active ally, you call yourself out when you catch yourself doing this because you are aware of (and troubled by) your own racism. You may also suffer a bit from White Savior Complex, presuming that your contributions are needed and will make an impact, without realizing the inherent racism involved in feeling a perhaps subconscious need as a white person to lead rather than to just simply offer your help humbly.

2

Ally

You feel legitimately awful about how America treats and has always treated black people. In fact, you support programs designed specifically to benefit black people, though the subconscious reason you support these programs is because you believe that black people need extra help, which is unquestionably a racist belief. You also commend, or feel the desire to commend, black people when they contradict negative stereotypes about black people, which you clearly would not do unless you have subconsciously bought into the stereotypes, and you also at times give black people a pass for bad behavior because you don't want to be thought of or perhaps more importantly to think of yourself as a racist, without recognizing that treating black people differently due to race is precisely the sort of thing a racist does. Additionally, unlike an Active Ally, you are blissfully unaware of your own racism and would strongly resent any such accusation.

3

Partial Ally

You recognize that racism against black people remains a major problem, so you "like" and "share" all the right Facebook posts, but you do sometimes feel at least a little bit anxious when interacting with black strangers, and you avoid black neighborhoods (especially "after dark") because your subconscious refuses to differentiate between "black" and "dangerous". You've also found yourself surprised by a specific type of positive behavior from a black person*. Additionally, as is the case with a 2, you are totally in denial about your racism and would defend yourself vigorously if someone suggested that you're a racist.

*A perfect example of this would be my old and dear friend Michelle. Michelle is black, and she is an absurdly talented linguist, and this surprises the stuffing out of a whole lot of white people, because they racistly do not expect an American black person to speak a whole bunch of languages. For the record, if you find yourself being "surprised" by any type of behavior from or attribute of a black person, you need to get out and meet way more black people, because there is no specific type of human behavior or attribute, positive or negative, that black people do not regularly embody. Please trust me; I promise that I am not making this up.

4

Fencesitter

You definitely don't hate black people, and you think of yourself as being racially tolerant because you not only don't say "nigger" but you have spoken up at least some of the time when you have heard someone else use that word in a purposefully offensive context; however, you still can't help wondering if there aren't at least some underlying issues in "the black community" that contribute to black people's troubles at least as much as racism. As a fencesitter, you don't think of yourself as being a racist, but you're more perplexed or amused by the allegation, rather than falling into anger or another state of high emotion.

5

Doubter

You don't hate black people, and you think of yourself as being racially open-minded, but you always "want more info" and find yourself reflexively doubting and disputing any evidence that paints the picture that racism remains a major problem in America, while tending to accept without question any data that can be used to try to explain away or justify racism. Also, you don't say "nigger" in a negative context, but you don't normally speak up when other people do; and you don't tell nigger jokes, but you have (at least at times) laughed at them. You do at least verbalize a recognition that racism still exists, but you feel pretty strongly that it's current effects are probably exaggerated, perhaps even grossly. As is the case with a fencesitter, you receive accusations of being a racist without a great deal of emotion.

6

Deflector

You get agitated and emotional about race. You still don't "hate" black people, but you shut down when people want to discuss the unequal treatment of black people in America, so you tend to mention all sorts of irrelevant deflections like "America has the best criminal justice in the world" or "you know, it was Africans who captured other Africans to sell as slaves" or "you really need to get over your white guilt", but the last thing on earth your comfort zone will allow you to do is have an open and honest conversation about race relations; and, if someone accuses you of being a racist, your agitation levels spike substantially.

7

Denier

While still not hating or even necessarily disliking black people, you do not verbally recognize that racism remains a major problem in America today, and you totally support racial profiling by the police because you don't want the "dangerous blacks" anywhere near your neighborhood. You have also quit caring about proportionality when it comes to consequences for poor choices when a black person was the one who made the poor choice- ie, you think that because Walter Scott made the poor choice to run from the police, it is totally OK that the police officer shot him in the back and killed him, as if failure to obey police commands in AMERICA does or should warrant a death sentence that is carried out on the spot without interference from pesky little matters like THE CONSTITITUTION OF THE UNITED STATES OF AMERICA. In your heart, you know that you're an overt racist, but you won't admit it, and you don't care for the accusation one bit.

8

Hothead

You feel anger toward black people that you can't necessarily explain (at least not rationally) and you get angry when the topic of race comes up in conversation or on social media. You probably still don't literally hate black people, and have likely even treated at least some black people with courtesy over the years, and you probably don't wish them any physical harm, but you are 100% belligerently convinced that black people are the problem with black people and that racism in 2017 is nothing more than a God Damn fucking excuse for black people's collective lack of character and work ethic and intelligence and values. In addition, you have crossed the line from denying the existence of modern racism to grossly misrepresenting or outright denying our nation's history on this topic. Finally, when accused of being a racist, your go-to response is to loudly spew, "I'M NOT A RACIST, I'M A REALIST!!" without the self-awareness to recognize the twin ironies of this comment: first, no one who doesn't hold racist beliefs feels the need to justify racist beliefs, and second, by asserting that your beliefs are valid because black people actually are inferior, you're only reconfirming your own obvious racism, while sprinkling in a little old-school white supremacy.

9

Zealot

You hate black people and even though you haven't personally caused a black person physical harm or death, you verbally support the extreme racist ideology that embraces violence, and you are eager to share and spread your hateful racist ideology to as many other white people as you possibly can. Interestingly, you normally do not admit being a racist, becoming angry when someone levels the accusation in your direction, even though your racism is incredibly obvious and offensive, even to other racists.

10

Devil

You hate black people and you personally have caused or intend to cause physical harm or death to black people, and when people accuse you of being a racist, it makes you proud, not angry.

Moving forward, please consider this scale as a reference point, because it should highlight racism's pervasiveness while making us as racist white people more open minded and more self aware so that we can gradually collectively work together to at long last fully participate in the true racial awakening and healing that our nation so desperately needs. Again, we're all a bunch of racists, and if we can't admit it, we will never be anything but.

CHAPTER 4

REALITY

Hopefully, this chapter shouldn't be too controversial or upsetting, as it mostly deals with math. I add some explanations and interpretations and conclusions about the math, but this chapter deals far more in objectivity than subjectivity. As such, I sincerely hope that the title of this chapter isn't misunderstood as a smug or judgmental remark.

Additionally, please believe that the title is meant to suggest "here are some incontrovertible truths you may not have previously considered" not "you're a delusional moron who doesn't or can't or won't understand the world around you." The chapter title "Reality" means that I am requesting that you please keep an open mind to new information that either supplements or contradicts what you may have previously assumed or believed to be true.

When reading this chapter, I implore you to please refrain from the reflexive compulsion to disbelieve or discredit race-related statistics that you haven't personally verified, unless you're going to actually spend the time to verify them. Our nation is way too full of RDT's (Racial Doubting Thomases), and I'm asking you to be aware of and fight against this tendency as you read this chapter.

Finally, this is as good a time as any to say that I am an individualist in many ways with several libertarian leanings, which means that I am not someone who thinks that 100% of poor black people are poor because of racism, nor do I think that 100% of incarcerated black people are innocent. I have long believed and am previously on the record that the overwhelming majority (90%+) of people who wind up in dire positions later in life made some bad decisions and formed some unhelpful habits along the way that greatly if not primarily contributed to their life outcomes. I believe in personal responsibility, totally. The old phrase "if it is to be, it is up to me" has always rung true to my ears.

Where we get into trouble is with either-or thinking, as if complicated things such as life outcomes only have 1 single cause. In other words, individual poor people can be poor due to racism and/or sexism and/or generational poverty and/or bad choices and/or bad luck and/or societal unfairness and/or a lack of intelligence and/or not having access to good schools and/or lack of work ethic and/or poor parenting and/or abusive parenting and/or no parents and/or addiction and/or sexual abuse and/or addiction to alcohol/drugs/sex/gambling/etc, plus a myriad of other reasons, and infinite combinations of the myriad of reasons. As such, there's no reason to think that pointing out other possible causes of disproportional black poverty proves that institutional racism doesn't exist. This just isn't an either-or topic, or at least it shouldn't be, so please consider the following information, with an open and soothed mind.

Incarceration

Here are three statistical facts:

1. Black people account for roughly 13% of the US population.

2. Black people account for roughly 42% of the US prison population.

3. Black people account for 63.3% of the American citizens who have been **exonerated**
    of a crime they had previously been convicted of based on DNA evidence.

Many people explain away the disparity between Fact 1 and Fact 2 by citing the disproportionate poverty in some black communities, while others either imply or state that the root cause is innate black criminality or black culture or the breakdown of black families and so on.

For the time being, let's accept any or all explanations. But what about Fact 3? What explains the huge disparity between Fact 2 and Fact 3?

Here are some more facts to consider according to the Substance Abuse and Mental Health Services' most recent study (2013):

Approximately 16.5% of black males over the age of 12 used illicit drugs in the past month.

Approximately 15% of white males over the age of 12 used illicit drugs in the past month.

Now, using 2010 Census data, approximately 100,000,000 white males over the age of 12 live in the US, compared with approximately 16,000,000 black males over the age of 12.

If you multiply the total population of each group by the percent that each group has used drugs in the past month, you will see that the raw number of active white male drug users is approximately 15,000,000 while the raw number of active black male drug users is approximately 2,640,000. This means that while black men use drugs at a slightly higher rate than white men, America has over 12,000,000 more active white male drug users than black male drug users.

Now, let's turn our attention to drug-related incarceration numbers. According to the most recent Bureau of Justice statistics, there are 516,900 black males in jail or prison on drug charges, compared with 453,500 white males in jail or prison on drug charges.

So, if you look at the raw numbers, black males are 14% more likely to be incarcerated for drug-related charges than white males (516,900 to 453,500), despite the fact that 568% more white males than black males use drugs (15 million to 2.64 million).

If you look at the math a different way, taking the incarceration numbers next to the drug use numbers, 19.5% of black male drug users wind up in jail or prison compared with 3% of white male drug users who wind up in jail or prison.

So, yes, it's true that black males use drugs at a 10% higher rate than white males, but that discrepancy alone can not explain why black males are incarcerated for drug offenses at a proportional rate that is more than 600% (19.5/3) higher than their white male counterparts (some white people try to explain away these statistics by claiming that the disproportionate arrests result from black people using/selling drugs less discreetly, but those white people have never been to a Phish concert or any other outdoor festival where countless white people publicly use/sell drugs about as flagrantly as could be imagined, and they've also clearly never spent much if any time on a mostly white liberal arts college campus, either).

I also recently ran some additional numbers that blew my mind. The incarceration rate for black men in the US is 4347 per 100,000, whereas the COMBINED incarceration rates for prison populations in the ENTIRETY of Sub-Saharan Africa is 3849.

In other words, I took the incarceration rates per 100,000 for each country in Sub-Saharan Africa, where every country but South Africa is almost 100% black, and added them together. Collectively, they still fell short of the USA's rate for incarcerating black men.

Additionally, would it surprise you to know that six of the top seven countries in the world in terms of incarceration rates per 100,000 are former European colonies that once imported large amounts of African slave labor? To expand this theme a bit further, 19 of the top 25 countries in the world in terms of incarceration rates per 100,000 are former European colonies that once imported large amounts of African slave labor.

Of course, one could argue that a commonality between these former colonies with unusually high incarceration rates is the presence of a large amount of (innately criminal) black people. However, this is why I pointed out the previous shocking statistic that shows that America out-performs all of Sub-Saharan Africa combined when it comes to locking up black men, and they have approximately 250,000,000 black males ages 12 and older while we have only 16,000,000.

One could also perhaps try to argue that the reason the Sub-Saharan African incarceration rate doesn't rank higher would be the economic realities in most of Sub-Saharan Africa. IE, maybe the "real" reason Sub-Saharan African nations don't incarcerate more people is that they can't afford to; however, were this a legitimate thought process, what accounts for the high incarceration rates in desperately poor 3rd world nations like Cuba and Panama, both of which are former European colonies that imported large amounts of African slaves?

Also, regarding this common excuse to explain away our crisis of (racially targeted) over-incarceration, consider that nine countries have a higher per-capita GDP than the US, with a combined per-capita GDP of $703,884 compared with the US per-capita GDP of $53,001; however, those nine countries' combined incarceration rates total 1025 compared with the overall US incarceration rate of 707; so, these countries are collectively 13 times wealthier per capita than the US, but their collective incarceration rate is just 1.45 times that of the United States- the point I'm making is that Sub-Saharan Africa's low incarceration rates and America's high incarceration rates aren't due to our respective economies.

So, we know that nations where African slavery existed on a large scale within the last 200 years disproportionately dominate the list of the world's top incarcerators. We also know that this trend holds true in former slave-holding nations regardless of those countries' relative wealth, and we know that other wealthy countries besides America don't share our appetite for incarceration. In fact, just three of the top 50 leading global incarcerators have a substantial black population without also having a history of importing African slaves, and two of those three nations are South Africa and Swaziland, which obviously had their own style of building and maintaining racial prejudice and unrest, and the third country is Rwanda, which has been engaged in civil war for nearly three decades.

It is hard for me to look at math like this and arrive at any other conclusion than being black in countries that enslaved your ancestors carries with it modern-day inherent additional disproportional risk of being arrested and incarcerated compared with your non-black countrymen.

Welfare

We also tend to make assumptions about statistics that the statistics themselves do not endorse. For example, we assume that a *70% out-of-wedlock birth rate for black children means that 70% of black children go through life fatherless (*the 2013 US Census had the actual rate at 67.8%).

However, we don't look at the 40% divorce rate in white families and assume that 40% of white children go through life fatherless. And why would we? It's beyond self-apparent that a man not being married to his child's mother does not preclude him from being involved in his child's life as a father.

We also look at the 70% out-of-wedlock birth rate for black children as a moral judgment against 70% of black biological fathers, as if a desire to be a low-character and irresponsible deadbeat is the only possible reason why a man might not be married to his child's mother at the time of the child's birth.

What if both expectant parents decide it's better to get married after they graduate from high school or college? What if the expectant parents are only teenagers, and one or both sets of soon-to-be grandparents forbids the marriage? What if they plan to get married, but are waiting to be able to afford a "proper" wedding (remember, birth mothers who are engaged rather than married are automatically included in the "out-of-wedlock" birth numbers)? What if the expectant parents want to wait until they have financial stability before they get married? What if an active duty boyfriend found out about his girlfriend being pregnant while he was deployed and couldn't marry her until he returned from his tour (black people serve in the US Armed Services at a disproportionate rate as well, which is sadly but not surprisingly an incredibly infrequently cited statistic)? What if the father-to-be wants to get married to fulfill his duty as a father, but the mother-to-be doesn't love him and turns down his proposal? What if they want to get married, but can't afford the hidden "marriage penalty" that exists in our tax and welfare systems?

And debunking the flawed assumption that a 70% non-marital birth rate means a 70% rate of absentee black fathers is not only a logical exercise of "what if?" like the previous paragraph, but rather also a matter of statistical evidence, as 58% of unmarried parents were cohabitating as of 2010. I suppose it goes without saying that a cohabitating father can not simultaneously be an absentee father.

Furthermore, it's important to consider that the out-of-wedlock birth rate is a SYMPTOM of disproportional black poverty, not a CAUSE of disproportional black poverty. Even the Heritage-Foundation-owned Daily Signal admitted that "non-marital births are even more closely associated with class and education than with race" which of course means that the out-of-wedlock birth rate is a poverty thing, not a black thing.

Consider these corroborating facts from the 2013 US Census that largely confirm what the Daily Signal found:

The white (non-Hispanic) non-marital birth rate is 26%, compared with the black non-marital birth rate of 67.8%, which means that black children are 2.6 times more likely to be born to an unmarried mother than white children.

The white (non-Hispanic) poverty rate is 9.6%, compared with the black poverty rate of 27.2%, which means that black people are 2.8 times more likely to be poor than white people.

The out-of-wedlock birth rate for impoverished women of all races is 68.9%.

In other words, poor people disproportionally have children out of wedlock, and black people are disproportionally poor, so of course black people will give birth out of wedlock disproportionally, but when you control for poverty, then black women actually give birth out-of-wedlock at a slightly lower rate than the average of all races of women who give birth out-of-wedlock.

Some people use the exact same figures I just used to reach an entirely different conclusion, instead arguing that the 70% out-of-wedlock birth rate in the black community explains disproportional black poverty, as if the out-of-wedlock birth rate is a cause of disproportional black poverty rather than a symptom. This train of thought struggles to answer a very basic question, which is that if a poverty-stricken woman gives birth before marriage, how did the out-of-wedlock birth cause the poverty that pre-dated the birth? It may have worsened the poverty, or extended the poverty, but as the poverty preceded the birth, the birth necessarily can not possibly have created the poverty. To use an analogy, if a person who has had diabetes for 20 years decides to start an all-Twinkie diet, clearly he is exacerbating the existing situation severely, but no one would blame the all-Twinkie diet for causing the diabetes, as a cause can not by definition occur after the alleged effect. That just isn't the way cause-and-effect conceptually works.

Additionally, in 1967, 33.9% of black families lived below the poverty line. As the out-of-wedlock birth rate has increased dramatically since 1967, the percent of black families living below the poverty line has actually decreased to 24%. How can we blame the spike in the black non-marital birth rate for disproportional black poverty when black poverty is actually less of a problem today than ever before? I'm not saying that the black non-marital birth rate isn't A cause of disproportional black poverty; I'm saying it clearly can't be THE cause, as the symptom doesn't fall precipitously in the face of the alleged cause worsening deeply (http://blackdemographics.com/households/poverty/).

Also, and this is a bit of a preview of Chapter 4, but we as a society need to quit non-empathetically deriding the "single black mother." We as Americans love to blame single black mothers with "fatherless" children for the plight of impoverished American black people. However, a lot of the time, an impoverished young woman sees nothing good in her life while noticing that her mother has at least one thing that brings her joy, and that is having a daughter. Why is it so hard to imagine that an impoverished and largely hopeless young woman might want to do the one thing that she knows based on her experiences would bring consistent joy and hope into her otherwise largely joyless and hopeless life?

And yet we keep scolding and deriding impoverished (black) single mothers for their "irresponsibility" and their "lack of intelligence", without even considering the imminent reasonableness of a hopeless and joyless young lady making a choice to bring hope and joy into her life. That is not only totally non-empathetic, but also a very silly deflection on the issue of disproportional black poverty, as we have already covered (as a reminder, again, the single black mothers who are poverty-stricken were overwhelmingly poverty-stricken **before** they became mothers, which means that the choice to become a single mother can not be responsible for an economic condition that pre-dated the decision to have a child).

Besides the incarceration data and the misperceptions surrounding the fabled out-of-wedlock birth rate in "the black community" (Jesus, I hate that phrase), we often mischaracterize what actually goes on within our social welfare programs. Here are some facts to consider about welfare:

In 2016, Temporary Assistance for Needy Families (TANF), which is the only direct cash assistance our nation provides, went to only 6.3% of families receiving some type of government aid (http://www.statisticbrain.com/welfare-statistics/).
According to a US Census study that examined welfare programs from 2009-2012, only 10% of direct cash assistance recipients (TANF) had been receiving benefits longer than three years.

We do help chronically poor or temporarily struggling Americans in other ways besides cash, such as SNAP (used to be called food stamps), housing subsidies, and medical care. In fact, 21% of Americans receive some sort of aid, and I have a feeling that 21% figure doesn't include corporate welfare. However, we receive and present images of the welfare queen, spitting out babies as fast as she can in order to keep getting those ever increasing government welfare checks to buy a new Cadillac and get her hair and nails done, with no plans to get a job or better her life, shiftlessly bilking the system indefinitely for all it's worth.

Look, don't misunderstand me, I agree that this awful metaphorical person does exist. However, the government-check-receiving welfare queen clearly falls under the logical fallacy of "Faulty Generalization" if you consider the math above. Again, we are talking about 10% of 6.3%, at most, which is .63%, or about 6 out of 1000 total welfare recipients. Not to mention, as only 21% of Americans receive welfare, we are talking about just .13% of the overall US population I hope we can agree that we should not allow .63% to get us upset, much less .13%, and we certainly shouldn't allow it to dominate our opinions or drive our policies.

"Crime Stats"

Crime stats are a complete misnomer- we don't keep crime stats, we keep arrest and conviction stats. For example, if the cops do a sweep through the projects and arrest 10 teenagers for smoking weed while not doing a sweep through the elite liberal arts college located three miles away and not arresting 10 college kids for smoking weed, did the 10 college kids not commit a crime? You see what I'm saying? We do not keep crime stats- there is no such thing- so please cease citing them.

In addition to the aforementioned drug-related incarceration stats, our so-called "crime stats" are often cooked in other ways as well, as our system (and our society) is highly discretionary in many subtle ways. For example, when I taught and coached in (mostly white) private schools, the powers that be called parents when kids got into a scuffle. When I taught at large public schools with a high percentage of black and/or brown students, the powers that be called the cops when kids got into a scuffle. At the private schools, no one got arrested or charged with anything. At the public schools, they usually arrested everyone who was involved and everyone got charged with something. The same thing is true on college campuses when drunk college kids get to fighting. At an expensive (and nearly all white at the time) private school like Trinity University in San Antonio, where I went, I saw plenty of drunken heated arguments and some drunken fights. No one ever got arrested. At historically-black college Huston Tillotson, where I worked as a part-time volunteer, kids who fought often got arrested.

Even homicide stats can be skewed, as homicides aren't counted in the official stats unless the death is legally ruled a homicide. This means that Mary Jo Kapechne, for example, never counted in the homicide data, despite the obvious truth that her death was caused by Ted Kennedy. It has also been normal for police departments to radically under-report homicides by police officers. In fact, a 2014 Wall Street Journal study found that 550 deaths caused by police officers between 2007 and 2012 went totally unreported, which means that those 550 homicides were not included in the oft-cited FBI homicide data.

Here are other examples of discretionary authority that skew all "crime" (and incarceration) stats:

1. Prosecutors have tremendous discretionary authority, and these decisions have a huge impact on the "crime" stats (11 of 18 studies analyzed by The Vera Institute found prosecutorial bias along racial lines in the "screening" phase where prosecutors decide what if any charges to file, three of five studies analyzed showed black defendants to be less likely to have their charges reduced or dropped compared with white defendants, and four of five studies analyzed found that black and brown defendants were more likely to be placed in pretrial detention and receive higher bails).

2. Judges have large amounts of discretionary authority when it comes to sentencing in many cases, and this discretion impacts incarceration stats a great deal (The Vera Institute analyzed six academic studies on racial bias in sentencing, and all six found sentencing discrepancies that hurt black and brown convicted defendants).

3. Legislators have total discretionary authority to draft laws, and their choices have a massive impact on both the "crime" and the incarceration stats. For example, in 1986, Ronald Reagan signed a law that made the prison sentence for 1 gram of crack cocaine equal to 100 grams of powder cocaine, despite the fact that crack is nothing more than diluted and therefore less expensive cocaine. Who was using expensive (and more potent) powdered cocaine? Rich white people. Who was using inexpensive (and less potent) crack cocaine? Poor black people. And to anyone trying to justify this shameful law by discussing the terrible harm that crack did to "inner city neighborhoods", they should take a look at what powdered cocaine did to Miami (and many other major

metropolitan areas all over the world) in the late 1970's and early 1980's.

4. Because poor people move from living place to living place much more often than middle class and affluent people, rich and middle class people are far easier to reach with a jury summons. This (and other factors) result in poor people being under-represented on juries, and of course any time poor people are under-represented, black people are, too. As we have shown that poor black people are over-represented as criminal defendants, it should be self-evident that a lack of representation of poor black people on juries has the potential to disrupt basic fairness.

5. Poor people normally can not afford a lawyer, which means they are represented by either a public defender or a court-appointed attorney. Either way, this often leads to inadequate representation based on inadequate and unequal resources compared with the prosecutor's office. My old friend Joanna Day is a former Public Defender in the Washington, DC area, and she can explain it much better than I can:

I was very lucky to work in one of the best funded offices in the country, although our resources paled in comparison to the US Attorney's office, which prosecuted our clients. My first year, I investigated my own cases, but had trained staff investigators that I shared with other trial attorneys after that. My case load was always very reasonable. For public interest work, we were well paid. But my experience is really an anomaly. In some offices, 100-120 cases per attorney is the norm. You can not be an effective advocate with 100 cases, or even 75. In some, you apply to a judge to pay for an investigator because there are no staff investigators. Judges can and will deny those requests. Being able to hire an expert, even in a homicide case, is practically unheard of in some jurisdictions. In jurisdictions where PD's have no resources, there is almost always tremendous pressure to plead cases. In all jurisdictions, there is pressure to plead because the criminal justice system could not function if everyone went to trial. You can not try cases effectively without good investigation. In fact, the Supreme Court has held that one of the duties of defense counsel is to investigate the facts of the case. In many cases in PD offices across the country, this investigation never happens. Compared to most PD offices, prosecutors seem to have limitless resources. They often have staff investigators, in addition to police officers who investigate cases. They have the resources of the Medical Examiner and the forensic units of the police departments. Defense counsel has to hire those people. When 80% of defendants are indigent and most jurisdictions have underfunded indigent defense systems, we do not have a fundamentally fair and equitable system. Add to that the racial disparities and we should all be taking to the streets. There are some great places to learn more about this. Gideon's Promise is an organization that was founded by one of my former colleagues. We also have to keep talking about these issues and the role race and class play at all levels of the criminal justice system. In my whole career as a PD, I had one white client. For less than five minutes. I went back to the lock up, introduced myself, started telling him what would happen next, and he said "Umm, I think I already have an attorney. My dad hired him." He handed me the card of one of the best criminal defense attorneys in town who is a regular commentator on a cable news channel. Every person charged with a crime should have access to the best defense possible, particularly in a system where racial bias clearly plays a role.

5. In addition to the understandable causes for the whitewashing of juries, we also have a nefarious history as a nation of deliberately excluding black jurors, particularly when the defendant is black. We tend to think that the whitewashing of juries ended around the time of the 1964 Civil Rights Act, but 20 years later in the landmark Batson v. Kentucky case, the Supreme Court ruled for the **first** time that striking a juror based on race was a Constitutional violation (obviously, had the whitewashing of juries ended in 1964, this 1986 Supreme Court ruling would have been unnecessary). However, even since the Batson decision, academic study after academic study from diverse regions such as Philadelphia, Long Island, Georgia, Alabama, North Carolina, and really anywhere else this topic has been studied have universally confirmed that the practice of striking black jurors when the defendant is black has continued to persist. And if you don't trust academic studies because you worry about liberal bias in academia, consider this quote from the Mississippi Supreme Court (not exactly a bastion of liberalism) in their ruling in the 2007 case of Flowers v. Mississippi: "racially-motivated jury selection is still prevalent twenty years after *Batson* was handed down."

6. It is also worth noting that prosecutors don't just tend to block black people from serving on juries, but they also tend to block any juror regardless of race who may be empathetic toward a black defendant. As my former classmate Mark Zwald noted:

I was selected for jury duty for a murder trial where the accused was a black man. During the prosecutor's interview I mentioned that I felt our judicial system is sometimes biased against African-Americans. Of course I wasn't selected for the jury.

My old friend Rick Oliver, who is a (white) defense attorney in Houston, made the following remark on this topic:

Racism in the criminal justice system isn't just pervasive. It's assumed. That's a part of the problem. If people of whatever color can not expect to be left alone as long as they follow the law, then why follow the law? As a society, we are developing behavior that is completely predictable. Broadly, whether black or white or whatever, we have no one to blame but ourselves.

The shared attitude between police and DA's is to protect the legitimacy of the arrest, whatever the cost. The systemic attitude corrupts both. Their intent is irrelevant in the face of societal perception. If those entrusted with enforcing a sense of true justice can't do it without party bias, race bias, or any other bias, there really is no sense of true justice. And no reason for those subject to it to respect it. The existence of honorable cops and DA's is a red herring. It doesn't even begin to address the real issue.

The point is that we should not only view the so-called crime stats cautiously, but we should actively consider the many ways in which these statistics can be highly skewed, deeply flawed, and dangerously biased rather than simply citing them as some sort of end-all-be-all sermon from the mount.

Protests

The #BlackLivesMatter movement and the accompanying protests have been broadly characterized as violent riots. This has been true in some cases, but not most, and this seems to be another good example of human beings giving in to the logical fallacy of "Faulty Generalization", allowing mathematically rare occurrences to distort our point of view.

Here's a list of the #BlackLivesMatter protests that have turned (at least partially) violent or destructive as far as I know:

Ferguson after Michael Brown

New York after Eric Garner

Los Angeles after Charley Leundeu Keunang

Baltimore after Freddie Gray

Chicago during the protests of the police chiefs' conference held there

Minneapolis after Jamar Clark

Baton Rouge after Alton Sterling

Dallas after Alton Sterling and Philando Castile

That's eight total, at least that I was able to identify. Maybe there are more, but there have probably also been many more than the 1000 or so overall #BlackLivesMatter protests I was able to identify as well, so there's no reason to expect the approximate ratio of violent and/or destructive riots versus peaceful protests to change all that much, even with more exhaustive research. Given this approximate ratio, how can 8/1000 constitute enough of a trend as to cause us to change our language from "protest" to "riot"?

Additionally, at the eight protests, the violent or destructive behavior was by no means universal. In Dallas, for example, it was a peaceful and productive protest until 1 person committed a horrific hate-based massacre. So, while the protest turned violent, the protestors were overwhelmingly non-violent. That is also the case in all eight examples I mentioned.

We as a nation need to stop arriving at mathematically unjustifiable "Faulty Generalizations". The Black Lives Matter movement is, by the numbers, overwhelmingly peaceful, and that is a statistical reality, not an opinion. So, while I think it's totally OK to criticize the protestors, let's do a better job of collectively characterizing them accurately as protestors and activists, not criminals and thugs. We as a nation must work harder to resist the temptation to let the media drive our thinking, especially as the modern media operates under a "if it bleeds, it leads" mentality, which means MSNBC and CNN and local affiliates of ABC, CBS, and NBC are all over-eager to show coverage of protests turned to riots, not just Fox News (we always let the media get away with this nonsense- Donald Trump holds hundreds of rallies, three or four featured threatening behavior toward people of color who were there to protest, and which three or four rallies did we hear about continuously? Surprise, surprise!!).

Deaths of and by Law Enforcement Officials

17 black men killed a police officer in 2015, out of 16,000,000 black males over the age of 12 living in the US. This means that a black man will kill a police officer at a statistical probability of .000001062.

102 police officers killed an **unarmed** black person in 2015 out of approximately 1.2 million police officers in the US. This means that a police officer will kill an **unarmed** black person at a statistical probability of .000085.

Clearly, this math demonstrates that both a black person killing a cop and a cop killing an **unarmed** black person are both enormously unlikely to occur. However, it should be noted that it is proportionally and mathematically 80 times more likely for a cop to kill an **unarmed** black person than for a black person to kill a cop (it is still over six times more likely even just using the raw number rather than making it proportional).

However, while it is less unreasonable by the numbers for black people to fear a violent death at the hands of the police than the other way around, both of these extremely common fears are nevertheless overwhelmingly unreasonable speaking strictly from a mathematical and statistical perspective.

Additionally, police officers killed 66 unarmed white people in 2015 compared with the 102 unarmed black people who lost their lives at the hands of the police in 2015. So, as a raw number, police kill unarmed black people at a 55% higher rate than the police kill unarmed white people. However, if you look at the numbers proportionally based on the total number of black men over the age of 12 (16,000,000) and the total of white men over the age of 12 (100,000,000), then the police kill unarmed black people at an astounding 965% higher rate than the police kill unarmed white people.

Summation

Having now been presented with this much factual information, we should hopefully no longer skeptically view the notion as controversial that American racism continues to thrive in the modern era and we should consequently accept the reality that American racism is not in fact "a thing of the past".

Again, if we can't admit it, we sure as fire can't fix it!!

CHAPTER 5

BIAS (AND BRAINWASHING)

We all know that bias exists.

Bias explains why a Dallas Cowboys fan and a New York Giants fan can watch the identical replay involving a controversial officiating decision and see two completely different things.

Bias places into context the seemingly incomprehensible current reality that most political conservatives spat fire about Barack Obama issuing so many Executive Orders that it appeared he was "ruling by fiat", while most political liberals defended President Obama's 2nd term end runs as necessary due to Republican obstructionism; today, with Donald Trump in the White House, the exact opposite is true in every single respect, with Democrats outraged by a President they think is trying to subvert our system of checks and balances, and Republicans defending President Trump's actions as necessary due to Democrats resisting rather than cooperating. Clearly, something this astoundingly ridiculous and mentally hypocritical would not be possible without human beings tending to be greatly affected by bias.

Bias also causes parents of objectively artistically talentless children to beam with wonderment at the artwork their children produce, even when the "artwork" is in fact so atrocious that I hesitate to even designate it as such (by the way, I am making this point through a self-deprecating inside joke, as this cited example involves my mother and me in the early 1980's, so please don't think I'm intending to be generally cruel to children by calling them talentless and their artwork atrocious- rather, I'm calling **my** "artwork" atrocious and my blessed mother's glowing assessment of it deeply if not totally bias-based).

In general, it is safe to say that bias is a pervasive or even universal human trait, and that bias tends to distort opinions in most if not all human beings. In this chapter, we will deal with five specific threads of bias (anti-black bias, anti-police bias, pro-police bias, bias displayed by the police, and anti-white bias), and we will take a look at some possible causes to explain these five forms of bias.

Bias Against Black People

From 2004 until 2006, I worked as a video assistant within the Georgia Tech athletics department. In the aftermath of Hurricane Katrina, we had 500 New Orleanians living in our gymnasium, and our school president, Wayne Clough, had given the order basically to disregard school protocols and go all in to lend a hand. My immediate boss Paul Hewitt did exactly the same, and the whole basketball staff and team were running around like crazy doing whatever we could think of to help. The school, and our basketball program, effectively shut down and did our best to help people who needed our help. It was a deeply moving display of humanity, in all regards.

As we were in the middle of trying to figure out how to coordinate everything that needed coordinating, Craig "Ironhead" Hayward called Coach Hewitt to offer his help when he saw that the Alexander Memorial Coliseum had become a hub for hundreds of displaced people (Mr. Hayward of course had a connection to the city of New Orleans through his time playing for the Saints). Within days, our gym had become way too full, so Coach Hewitt reached back out to Mr. Hayward, who immediately and graciously agreed to accept a crew of complete strangers into his suburban Atlanta home.

I do not remember how, but some way or another, I wound up being involved in providing transportation to the 100 or so people who we could not accommodate at Georgia Tech. I vividly recall giving three elderly black men a ride to Mr. Hayward's house. All three of them had tears in their eyes of appreciation as they thanked me for giving them a lift, and I had tears in my eyes as well, both in the moment and now as I write this. It was a genuine moment of love, one of the few times I have felt love from or given love to a complete stranger, and it is an experience I will not forget as long as I live.

However, I also remember that there was one really loud-mouthed and ignorant woman among the huge crowd of people back at Georgia Tech, wagging her finger at everyone in sight, shouting things like, "Where my motherfucking check at?" As I started to notice that lots of Georgia Tech kids had sort of quit working and were just gawking at her and talking about her as she continued to loudly make a fool of herself, I approached her and asked her very politely if I could have a word with her in private.

About one minute into me calmly telling her that she was being rude and inappropriate and that she would be the only thing that any of these college kids would remember about this whole experience if she didn't stop embodying every single negative stereotype out there, she started *going off on me. Well, Coach Hewitt came over to see what on earth was going on, and she basically berated him, too. Eventually, we sort of calmed her down, or at least went our separate ways (*Although I was not aware of this term at that time, I was definitely "whitesplaining" here, which is the act of a white person paternalistically and condescendingly-and racistly-lecturing a black person, especially a black stranger; and this egotistical and obnoxious-and racist-tendency could very well have played a partially causal role in her negative reaction toward me. I generally try to avoid whitesplaining in this book, although I have no doubt that I fall short of this goal at least some of the time. That having been said, as an American white person, I feel extraordinarily well qualified to write a book about racism, just as a chef is well qualified to write a cookbook).

Later that night, I turned on the local news (I could not afford cable at that time, so I had about five channels), and they had some coverage about Katrina from Georgia Tech. Well, take a wild guess who was the ONLY person they interviewed and showed on TV? 500 people in that gym, 499 of whom were decent and humble and grateful. She was the ONLY person acting like a jerk... THE... ONLY... ONE... and yet she was the lone person the local news chose to feature.

I burst into tears when I saw that, and I couldn't stop for about 20 minutes. It was as if every negative media image of black people I had ever seen in my life came flashing back into my mind, and for the first time, I realized the true destruction the biased media causes by perpetuating negative stereotypes about black people. I immediately recognized that many white people (especially in their 50s and 60s and 70s and 80s, since most younger people don't watch local news) all over the city of Atlanta saw her AND ONLY HER and likely thought to themselves, "typical".

At first, anger pumped through my veins, and I vowed that I would neither forget nor forgive that news network for that destructive and shameful and I believed at the time deliberate little piece of "journalism". After further reflection, though, I became less angry and more troubled, as it started to make more and more sense in my mind that the actions of that news network were probably in fact more subconscious than deliberate. I don't now think that some old white racist producer instructed that news crew to find the worst-behaving black person at Georgia Tech in order to highlight them and perpetuate racism; rather, I think that they went to Georgia Tech **expecting** to find belligerence and chaos and ingratitude, so they gravitated to the 1 person who actually met their bias-based expectations.

Probably at least partially because of this experience, it upsets me to the core of my soul as a person to this day how often white people shrug and think or say "typical" about black people broadly based on the bad behavior of ONE individual black person or a very small group of black people. There are just so many things that a lot of white people believe are "typical" of black people that are in fact ATYPICAL.

Unfortunately, in my experiences and based on a mountain of supporting data, anti-black bias contaminates the vast majority of American white people (by "vast majority", I mean "virtually all" if not "all". For example, I remember personally taking the Harvard racial implicit bias test, and they basically told me to take off my white hood, stop burning crosses, and that the Department of Justice would be wanting to talk to me soon. At the time, the results of the test shook me up. I mean, I'm a basketball white person, not a regular white person. I have more black friends than I can count, and all that stuff. I couldn't believe it.

I mention this because it is important to reiterate that when I call a white person out for being racist, I'm not necessarily saying YOU are a racist. I'm saying WE have been brainwashed to believe that black people are less than (plenty of American black people have also been brainwashed into believing that black people are less than).

Brainwashing and bias are the reasons why a white person like me who is not particularly likely to be identified as a racist (prior to this book, anyway) catches myself getting emotional when I'm driving down Elgin in 3rd Ward (an historically black neighborhood in Houston) and I see a black father holding his child's hand, and I find myself wanting to stop the car and congratulate that black man for being "a good father". And then I want to slap the shit out of myself, because I have about 50 black friends who are fathers, and I can think of exactly 1 black friend of mine who is anything other than an excellent father. As such, I feel like I am supposed to know better than that, and be better than that- but it's obviously harder than it sounds, or I wouldn't subconsciously view black fathers as unicorns. As my old friend Aisha Crumbine wrote:

Please consider the undeniable lens through which black males are seen. For hundreds of years, black men have been portrayed as animals, barbarians who rape and kill, who terrorize and self-sabotage their own ability to be contributing citizens of this country. Everywhere you turn, we are bombarded with images of the angry, aggressive black man from news interviews to fictitious movie characters. In the same way people shout from the mountain tops that music and video games subliminally impact our thinking, these images cause many to see black men through a lens of fear.

Or as my friend Kyle Martin candidly wrote:

What frustrates me is the inability for people to get on the same page with this conversation. People think it's black people versus the police, but police officers are just reflecting the society they serve. Our society assumes things about black men that we don't about all other races. It's a hard truth, one that I've faced in myself at times. That knee jerk reaction that I didn't choose to have, but have had nonetheless, then the poor black kid had to prove me wrong. I hate that part of myself, and I fight against it. But, I know that others don't necessarily distrust their knee jerk reaction and in fact rely on it, even when it's based in ignorance and misunderstanding.

When I think back to so many of the images from my childhood, it isn't hard to figure out why I often reflexively can't help but feeling a certain kind of way about black people.

One of my favorite movies of all time is "The Principal" starring Jim Belushi as a white principal who goes in to save a black school from a sociopathic teenage black drug dealer who had taken over the school.

Or what about the "Do you mind if we dance with your dates?" scene from "Animal House" where a giant black man and his cohorts essentially stole a group of white women from their terrified but powerless white escorts.

I also adore the original "Vacation", with Chevy Chase- remember how they took a wrong turn and found themselves in East St. Louis and Chevy Chase had the windows down, much to the chagrin of his nervous wife, and then they immediately heard gunfire and Chevy Chase delivered the classic line, "Roll 'em up!!"

And of course I was influenced by maybe my favorite movie scene of all time, toward the end of "Revenge of the Nerds" when UN Jefferson and the big, black, sullen-looking men of Lambda Lambda Lambda confronted and clowned the (all white) football team that had been bullying the nerds.

I still love those movies, and those scenes, and as I don't think I can help it, I don't apologize for it. But I do recognize the extent to which images like these affect people, because they're so pervasive- in "The Principal", a white man is a savior and hero to the violent and ignorant black people; in "Animal House", the lustful black men aggressively forced themselves on the white women; in "Vacation", an innocent white family needing a helping hand instead got cussed out, lied to, taken advantage of, and shot at, all in the space of their three minute detour through a black neighborhood; and in "Revenge of the Nerds", the very scary and potentially violent black men intimidated and threatened the now visibly shaken all-white football team. So, as a boy in the 1980's, I learned that black men are angry, violent, drug-addicted, untrustworthy, insane, and insatiably lustful toward white women- and three of those four movies are comedies. We really never notice this sort of thing until we've been made aware of it and until we make a conscious choice to pay attention to it moving forward.

My friend Jen Talley brilliantly explained it this way:

I see a lot, in response to an article or post about racism, comments like: "But I'm not racist! I didn't grow up that way, I was taught that everyone is equal! I don't see color! My parents didn't tolerate any racism!" I see it a lot from people my age -- Gen X'ers who thought that all these problems would have been solved by now, but also from those above and below me on the generational curves.

It might actually be true that you grew up in a family that actively taught you not to be racist. But guess what? Even if you grew up a white person in a white home with UTTERLY NON-RACIST white parents (questionable because they grew up in an EVEN MORE RACIST world than you have, no matter how old you are), you grew up in a racist world in a racist country in a racist state/county/town. You have spent your life consuming racist media and seeing racist images. You have watched movies in which the black people are sidekicks, poor, criminal, "magical," slaves, sharecroppers, gangsters. The Asian people in your media are sidekicks, kungfu masters, dragon ladies, geishas, delivery boys, emasculated males. The brown people you see on screen are sidekicks, maids, criminals, illegal immigrants, food service workers, gangsters. You see memes making fun of the black people interviewed on the news because they don't talk like you. You see local news where another black person was shot, another black child was killed, another black person is going to jail.

So no matter how actively anti-racist you were raised, no matter how many black and brown friends you have had, no matter how much you think you sympathize with Black Lives Matter, even- you started out racist (and developed bias). Maybe a little, maybe a lot. Maybe you still get a little nervous when you see a black man walking down the street toward you. Maybe you roll your eyes when you see a black woman dressed a certain way or hear certain slang in conversation. Maybe you secretly wonder why people don't just comply with the police, or if it's REALLY as bad as they say it is. That's still bias. There's a system in place we benefit from, asked for or not. That's racism.

Before we can change it we have to acknowledge it. We have to own it. And then WE have to change it. Racism (and bias) is our problem, fellow white people. We didn't ask for it, we didn't necessarily create it, but we perpetuate it and we have to stop it. Because it is literally killing people. And it has to stop.

The truth is that we collectively constantly get fed negative images and stereotypes about black people from a very early age, and this reality creates at least some degree of anti-black bias in nearly all of us. This isn't meant to be insulting, but rather just a plea to acknowledge the existence of anti-black racial bias so that we can begin trying to reduce it or even overcome it.

Bias Related to Our Criminal Justice System

To begin with, the previous chapter "Accept Reality" touched on our criminal justice system, and bias plays a big role there as well. After all, a lot of people have deeply held but unacknowledged and possibly even sub-conscious feelings about black people, which are unfortunately reinforced constantly. As previously discussed, quite a few white people draw the conclusion that more black people are in prison because black people commit more crimes without recognizing how broadly that all-too-common biased train of thought poisons a black defendant's chances in the minds of many white jurors, judges, and prosecutors.

For example, in looking at homicides and the death penalty, we see that roughly 50% of homicide victims are black, yet only 15% of death-penalty cases involve a black victim. Furthermore, when the homicide victim is white, a black defendant is three times more likely to receive the death penalty than a white defendant (http://www.amnestyusa.org/our-work/issues/death-penalty/us-death-penalty-facts/death-penalty-and-race). To continue with the theme of racial bias in death penalty cases, we ran the numbers over the last five years and discovered that black people kill on average 437.8 white people per year, while white people kill on average 200.4 black people per year (source: 2009 to 2013 FBI expanded homicide data). Examining post-1976 capital cases that resulted in executions, 293 involved a black defendant and a white victim, while only 31 involved a white defendant and a black victim (http://www.deathpenaltyinfo.org/race-death-row-inmates-executed-1976). This means that black people are 2.2 times more likely to commit an interracial homicide but are 9.45 times more likely to receive the death penalty for doing so.

This again isn't to say that there are no black criminals, or that all white jurors and officers of the court have been severely impacted by this common mental phenomenon; but this phenomenon is a real thing, and if we at least acknowledge it, then we can perhaps start trying to deal with it.

One strain of bias that affects law enforcement involves the bias that police officers often themselves carry into their work, as even law enforcement officials who are in a position to examine a large amount of data confess. For example, please consider this statement from former FBI Director James Comey:

After years of police work, officers often can't help but be influenced by the cynicism they feel.
A mental shortcut becomes almost irresistible and maybe even rational by some lights. The two young black men on one side of the street look like so many others the officer has locked up. Two white men on the

other side of the street—even in the same clothes—do not. The officer does not make the same association about the two white guys, whether that officer is white or black. And that drives different behavior. The officer turns toward one side of the street and not the other. We need to come to grips with the fact that this (biased) behavior complicates the relationship between police and the communities they serve.

Additionally, as Americans, we also tend to allow bias to cause us to miss the mark completely when it comes to our feelings toward police officers, and we do it almost universally, just in radically different yet almost equally biased ways.

For many white people, especially white people who lean right politically, the police can do no wrong. Conversely, for many black people, especially black people who lean left politically, the police can do no right. Both sides are wrong, with bias and emotion being the top 2 reasons why we struggle so badly to have a beneficial conversation on this topic.

We will begin by addressing the pro-police bias held by many Americans, who rightly point out that cops put their lives on the line to protect us. Although this is true, we often elevate cops in our minds to the level of soldiers, because both groups of Americans make the ultimate sacrifice. While this correlation makes sense on the surface, 2013 figures say that over 6500 soldiers died in combat, while 27 cops were murdered in the line of duty. As such, it isn't mathematically justifiable to compare the sacrifice of soldiers and cops, and I could even argue that making the comparison is disrespectful to soldiers. But regardless of the comparative sacrifices of cops and soldiers, let's remember that a huge majority of Americans (left and right) largely condemned what happened at Abu Ghraib. Sure, you had some fringe people decrying the "liberal attacks on the soldiers", but they truly were people on the fringe. However, in the case of cops, people I don't consider to be generally unreasonable have an automatic and universal and unshakeable default position in defense of cops, seemingly no matter what they've been caught doing. I can't understand why or how cops have been elevated to that singular position in American society, where (it seems) easily over half of us will blindly defend cops and make excuses for them regardless of what they've done.

Now, I'm not saying policing isn't a dangerous job. In fact, 102 police officers died in the line of duty in 2015 according to Department of

Labor statistics (according to the FBI, 41 of the 102 deaths were homicides). For context, it is worth considering the following information as well from the Department of Labor statistics on work place fatalities:

546 truck drivers lost their lives in 2015.

937 construction workers lost their lives in 2015.

252 farm and ranch workers lost their lives in 2015.

Is policing dangerous? Yes.

Is policing vital? Yes.

Are farming, construction, and trucking also vital to America? Yes.

Do more farmers, construction workers, and truck drivers die each year on the job more than police officers? Yes.

The point is that while policing is dangerous and policing is vital, policing is not the most dangerous profession in America, nor is it the only often unpleasant profession that is vital to America. Yet, for some reason, many Americans have attached a universal and singular nobility to police officers, which prevents many of us from examining at least arguably questionable police behavior either thoughtfully or objectively or productively (the thought has often occurred to me that the subconscious reason so many white Americans have elevated police officers even above soldiers to a unique pedestal is that soldiers protect them from unseen and far-a-way threats whereas the police protect them from niggers).

For example, if a criminal chooses to run from the police to evade arrest and the video captures a police officer beating the shit out of the suspect after tackling him, many Americans will look at the video, shrug, and say, "that's what you get for running from the police." To be clear, I agree that running from the police is unadvisable, and I understand why a police officer would be angry about a suspect choosing to flee. However, under our system of laws, it is a police officer's job to pursue the suspect, tackle the suspect, handcuff the suspect, arrest the suspect, and book the suspect. It is not a police officer's job to mete out violent vigilante justice on the spot; even if we find the arresting cop's behavior to be understandable, it is still not acceptable (or legal!!) in a free society, and any attempt to argue otherwise simply demonstrates bias and a total lack of objectivity.

To look at some data on this topic, the Cato Institute found that 11,000 police officers in 2010 were involved in credible allegations of police misconduct. Of the 11,000, 3238 were formally charged and 1063 were actually convicted in a criminal court of law. For starters, it should concern all of us that only 29% of credible reports of police misconduct produced any actual criminal charges, and it should concern us that only 33% of charged police officers were actually convicted (compared with 68% of the general public when charged with a crime). These factors speak to a gigantic bias within the system toward police officers on the part of prosecutors, judges, and juries. However, we still must look at the 1063 criminally convicted police officers and admit that police officers are not infallible and should not be blindly and automatically defended based on bias.

On the other hand, many Americans have deeply held anti-police bias, which also isn't particularly well supported by the numbers. The truth is that cops do perform vital work that not many people are willing to take on, and they do have a very tough job, and they do discharge their duties heroically far more often than criminally.

Consider the Bureau of Justice statistics from 2002 regarding citizen complaints of police use of force, which reveals that 22,238 complaints were leveled against police officers in large urban police departments. Sadly, and frankly infuriatingly, our government apparently hasn't bothered to keep any data whatsoever on this topic since 2002, so we will have to use the data from 15 years ago.

Also, the number of complaints dealt with only 59% of the police population- given the data gap, we are going to assume the complaints per officer would stay roughly the same proportionally, so we will use the presumed number of 37,692 complaints about police use of force.

Obviously, as a raw number, 37,692 complaints is a large number. However, when we also consider that we have 1.2 million police officers in America, we see that the probability of a police officer committing an act of unjustifiable force is .03141, and that is assuming that 100% of complaints were legitimate, which can not possibly be true (in fact, only 8% of complaints were found to be valid, but given that our government can't even be bothered to regularly compile this information and the people who did the investigating into the claims of excessive force are the same people who failed to keep records on this topic, I think we can fairly reasonably assume that the actual number of legitimate claims was higher than 8%).

Also, in order to fight anti-police bias and be as fair as possible, we must also consider the opposite side of the same coin, which is the number of times police officers have been assaulted. On this topic, of course, the FBI keeps very updated stats, so we know that 50,212 police officers were assaulted in 2015. As is the case with the citizen complaints, we know that some of these alleged assaults did not in fact occur, as police officers who use excessive force will sometimes claim self-defense and charge the victim with assaulting a police officer in order to protect themselves. However, given that we just can't know what percent of assault claims by citizens or by the police are fraudulent charges, we are going to assume that the respective percentages of false allegations are roughly the same and leave the raw numbers alone.

So, first, based on the raw data, police officers are 33% more likely to be assaulted by a citizen than the other way around. However, when we turn the raw data into proportional data, we find that the probability of a police officer being assaulted by a citizen is .0418 (50,212 divided by 1.2 million), while the probability of an adult male citizen being assaulted by a police officer is .000316. This means that a police officer is more than 132 times more likely to be assaulted by a citizen as to commit assault against a citizen.

As we are considering the subject of law-enforcement-related bias, now might be a good time to share the results from my own (often drunkenly administered and "recorded") informal study over the course of the past 15 years or so. Wherever I go, any time the subject of how the police treat black people comes up and one of the participants in the conversation is black, I always inquire directly about their personal experiences dealing with law enforcement officials. In this (very non-academic) "study", three truths emerged literally 100% of the time:

100% of black men reported to me experiencing at least one negative interaction with a police officer (at least 75% reported to me multiple negative interactions with the police, not just one).

100% of black men reported to me having experienced at least one interaction with a police officer that they felt was racially motivated or had racial overtones (at least 75% reported to me multiple interactions they felt was at least somewhat racial, not just one).

100% of black men admitted that way more than 50% of their overall interactions with the police had been reasonable or positive with a racially neutral tone.

In other words, my informal study largely predicted what my data-based research later substantiated. Yes, some cops exhibit racist attitudes and behavior some of the time, despite what people who hold a pro-police bias desperately want to believe. But, no, racism insofar as how the police treat black people on a daily basis has not permeated even close to a majority of the police force, despite what people who hold an anti-police bias tend to insist.

The point is that while all forms of police-related bias are understandable, none is defensible or justifiable. Some police officers behave criminally, and do not deserve to be defended, especially not blindly or universally. Some police officers carry racially biased fears of black men into their jobs, despite the incredibly low probability statistically of a black person actually harming a police officer (remember the .000001062 probability of a black person killing a cop from the previous chapter "Accepting Reality"). Finally, as we have seen, the math also does not support the extent and prevalence of the anti-police bias we see in America.

Bias Against White People

I think it also very important to consider that white people are not the only racial group in America that has the capacity to exhibit bias. My old friend Aisha Crumbine once wrote:

I'm going to be vulnerable and honest. I've lost something this election season, and it makes me sad.

While driving home yesterday, a big white pickup truck pulled next to me. My windows were down. I looked over, and when I saw the tint was super dark, I slowed down concerned the driver might be one of those people.

The thought gave me pause.

I kept driving, later arriving at the gas station. As I walked inside, an older white man was walking out. I thanked him for holding the door. But before I crossed the threshold, I wondered whether he was one of them--one of those white men who want to make America great again, one of those who think Black lives mattering is a bunch of bullshit, one of those who looks at me as an outsider who can "go back to where I came from" if I have so many problems with this here country.

I got back in my car and sat for a minute. I have become suspicious of every passing white person. The way I feel towards them, with this sense of mistrust, is exactly how many whites have long looked at blacks. This prejudice is what blacks have been fighting against for decades. And yet, here I am.

I took exception to her post, and decided to engage in a dialogue with her:

I cherish your honesty, and I have long said that unlike white-on-black racism, black-on-white racism is not irrational. However, while being understandable in my view, it still isn't OK.

I don't think we as people can necessarily help how we feel, so I don't judge you one iota for having or sharing your feelings honestly. I do hope, however, that you do your level best to fight against your racism and bias because I just don't see hypocrisy as being a helpful step toward fixing white people (and I agree that we need fixing).

Your post (and the replies) don't make me angry, or upset, or fearful, but like you, it sure did make me sad and less hopeful.

Aisha next thoughtfully replied:

I'd originally written, "I am a fighter. I'm going to call out this feeling when I have it, so I can acknowledge it for what it is: fear of the unknown. Then I am going to remind myself that who I am is too bright, too powerful, to succumb to the darkness. I will have to choose to live in the light. It will be- it is already- hard. Not knowing who I can look in the eye without seeing the illusion of disdain, is already hard. But you're damn right- I'm going to do what I'd want someone to do when they see me- see our shared humanity."

Thanks for making sure I wasn't giving in to the dark side.

To me, Aisha's reply was perfect. She recognized that she was wrong without getting defensive. I think we should all take a page from her book, as honest engagement without defensiveness goes such a long way toward solving our racial issues as Americans.

As a basketball white person, I have also personally experienced anti-white racial bias. Frankly, by way of full disclosure, I have also practiced anti-white racial bias, as the truth is that the vast majority of white people who give basketball a shot are either too soft or too unathletic to excel in the sport I love. Please note that I am not trying to throw a pity party or attempt to equate the consequences of the anti-white racial bias I've experienced with the consequences of anti-black racial bias that all of my black friends have experienced. Rather, I am simply giving voice to an existing reality, namely that black people are not the only Americans who have been touched by racial bias, and white people are not the only Americans who have perpetuated racial bias.

Possible Causes of Bias

Not surprisingly, the media plays a major role in the formation of bias and the brainwashing of our citizenry. This idea shouldn't be too controversial for anti-media Americans to accept, given that one of the main pillars of our feelings against the American media relates to their attempts to program the American people through biased propaganda.

Think, for example, about the story I began this chapter with from my days at Georgia Tech where the media's bias caused them to find the only black person who was acting like an idiot and interview her and only her, thus broadcasting and disseminating their bias into the homes of the American people. Or, I'm sure many of us can remember during Hurricane Katrina how our media referred to white people who stole from Wal-Mart as survivalists but black people who stole from Wal-Mart as looters? These types of subtle differences in how the media comparatively treats black people add up to collectively help foment a decidedly unsubtle amount of anti-black racial bias.

And who could forget Cokie Roberts on Meet the Press during the 50 year anniversary of Dr. King's March on Washington, when she became visibly shaken recalling how afraid white people were about potential violence. I will never forget this example of how deeply ingrained the stereotype of black men being violent truly is, because there was no violence, which means that her fear was totally unfounded, yet she still trembles in fear 50 years later about violence that never even occurred. Talk about being brainwashed!!

Interestingly, ironically, and I suppose fairly unsurprisingly, the media as well as our popular culture have also played a major role in the formation of both the pro-police and the anti-police biases so many Americans possess. For example, most older Americans carry a pro-police bias, which makes sense considering that the only police-related images they were ever presented with were of wholesome and humble and unimpeachable public servants like Joe Friday from the TV show Dragnet. On the other hand, most Americans who harbor anti-police bias belong to younger generations that grew up watching and listening to images from a movie like Serpico in the 1970's to a TV show like Hillstreet Blues in the 1980's to a song like Fuck the Police in the 1990's to a movie like Training Day in the 2000's. Considering this, it should not be too surprising that younger Americans hold much more varied opinions and different types of bias regarding the police, as they have absorbed images of the police that vary from heroic to tragically but relatably flawed to nakedly despicable.

Oral traditions also play a giant role in the formation of bias- as illogical as it sounds, experiences are in many ways inherited.

If you're around 40 years old and a 3rd plus generation American like I am, your grandfather likely served in World War II. Many of us were lucky enough to know our grandfathers, and our grandfathers naturally shared stories and world views with us.

When discussing bias, it's important to think about the wildly different experiences of our grandfathers who served in World War II depending on what race they were. Our white grandfathers returned to a grateful nation as heroes who deservedly benefited from the GI Bill to become home owners and college graduates, often for the first time in the history of their families. Our black grandfathers, on the other hand, served in segregated military units that were often relegated to either demeaning supporting roles or suicide missions, and they returned to a segregated nation that systematically denied them the vast majority of their rights under the GI Bill that largely created the thriving white middle class of the 1950's (as we will cover more thoroughly 2 chapters from now).

What stories did our grandfathers tell our mothers and fathers? What opinions did they bestow upon our parents? How does this affect us? Whether overtly or discreetly, deliberate or unintentional, willful or subconscious, no human being can fully detach themselves from our early childhood upbringing and experiences. Being biased isn't a moral failing, it's a psychological inevitability.

A far less obvious and less discussed cause of racial bias in America is basic geography. Simply stated, in general, the poorest and least educated black people are concentrated in urban neighborhoods and housing projects, whereas the poorest and least educated white people are concentrated in rural areas and trailer parks. As such, the poorest black people are so much more visible than the poorest white people because the poorest black people are geographically located a matter of a few miles or even a few blocks from our major media centers inside of our major population centers. Consequently, the comparative over-visibility of the poorest black people based on geography tends to pervert our perceptions of black people in general.

Finally, one key element that does not necessarily cause bias but badly exacerbates it is simply human nature. Sadly, it's a terribly common aspect of the human condition that we tend to remember instances that confirm our stereotypes and prejudices far more than we remember instances that contradict our stereotypes and prejudices, even when the number of contradictory instances FAR OUTWEIGH the number of confirmatory instances. My favorite example of this comes from a joke that goes like this:

Many years ago, a young Scotsman named McGregor moved to London to make his fortune, and make his fortune he did, establishing himself as a business magnate. One year, as he was getting older, he told a younger lad at the bar (in an increasingly bitter tone), "You know, lad, I've built over 100 bridges for the people of England. But do you think the English would ever call a Scotsman from humble origins McGregor the Bridge Builder? Noooooooooo. And, laddy, my business also laid the railroad tracks that cover this great land, but do you think the English would ever call a Scotsman with my family background McGregor the Rail Layer? Noooooooooo. And later in life, after I had made my fortune, I gave money to build 30 hospitals for poor children, but do you think the

English would ever call the son of a Scottish blacksmith McGregor the Generous? Noooooooooo. But you fuck just one sheep…"

As people, we do that to one another at alarming rates, casually dismissing an incalculable tonnage of good in each other because a small amount of bad better conforms to our pre-existing biases and stereotypes. We should really do our level best to stop doing this to one another.

Summation

Given the pervasive and destructive nature of bias in America, our country can not and will not be a fair or equal place until we all force ourselves to be aware of the possibility of at least some implicit bias within ourselves. Then, once we're aware of it, the good-hearted and fair-minded among us will fight against it within our own mental dialogue, which will (over time) make America (at least closer to) the fair and equal place we all want it to be. In my heart, if we collectively made the choice to vigorously fight bias and brainwashing, our nation and our world would be such a far better place.

CHAPTER 6

EMPATHY

As human beings, all over the world, we often struggle with the concept of practicing empathy toward each other.

Before continuing, let's make sure we don't conflate empathy with sympathy. Simply put, empathy means you try to walk a mile in someone else's shoes, while sympathy means that you feel sorry for them. Sometimes, there's overlap, but that definitely doesn't need to be the case.

For example, if you encounter a celebrity at a restaurant and they snub your polite request for an autograph or a picture, we tend to understandably react negatively to the celebrity's rudeness (I once stole Goldie Hawn's shoes in a Japanese restaurant out of anger that one of my earliest crushes brushed me off curtly). However, can you imagine living life where every single time you went out in public, multiple strangers interrupted you during a conversation at dinner and imposed on your time? What if the conversation was a contentious business meeting that wasn't going well for the celebrity? What if the celebrity had just discovered their mom has cancer? Do celebrities lose all rights to enjoy a private dinner or be visibly annoyed by a stranger's intrusion because they're rich and famous?

Now, do I feel sorry for celebrities because we allow them no privacy and hold them to unreasonable expectations about the percent of time-intruding requests they are expected to cheerfully grant as well as their levels of social politeness when they're being interrupted? No, I sure don't. They're rich and famous, and it comes with the territory, and I, like most people, would gladly trade my problems for theirs. But, do I (at this point in my life) have enough empathy to at least consider how annoying it must be at times to be a celebrity and consequently cut them some slack? Yes, I do.

Or think about our lack of collective empathy we as men display toward women. It is so easy to brush off the cat calls, the crass pickup lines, the drunken heavy petting or groping, the "playful" ass slapping, and so on and so forth. Believe me, I've been guilty of all those all-too-common behaviors myself, and worse (#ItWasMe), and I never even tried to think about how my words and actions actually made the girls feel until I was in my mid 20's. However, as I've matured (somewhat), I've tried to put myself in their shoes.

I weigh 300 pounds. Let's assume some attractive woman walked by me who weighed 150 pounds, and I hollered at her, "Want some fries with that shake?" Between the ages of 12 and 25, I definitely would have described my remark as a compliment, or a joke, but by my late 20's, I knew that I was never in fact "joking" because if she had inexplicably accepted my juvenile sexual advances, we would have been butt naked in very short order.

As my thoughts on this topic have been somewhat reshaped in the last decade plus, I've tried to think how I would feel if a homosexual man who weighed twice as much as I did said the identical thing to me as I walked by.

Would I find it funny? Charming? Acceptable?

Or would I find it offensive? Threatening? Angering?

I think we can all agree as heterosexual men that having a homosexual man who owned a clear physical power imbalance over us making sexually suggestive comments toward us after lustfully undressing us mentally as we walked by would make us terribly uncomfortable at best. As such, we should have enough empathy toward women to not put them in a position that we would strongly dislike being in ourselves.

With this premise in mind, I must confess that I'm so incredibly frustrated and saddened by the non-empathetic words that spill out of some white people's mouths when the subject of racism in America comes up.

"I never enslaved anyone."

"Slavery was a long time ago."

"Get over it."

If we as American white people strived toward greater collective empathy, we'd keep in mind that had we (we meaning white people in our late 30's/early 40's) been born black, our MOTHERS would have been disallowed from using the indoor restrooms on family road trips. Our MOTHERS would have been forced to use the restroom in the woods, like an animal, because the hostile and bigoted gas station attendant would not allow little black girls to use the indoor toilet like the rest of the human beings. Every black friend I have who is around my age has a MOTHER who was systematically discriminated against and treated like crap for no reason other than her skin color. And yet millions of white people callously demand that black people should fully forget and forgive the way our country treated their MOTHERS. Inexplicably, millions of white people brush aside this damn recent family history as somehow irrelevant and expect black people to just "get over it". That's just such a mean and ignorant and absurd and non-empathetic way for us as white people to feel about black people, because there's NO WAY I could or would cheerfully or quickly absolve a society that had consistently and deliberately and systematically treated my MOTHER like shit. What about you?

Now, let me address what some people are thinking: "Yeah, Peter whatever the hell your last name is, you just admitted our whole argument- their MOTHERS were abused, NOT them, which is why THEY should get over it!!"

Please understand that I mention their mothers' experiences instead of theirs because even the deeply and hatefully and totally racist white people now admit there was widespread abuse of black people in America prior to 1965, whereas millions of white people in America largely deny or dispute that racial abuse against black people continues into the current day, so in a chapter on empathy, it makes a lot more sense to focus on supporting points that are not disputed factually in order to drive the main point home.

Additionally, please do not take my citing an example of racial abuse and animosity from the historical past as any sort of tacit admission that racial abuse and animosity exist only in the past. Please consider my friend Craig Brownson's perspective here, as he is the real life White Shadow, a white high school basketball coach with a nearly all-black team (of kids who were born and grew up in the 2000's):

This has been bothering me for at least a week...what is it about young black males that is so threatening? And what does it say about our society that this is almost universally accepted?

Why is it so hard for white America to understand the fear and paranoia of many blacks when dealing with police and the criminal justice system, when their parents and grandparents have seen these things happen for decades?

I grew up in upper middle class white America and am so thankful I have been blessed to teach and coach young people of all races for the last 19 years because coaching hundreds of young black males gave me a perspective and an empathy my upbringing never could.

These young black men are wonderful, caring, and joyful. They treat my wife like their mom and they treat my kids like their little brothers. Some of them have had upbringings that are less than ideal, parents who aren't home because they are always working, empty refrigerators and electricity that's been cut off. They don't complain about these things, they don't act like victims because this is their life and they own it. And I could never understand these things growing up in Midland, Texas, because I never experienced it.

I guess I am asking for more empathy, the thing that this world needs more than anything. It's not natural to our society, it doesn't fit in with a society that is based on competition above everything else. But it is something sorely needed to heal the wounds of the black community.

I hope that Craig's call to empathize is heeded, or at least considered. As a general rule of thumb, expert counsel should be adhered to, unless the advice receiver also has expert qualifications on the subject at hand. However, even if the advice receiver is an expert on the subject, wise experts at least consider the counsel of fellow experts. To reiterate a key point from Craig's thoughts, he has (or has had) literally hundreds of close relationships with black people. If you do not also have literally hundreds of close relationships with black people, you should adhere to Crag's call for more empathy out of respect for his expertise on the subject. However, even if you do match Craig's experience in this area, you should still at least consider his call for empathy, as that is what sensible fellow experts do.

For a long time, I have felt like most white people don't even try to see things from the perspective of a black person. The OJ verdict was probably the first time I noticed this, as a racist white cop unconstitutionally scaled OJ's fence, planted the glove, lied about it, got caught, got asked about calling black people "niggers", lied about it, got caught, and yet practically no white people could wrap their heads around how the black jurors possibly could have bought into a police conspiracy. Yes, OJ did it, and believe me when I tell you that nearly all black people think he did it as well, but the state can't prove that beyond a reasonable doubt when an overzealous and racist moron mucks things up the way Mark Furman did. If you look at the case from an empathetic lens, it would be totally unreasonable for any American black person not to have at least a degree of reasonable doubt, given Mark Furman's idiotic and racist behavior that largely validated the main thrust of the defense's theory.

Another aspect of the OJ trial that highlighted the lack of white racial empathy involved not only the white reaction to the verdict, but the white reaction to the black reaction to the verdict.

"Those animals are celebrating that a murderer went free!!"

But those sorts of remarks missed the point completely. The truth is that black people were celebrating the promise of the American justice system, as black people had been watching guilty white people go free based on "reasonable" doubt for centuries, especially when the victim was black and the suspect was rich. The OJ trial showed black people on a national level, for the very first time, that America had evolved into a nation where a guilty black man could go free based on "reasonable" doubt, too, even when the victims were white. As such, black people's celebrations of the OJ verdict had nothing to do with supporting OJ or condoning his heinous crimes. In fact, the black reaction to the OJ verdict had absolutely nothing to do with OJ at all, and everything to do with a partial validation of their deep and abiding hope and faith in the promise of America, that all men are created equal and will one day be treated as equals in the eyes of the law. The OJ verdict showed black people that a rich black man and a rich white man could be the same in the eyes of the law, and after everything black people had seen happen within the criminal justice system previously, it was cause for celebration and continued hope because, after all, if a rich black man can be treated equally, maybe one day all black people will be treated equally (it should also be noted that hundreds of thousands if not millions of black people were outraged by the OJ verdict; they just weren't the black people the media chose to plaster all over television screens).

I'd also like to share what my old friend Jamaal Moore had to say during the time that the University of Missouri's football team was threatening to boycott playing games due to the unaddressed racial issues that had been occurring on Missouri's campus, as it offers an additional reliable personal testimonial to suggest that racism does in fact persist into the current era of American life:

I LOVE MY STATE (Missouri)! You can take me out of the state, but you can't take the state out of me.

However, the same state that I love to death is the same state where I can remember at least three times on my bike being called the N-word by grown men from the back of a pick-up. I can name four times being called the n-word by other children while also riding my bike.

I can remember being at a party, and having a grown man yelling, "I'm going to shoot the next n-word I see" and then cocking the gun and firing and me and my friends running as fast as we could to our cars and praying we made it home safe.

I can name a time of getting our tires slashed in a little small town and calling the police and the police officer telling us "we shouldn't be there anyway" before refusing to offer any assistance.

My point is this, from my experiences, where there's smoke, there is usually fire, so let's try to understand each other better so the flame doesn't engulf us all. There are documented events that led these kids to boycott. Instead of being distracted by focusing all our attention on the end results and by casting blame on who's right or wrong, let's focus on the issues/events that led to these students to feel the need to voice their concerns. Understanding the cause of their concern is much more important than analyzing the effects of them. There in lies the growth opportunity for us as a state and as a country.

Racially empathetic American white people feel devastated reading Jamaal's words. American Racial Fencesitters (ARF's) or Racial Doubting Thomases (RDT's) read Jamaal's words and want more information and data and context out of a reflexive tendency to view accounts such as these with skepticism. And outright racists feel anger flushing through their faces when they read Jamaal's words and think to themselves, "Toughen up!! Everyone has mean words said to them!! This is the problem with the black community- they're so busy dwelling on perceived racial slights and accusing everyone of being a racist that they value a grievance culture over a success culture and a victimhood culture over a personal responsibility culture!!"

If you fall into either of the second two categories of American white people, and Jamaal's words either made you doubtful, or half-curious (half-curious means that you expressed or felt curiosity, but not enough to actually do the work to find out more information), please ask yourself why you feel the reflexive need to question the veracity of Jamaal's recollections from his childhood. Do you normally view stories from people's childhoods with suspicion? Or only the stories that make you uncomfortable? Or only when the story teller is black? Or what? There must be a reason why you "need more information" and it's probably the same reason why you don't typically actually then spend the time to find more information, which is readily available.

If, on the other hand, Jamaal's story made you feel angry, or condescending, or defensive, please consider the difference between white racism-related anger and black racism-related anger. White people get angry about discussions of racism, and wish conversations about racism (and the race agitators who engage in these discussions) would just go away, whereas black people get angry about actual racism, and wish that actual systemic racism would just go away (criminal justice, banking, real estate, education, etc).

Whose anger is more justified? Whose cause is more important? Whose priorities are more just? Whose heart is more in the right place?

If a white person wants to get angry about "reverse" racism, such as Affirmative Action, fine. I get it. Affirmative Action doesn't make me angry, but I do think it's flagrantly unconstitutional, as the 14th Amendment requires equal protection under the law, and Affirmative Action provides extra protection under the law, which by definition isn't equal (more on this later, but we should note right here that Affirmative Action was enacted into law by a Democrat-controlled white Congress and a Republican white President, so being pissed off at black people about Affirmative Action is a total misplacement of blame).

And I can understand why a white person might be angry about white-on-black (or society-on-black) racism, because I'm angry about it. The combination of seeing the huge number of black people who get hurt by racism while hearing so many white people deny that racism exists "anymore" does tend to make me furious.

However, the far more common brand of anger that white-on-black racism inspires in white people relates to how white people react when someone else tries to point out an example of racism or even have any sort of discussion on the topic of race in America. Honestly, there is no greater "tell" about what's inside a person's heart on this topic than when they react angrily or agitatedly, not about racism itself, but because someone else shared an opinion about racism that made them uncomfortable. In my experiences, only overt racists react this way.

If you fall into this category, I want you to please earnestly try to imagine the following conditions:

You are 10 years old.

You own a red bicycle that you ride around your town.

Your family has always ridden red bicycles, and although you're not sure why, you've noticed and your parents and grandparents have warned you that some of the people in the town have open hostility to people who ride red bicycles and a very small percentage of the people who don't like red bicycle riders have even harmed or killed red bicycle riders.

On three separate occasions when you were a **child** riding around on your red bicycle, different groups of grown men in pickup trucks threatened you and harassed you for no reason other than your red bicycle.

How would you have felt?

Do you think those instances might stick with you?

Even if you think they would not have stuck with you, do you recognize that traumatic childhood events do have at least some lasting effect into adulthood for most human beings?

Would you have quit riding the red bicycle? I sure as hell would have!!

The simple truth is that we as American white people should accept that Jamaal's stories are real, as virtually all American black people have very personal stories that mirror or at least resemble Jamaal's. And unlike the red bicycle riders, who could have chosen to quit riding the red bicycles, black people can't quit being black, so we should therefore have enough empathy to be pissed off at the right people when we hear these kinds of stories. In other words, if Jamaal's words are going to make us angry, they should make us angry at the hostile racists who harassed him periodically (but repeatedly) throughout his life, and if Jamaal's words are going to make us defensive, we should be defending Jamaal.

Unfortunately, too many white people get very defensively upset when the subject of racism against black people in America comes up without being even remotely upset about the subject itself. This occurs in some cases because the emotional and defensive white person thinks that racism against black people no longer exists or may even have adopted the victimhood mentality by incorrectly (and absurdly) asserting that the "real racism" in America today is against white people. However, what's most frustrating is that most white people do at least sort of recognize that we have not totally successfully stamped out anti-black racism in our country, while **still** getting upset about anti-black racism only in the context of defensively arguing against black people and white allies who point out that we have race-relations-related work left to do. We need empathetic ears and hearts, not defensive mouths and brains, and I certainly believe that the time has come for all Americans to listen to the cries of American black people with eager ears and open minds. Black people aren't making excuses and making things up- they're sharing real stories from deep inside their broken hearts, and we should view the broken-hearted with empathy, not derision.

Changing gears a bit, let me admit that despite being raised as a Christian, I am not much of one. Ever since a Christian preacher presiding over one of my best friend's funerals shared his belief that my friend was going to burn in hell forever because he took his own life, I haven't made a whole lot of time for the church.

However, I don't like it (at all) when essentially Godless liberals throw arbitrary (and often out of context) Bible verses into the faces of conservative Christians as a way to exalt themselves as being morally (and intellectually) superior and insult conservatives as being a bunch of hypocritical morons.

However, as I kept re-reading this chapter, something was missing. I just didn't feel my call for empathy was being worded convincingly enough, so I decided to Google "quotes on empathy", and I accidentally discovered pages and pages of Biblical quotes on this subject. As I started to read them, I began to cry, and as I found The Bible's thoughts on this topic to be profound, persuading, and deeply moving, I wanted to share them with you.

1st Peter 3:8

Finally, all of you, have unity of mind, sympathy, brotherly love, a tender heart, and a humble mind.

Ephisians 4:29

Let no corrupting talk come out of your mouths, but only such as is good for building up, as fits the occasion, that it may give grace to those who hear.

Ephesians 4:32

Be kind to one another, tenderhearted, forgiving one another, as God in Christ forgave you.

Romans 12:15

Weep with those who weep.

1st Corinthians 12:26

If one member suffers, all suffer together.

Colossians 3:12

Put on then, as God's chosen ones, holy and beloved, compassionate hearts, kindness, humility, gentleness, and patience.

Galatians 6:2

Bear one another's burdens, and so fulfill the law of Christ.

Hebrews 13:3

Remember those who are in prison, as though in prison with them, and those who are mistreated, since you also are in the body.

Proverbs 21:13

Whoever closes his ear to the cry of the poor will himself call out and not be answered.

Mark 12:31

You shall love your neighbor as yourself.

Isaiah 66:13

As one whom his mother comforts, so I will comfort you; you shall be comforted in Jerusalem.

Psalms 34:18

The LORD is near to the brokenhearted and saves the crushed in spirit.

Romans 15:1

We who are strong have an obligation to bear with the failings of the weak, and not to please ourselves.

James 2:1-26

My brothers, show no partiality as you hold the faith in our Lord Jesus Christ, the Lord of glory. For if a man wearing a gold ring and fine clothing comes into your assembly, and a poor man in shabby clothing also comes in, and if you pay attention to the one who wears the fine clothing and say, "You sit here in a good place," while you say to the poor man, "You stand over there," or, "Sit down at my feet," have you not then made distinctions among yourselves and become judges with evil thoughts? Listen, my beloved brothers, has not God chosen those who are poor in the world to be rich in faith and heirs of the kingdom, which he has promised to those who love him?

1st Thessalonians 5:11

Therefore encourage one another and build one another up, just as you are doing.

Please understand that I am not using Bible verses to imply that American Christians are "the problem". I think I've been very clear throughout this book that I think virtually all Americans are racist in one way or another, not just Christians, but Jews, Muslims, Hindus, Buddhists, Agnostics, Atheists, and all the other religions and non-religions not mentioned here. Also, I am not trying to use The Bible as a cheap stunt to manipulate people, which should be obvious based on the admissions I've already made about my lack of expertise on the subject of Christianity (IE, someone who intends to use The Bible to manipulate wouldn't typically begin by admitting to being a largely non-practicing "Christian"). Rather, I am quoting The Bible in this chapter simply because it has so much to say on the topic of empathy, and because it calls for empathy in a deeply moving and convincing manner.

The bottom line is a very simple one- American black people deserve our empathy, not our scorn. However, it's important in my view for all Americans to work harder to establish an empathetic view toward our fellow Americans, not just white Americans who exhibit a lack of compassion toward black Americans.

For example, many people (myself included at times) express broad frustration toward the police without earnestly trying to think what life must be like as a police officer. FBI Director James Comey said it well:

Police officers on patrol in our nation's cities often work in environments where a hugely disproportionate percentage of street crime is committed by young men of color. Something happens to people of good will working in that environment.

And my friend Aisha Crumbine largely echoed Director Comey's sentiments:

Police officers encounter the worst of us on a regular basis. From domestic violence calls to gruesome murders, the police are always the first on the scene. Their job is essentially manning the trash and putting their lives on the line in the process. And what do they get in exchange for this? Gratitude? Hefty paychecks? No.

Considering what they have to deal with, it's not unreasonable for police officers to become jaded. Just like garbage workers who can never wash the stench from their clothes, officers often find it hard to rid themselves of the filth they encounter. So when something goes wrong, like it did for Eric Garner, officers and the people who understand them best, prosecutors, stand together. Even if it means leaving a chasm of hurt and pain in their wake, they do what every surviving species does- they stand together.

On a personal level, my anger toward the police in general stems from their broad collective refusal to cooperate with an investigation into one of their fellow officers, even when they know that the officer in question behaved illegally or immorally or both. However, while the Blue Wall of Silence will infuriate me until the day it finally crumbles because the police took a solemn oath to uphold the law, and that oath did not include their assumed and deeply hypocritical self-exemption, I must recognize that the moral code of not ratting on your friends is enormously human, and it is in fact one that I live by personally, which means that my feelings on this topic toward the police are not only thoroughly non-empathetic, but every bit as hypocritical as I just accused them of being, so I too need to seek greater understanding and more empathy.

I also believe that American black people should try to empathize more with American white people on the topic of race relations. For example, I am a racist, but I certainly didn't choose to be one. In fact, I have tried quite hard to unchoose being a racist, with only limited success. I view myself as being brainwashed, not evil, and I think I need empathy from black people, and direct help from black people in the form of conversations to set me right and help me to understand. I do not need scorn. I do not need to be told, "you don't understand" seemingly without recognizing the whole truth of your own words, as not understanding something should not and does not imply maliciousness. People who have been brainwashed are victims, not monsters, and American white people for about the last 30 or 40 years have been doubly brainwashed, as it is terribly confusing to live in a country that simultaneously tells us that black people suck but racism is wrong.

When I have shared these sentiments in person to a black person's face, it has rarely received a receptive audience. However, I do believe with all my heart that it's fundamentally unconvincing to ask for something that you are not interested in reciprocating. This principle applies very broadly, not just to race relations, as General Patton was famously known for being unwilling to send his troops into a situation that he would not venture into himself, and I think that's a useful lesson for the countless brave American black people who continually step up into leadership roles regarding race relations: personally embodying the behavior you wish to see in others moves the needle most effectively because an audience is always most receptive to a given message when the person delivering the message is themselves personally un-reproachable on the subject at hand.

I am going to let the legendary Steven R. Covey have (almost) the last word here:

When you show deep empathy toward others, their defensive energy goes down, and positive energy replaces it. That's when you can get more creative in solving problems.

Race relations in America has been an intractable problem thus far, but if we would truly strive for empathy toward each other as Americans, we could quit being defensive and disagreeable and hypocritical and finally work together toward a lasting solution.

NOTE: I hope this is already clear by now, but I am not and do not blame American black people for white racism or for white people lacking empathy toward black people- I blame American white people for that. But I do blame American black people for their racism toward white people, and for their lack of empathy toward white people.

NOTE 2: This must be clear by this point in the book, but just to say it again, I do not at all think that white-on-black racism and black-on-white racism should be discussed on an equal footing, because the actual damage done by white-on-black racism exceeds the damage done by black-on-white racism by infinity fold.

CHAPTER 7

HISTORY

There is no reason to read this chapter as an indictment of America. I have never and would never do that, and I don't like people who do. That having been said, it is not unpatriotic at all to criticize your nation. I agree with my old friend Matt Henry, that too many people think we are supposed to love our country as a small child loves a parent, with a blind devotion that sees literally zero flaws, whereas Matt and I think that we should love our country as a parent loves a child, with total devotion while constantly encouraging and criticizing and pushing and prodding and doing whatever it takes to make sure that we see consistent excellence **and** constant improvement.

To the extent that this chapter criticizes, rather than reports, the condemnation applies much more to our politicians and our patricians, and much less to our nation or to us the American people as a whole. As such, please do not allow yourself to become defensive as we present and discuss some historical facts and context, some of which will be new information to you, but some of which will also directly contradict what you've previously been taught to believe.

Slavery ended in 1865 with the ratification of the 13th Amendment to the United States Constitution. But for the next 100 years, overt discrimination against black people continued through the Jim Crow laws that created segregation in the South and the various housing and banking practices that largely prohibited minority home ownership in Northern cities like Chicago and New York.

Nobody disputes this history. And yet many people seemingly continue to believe that racism against black people ceased to exist as a major problem in America at the legislative conclusion of the Civil Rights Movement in 1965.

We also see, on a fairly regular basis, that some Americans look at the statistics of current black poverty and can not help but wonder if there isn't some cultural issue or a lack of collective work ethic or intelligence that keeps black people poor. After all, slavery was a long time ago.

However, please consider that the abolitionist movement existed since the birth of our nation. Legendary Founding Fathers like John Adams and Ben Franklin were staunch abolitionists, for example. From 1775 until 1865, the growing and ever more diverse abolitionist movement worked and eventually won their fight, as slavery ended. But we know from the next century of agreed upon historical record that the end of the abolitionist movement did not mean the end of black people's struggles in this country. Ask yourself this question- if we all agree that the Civil War wasn't able to create an equal or fair America for black people, as we all recognize that it failed to do so for at least the next century, how is it that so many people have successfully convinced themselves that a couple of federal laws in 1964 and 1965 instantly created total equality for American black people? Have you ever known another example where a new federal regulation instantly and permanently solved what had previously been an intractable problem for centuries?

It is truly ironic for anti-government Americans, who will not stop talking about the utter incompetence of the federal government, to inexplicably assume that the Civil Rights era federal legislation was so perfectly drafted and flawlessly implemented that it immediately ended racism in the United States of America. It is also ironic that people on the political right are eager to point out that people on the political left are the "real racists" because they promote the "plantation mentality" with all the promises of "free stuff", while those same exact right-leaning people generally tend to dispute that racism remains a major issue in the modern era. I just don't know how so many people can make the claim that left-wing politicians are currently and aggressively engaged in a racist conspiracy to keep the black man down, while at the same time denying that racism continues to be a serious problem in this country. You can't simultaneously argue that half the country is purposefully screwing black people while also arguing that black people aren't being screwed.

Of course racism persists, and of course the past effects the present. Think about history's current impact on a very basic level- does past family wealth, especially land ownership, impact current family wealth? If the answer is yes, which we know it is (at least in many cases), then of course past financial and educational discrimination will continue to play a role in current levels of poverty.

The numbers presented in a 2013 study conducted by a group of Brandeis professors very much confirm this self-evident reality, as they found that 36% of white families benefit from some level of inheritance compared with 7% of black families. Furthermore, the study discovered that white families inherited an average of 10 times more than black families, which should also not be surprising if we are willing to connect history.

Perhaps no single legislative package in US history better exemplifies the extent to which our racial past effects our racial present quite like the legendary post-World-War-II GI Bill. By offering educational assistance, job training and placement, plus guarantees on home mortgage loans, a consensus amongst historians and economists has developed that the GI Bill largely created, or at least substantially expanded, the American middle class.

Technically, the GI Bill was race-neutral. So, the issue wasn't the Bill itself, but rather the implementation. For example, in the American South, black veterans had a hard time finding a college that would accept them due to segregation in higher education (and most other things). In the American North, on the other hand, while nearly all institutions of higher learning would at least admit black students, the vast majority of them observed a strict cap of black students they were willing to accept (in 1946, for example, far-left liberal icon UPENN had 46 black students out of a total body of 9000-http://www.nytimes.com/2005/08/28/books/review/when-affirmative-action-was-white-uncivil-rights.html).

Problems were nevertheless worse in the South, though, as 94% of public expenditures in higher education went toward colleges and universities that could not by state law accept black students. The black schools had always understood creative problem solving and they knew how to stretch a dollar, but with 6% of the public money coming their way and not a single bank willing to lend them money, how on earth could these schools have been expected to finance the land purchases and the on-campus residential construction that would have been necessary in order to accommodate the boom of black students now able to afford tuition thanks to the provisions of the GI Bill?

It is also important to understand that the GI Bill had massive racial inequality with far-reaching consequences in its implementation across the board, not just regarding the educational provisions. For example, a government study from October 1946 examined the GI Bill's job placement provision's implementation in Mississippi and discovered that 86% of the higher-waged skilled and semi-skilled jobs had gone to white veterans, with 92% of the lower-waged unskilled jobs going to black veterans (keep in mind that the GI Bill applied only to veterans, which means that 100% of the black veterans being forced into unskilled jobs were not in fact unskilled, just in case you were wanting to explain away this study by assuming, with no evidence, that a lack of skills amongst the black job seekers caused this outrageous discrepancy- again, we know that 100% of US Armed Services veterans have "skills"). Also, historian Ira Katznelson looked at the GI-Bill-backed home mortgages in New York and New Jersey and discovered that of the first 67,000 government-backed mortgages that NY/NJ banks issued, fewer than 100 went to black veterans (http://www.nytimes.com/2005/08/28/books/review/when-affirmative-action-was-white-uncivil-rights.html).

As a reference point, in case you are the classic RDT (Racial Doubting Thomas), New York City alone was home to more than 450,000 black people in 1940, so please don't allow yourself to wonder if the problem may have been related to an overall lack of black people in those 2 states at that time. Particularly on Long Island and in Queens, the US government-backed mortgages for veterans led to an unparalleled home construction boom and a sharp spike in the home ownership rates, but the banks wouldn't lend black veterans money to become home owners, even though the loan was guaranteed by the United States Treasury. The government provided the banks with every investor's dream- real upside and literally zero risk- and the banks, to the point of being systemic, overwhelmingly refused to issue the federally-backed loans to black veterans who had just risked their lives for their country. The banks were essentially being offered a chance to gamble with casino house money, and their nearly universal reaction was, "Sounds good, but there better not be any niggers in the casinos."

It is hard to fully understand the total frustrations black veterans must have felt after serving patriotically during World War II only to return home to find themselves largely locked out of the universally made but selectively kept government promises. The government said "we will help pay for your college education" and "we will help you find a job" and "we will help you become a homeowner for the first time" without establishing any guidelines or provisions whatsoever requiring the (white) people actually in charge of administering the programs to keep the promises to black veterans.

So, we know that the GI Bill created an entire generation of college-educated, home-owning Americans while in practice largely excluding American black people from fully participating in those benefits. As should be intuitively understood, if your parents owned a home and graduated from college, the odds spike substantially that you will also be a college-educated home owner. This is why it should not be a controversial notion that historical discrimination carries with it lasting effects into current situations (by the way, I know of no American black people who are angry about slavery- my black friends are angry about the racist bullshit they and their immediate family members have been forced to endure in their own lives).

If you look at the historical life trajectories of living in America as a never-ending race, we all know that white people were allowed to begin the race 200 years ago while black people were forced to wait in the blocks at the starting line until (at least) 1965. We as white people must stop congratulating ourselves for being ahead while deriding black people for being behind, as if somehow having a 200-year head start has had zero impact on how far we are currently out in front (on average). After all, white people weren't voluntarily hanging around the starting line just because black people were forced to- we were, of course, in many cases, out there busting our ass and getting ahead and living the American Dream. And the thing is, because nearly all of us belong to families, this never-ending race is in fact a relay race, which means that we all get handed the baton from our parents and begin our leg of the never-ending race wherever they left off. Many white families fucked up the 200-year head start, and many black families have recently made up the gap and surpassed some or even many white families. However, on average, we know that American white people have been benefiting from inherited property ownership for centuries, while black people really weren't even allowed to own homes on a large scale until the 1970's, which means the first generation of black home owners hasn't even died yet, resulting in the obvious fact that the first wave of mass black inheritance hasn't yet occurred; and as we know the impact of inheritance on comparative white wealth, we should not pretend as if the systematic denial of black wealth accumulation, which by definition has prevented black inheritance, somehow managed to have absolutely no effect on the current economic condition of American black people.

I suppose one of the reasons we struggle to connect history is because we misunderstand history in the first place.

One of the central historical facts that many American white people dispute is the cause(s) of the American Civil War. There still seem to be a whole bunch of revisionist "historians" out there who feel compelled to convince themselves that The Civil War was primarily about something other than slavery, citing alternative theories ranging from tariffs to states' rights to Northern aggression. However, we are very fortunate in this case that we don't need to guess what was actually on the minds of the Southerners who made the decision to secede because they put their reasons in writing by way of their formal declarations of secession. For example, here is the exact verbiage of the actual notice of secession by South Carolina (the subsequent notices of secession do not differ substantially from South Carolina's- we are citing theirs because they were the first state to secede):

The people of the State of South Carolina, in Convention assembled, on the 26th day of April, A.D., 1852, declared that the frequent violations of the Constitution of the United States, by the Federal Government, and its encroachments upon the reserved rights of the States, fully justified this State in then withdrawing from the Federal Union; but in deference to the opinions and wishes of the other __slave__holding States, she forbore at that time to exercise this right. Since that time, these encroachments have continued to increase, and further forbearance ceases to be a virtue.

And now the State of South Carolina having resumed her separate and equal place among nations, deems it due to herself, to the remaining United States of America, and to the nations of the world, that she should declare the immediate causes which have led to this act.

In the year 1765, that portion of the British Empire embracing Great Britain, undertook to make laws for the government of that portion composed of the thirteen American Colonies. A struggle for the right of self-government ensued, which resulted, on the 4th of July, 1776, in a Declaration, by the Colonies, "that they are, and of right ought to be, FREE AND INDEPENDENT STATES; and that, as free and independent States, they have full power to levy war, conclude peace, contract alliances, establish commerce, and to do all other acts and things which independent States may of right do."

They further solemnly declared that whenever any "form of government becomes destructive of the ends for which it was established, it is the right of the people to alter or abolish it, and to institute a new government." Deeming the Government of Great Britain to have become destructive of these ends, they declared that the Colonies "are absolved from all allegiance to the British Crown, and that all political connection between them and the State of Great Britain is, and ought to be, totally dissolved."

In pursuance of this Declaration of Independence, each of the thirteen States proceeded to exercise its separate sovereignty; adopted for itself a Constitution, and appointed officers for the administration of government in all its departments-- Legislative, Executive and Judicial. For purposes of defense, they united their arms and their counsels; and, in 1778, they entered into a League known as the Articles of Confederation, whereby they agreed to entrust the administration of their external relations to a common agent, known as the Congress of the United States, expressly declaring, in the first Article "that each State retains its sovereignty, freedom and independence, and every power, jurisdiction and right which is not, by this Confederation, expressly delegated to the United States in Congress assembled."

Under this Confederation the war of the Revolution was carried on, and on the 3rd of September, 1783, the contest ended, and a definite Treaty was signed by Great Britain, in which she acknowledged the independence of the Colonies in the following terms: "ARTICLE 1-- His Britannic Majesty acknowledges the said United States, viz: New Hampshire, Massachusetts Bay, Rhode Island and Providence Plantations, Connecticut, New York, New Jersey, Pennsylvania, Delaware, Maryland, Virginia, North Carolina, South Carolina and Georgia, to be FREE, SOVEREIGN AND INDEPENDENT STATES; that he treats with them as such; and for himself, his heirs and successors, relinquishes all claims to the government, propriety and territorial rights of the same and every part thereof."

Thus were established the two great principles asserted by the Colonies, namely: the right of a State to govern itself; and the right of a people to abolish a Government when it becomes destructive of the ends for which it was instituted. And concurrent with the establishment of these principles, was the fact that each Colony became and was recognized by the mother Country a FREE, SOVEREIGN AND INDEPENDENT STATE.

In 1787, Deputies were appointed by the States to revise the Articles of Confederation, and on 17th September, 1787, these Deputies recommended for the adoption of the States, the Articles of Union, known as the Constitution of the United States.

The parties to whom this Constitution was submitted, were the several sovereign States; they were to agree or disagree, and when nine of them agreed the compact was to take effect among those concurring; and the General Government, as the common agent, was then invested with their authority.

If only nine of the thirteen States had concurred, the other four would have remained as they then were-- separate, sovereign States, independent of any of the provisions of the Constitution. In fact, two of the States did not accede to the Constitution until long after it had gone into operation among the other eleven; and during that interval, they each exercised the functions of an independent nation.

By this Constitution, certain duties were imposed upon the several States, and the exercise of certain of their powers was restrained, which necessarily implied their continued existence as sovereign States. But to remove all doubt, an amendment was added, which declared that the powers not delegated to the United States by the Constitution, nor prohibited by it to the States, are reserved to the States, respectively, or to the people. On the 23d May , 1788, South Carolina, by a Convention of her People, passed an Ordinance assenting to this Constitution, and afterwards altered her own Constitution, to conform herself to the obligations she had undertaken.

Thus was established, by compact between the States, a Government with definite objects and powers, limited to the express words of the grant. This limitation left the whole remaining mass of power subject to the clause reserving it to the States or to the people, and rendered unnecessary any specification of reserved rights.

We hold that the Government thus established is subject to the two great principles asserted in the Declaration of Independence; and we hold further, that the mode of its formation subjects it to a third fundamental principle, namely: the law of compact. We maintain that in every compact between two or more parties, the obligation is mutual; that the failure of one of the contracting parties to perform a material part of the agreement, entirely releases the obligation of the other; and that where no arbiter is provided, each party is remitted to his own judgment to determine the fact of failure, with all its consequences.

In the present case, that fact is established with certainty. We assert that fourteen of the States have deliberately refused, for years past, to fulfill their constitutional obligations, and we refer to their own Statutes for the proof.

The Constitution of the United States, in its fourth Article, provides as follows: "No person held to service or labor in one State, under the laws thereof, escaping into another, shall, in consequence of any law or regulation therein, be discharged from such service or labor, but shall be delivered up, on claim of the party to whom such service or labor may be due."
*This stipulation was so material to the compact, that without it that compact would not have been made. The greater number of the contracting parties held **slaves**, and they had previously evinced their estimate of the value of such a stipulation by making it a condition in the Ordinance for the government of the territory ceded by Virginia, which now composes the States north of the Ohio River.*

The same article of the Constitution stipulates also for rendition by the several States of fugitives from justice from the other States.

*The General Government, as the common agent, passed laws to carry into effect these stipulations of the States. For many years these laws were executed. But an increasing hostility on the part of the non-**slave**holding States to the institution of **slave**ry, has led to a disregard of their obligations, and the laws of the General Government have ceased to effect the objects of the Constitution. The States of Maine, New Hampshire, Vermont, Massachusetts, Connecticut, Rhode Island, New York, Pennsylvania, Illinois, Indiana, Michigan, Wisconsin and Iowa, have enacted laws which either nullify the Acts of Congress or render useless any attempt to execute them. In many of these States the fugitive is discharged from service or labor claimed, and in none of them has the State Government complied with the stipulation made in the Constitution. The State of New Jersey, at an early day, passed a law in conformity with her constitutional obligation; but the current of anti-**slave**ry feeling has led her more recently to enact laws which render inoperative the remedies provided by her own law and by the laws of Congress. In the State of New York even the right of transit for a **slave** has been denied by her tribunals; and the States of Ohio and Iowa have* *refused to surrender to justice fugitives charged with murder, and with inciting servile insurrection in the State of Virginia. Thus the constituted compact has been deliberately broken and disregarded by the non-**slave**holding States, and the consequence follows that South Carolina is released from her obligation.*

The ends for which the Constitution was framed are declared by itself to be "to form a more perfect union, establish justice, insure domestic tranquility, provide for the common defence, promote the general welfare, and secure the blessings of liberty to ourselves and our posterity."

*These ends it endeavored to accomplish by a Federal Government, in which each State was recognized as an equal, and had separate control over its own institutions. The right of property in **slave**s was recognized by giving to free persons distinct political rights, by giving them the right to represent, and burthening them with direct taxes for three-fifths of their **slave**s; by authorizing the importation of **slave**s for twenty years; and by stipulating for the rendition of fugitives from labor.*

*We affirm that these ends for which this Government was instituted have been defeated, and the Government itself has been made destructive of them by the action of the non-**slave**holding States. Those States have assume the right of deciding upon the propriety of our domestic institutions; and have denied the rights of property established in fifteen of the States and recognized by the Constitution; they have denounced as sinful the institution of **slave**ry; they have permitted open establishment among them of societies, whose avowed object is to disturb the peace and to eloign the property of the citizens of other States. They have encouraged and assisted thousands of our **slave**s to leave their homes; and those who remain, have been incited by emissaries, books and pictures to servile insurrection.*

*For twenty-five years this agitation has been steadily increasing, until it has now secured to its aid the power of the common Government. Observing the forms of the Constitution, a sectional party has found within that Article establishing the Executive Department, the means of subverting the Constitution itself. A geographical line has been drawn across the Union, and all the States north of that line have united in the election of a man to the high office of President of the United States, whose opinions and purposes are hostile to **slave**ry. He is to be entrusted with the administration of the common Government, because he has* *declared that that "Government cannot endure permanently half **slave**, half free," and that the public mind must rest in the belief that **slave**ry is in the course of ultimate extinction.*

This sectional combination for the submersion of the Constitution, has been aided in some of the States by elevating to citizenship, persons who, by the supreme law of the land, are incapable of becoming citizens; and their votes have been used to inaugurate a new policy, hostile to the South, and destructive of its beliefs and safety.

*On the 4th day of March next, this party will take possession of the Government. It has announced that the South shall be excluded from the common territory, that the judicial tribunals shall be made sectional, and that a war must be waged against **slave**ry until it shall cease throughout the United States.*

*The guaranties of the Constitution will then no longer exist; the equal rights of the States will be lost. The **slave**holding States will no longer have the power of self-government, or self-protection, and the Federal Government will have become their enemy.*

Sectional interest and animosity will deepen the irritation, and all hope of remedy is rendered vain, by the fact that public opinion at the North has invested a great political error with the sanction of more erroneous religious belief.

We, therefore, the People of South Carolina, by our delegates in Convention assembled, appealing to the Supreme Judge of the world for the rectitude of our intentions, have solemnly declared that the Union heretofore existing between this State and the other States of North America, is dissolved, and that the State of South Carolina has resumed her position among the nations of the world, as a separate and independent State; with full power to levy war, conclude peace, contract alliances, establish commerce, and to do all other acts and things which independent States may of right do.

Adopted December 24, 1860

I am sensitive to the idea that many of us grew up being taught that the Civil War had "many causes" and that slavery "but one piece of the overall puzzle". In fact, I personally taught this idea to my students as a US History high school teacher in 1999, as that is the history I had learned growing up (is there a more effective propagandist than a nondeliberate one?). However, now that we have read the above secession document, we should have noticed that while it actually does discuss states' rights repeatedly, it also mentions a derivative of the word "slave" (slave, slaves, slave-holding states, slavery) 18 times in a fairly brief document. It mentions the word "tariff" 0 times, and it does not in fact mention any SPECIFIC states'-rights-based grievances whatsoever that are not slavery-related. So, let it be known once and for all that the only "state right" that South Carolina held so sacred as to justify secession in their minds was slavery, rendering preposterous the argument that The Civil War was chiefly about something other than slavery. Again, the people who actually made the decision to secede made it absolutely clear that a desire to continue owning slaves was their primary motive for secession, and that should be the end of the discussion (only Texas mentioned any specific issue other than slavery in a secession document- they also spelled out a grievance due to the Federal Government not doing enough to help Texans fight Comanches on the Western frontiers).

Consider this analogy:

Let's say a woman owns a bunch of dogs and loves them dearly, and she decides to author a book in which she exhaustively describes herself broadly as an "animal lover" but doesn't mention even one single animal in the whole book except for dogs.

Would you say that she is more of a dog lover or more of an animal lover?

I think she's pretty clearly a dog lover, and since slavery was the ONLY states' right mentioned in ANY of the secession documents, we can very safely and factually deduce that the Southern aristocracy were not generally states' rights lovers, they were specifically slavery lovers.

However, even given that we are fortunate to have primary-source, first-person historical documents regarding the specific motives of the people who seceded, many people nevertheless continue insisting that the Civil War was about something other than slavery, pointing out that Lincoln didn't issue the Emancipation Proclamation until the Civil War had been going on for 2 years or pointing to Lincoln's own words at the time in which he makes clear that preserving the Union was his initial goal, not ending slavery ("if I could preserve the union without freeing a single slave, I would do it").

Here's the thing- yes, it is true that Lincoln was a whole lot less interested in ending slavery than he was in preserving the Union (at least at first), and that's a very relevant historical point that often gets missed.

But why did the Union need to be preserved in the first place?

BECAUSE THE SOUTH SECEDED.

And why did the South secede?

BECAUSE OF SLAVERY.

Slavery begat secession and secession begat The Civil War, therefore slavery begat The Civil War.

To illustrate the point, let's say Jimmy steals a car and he gets caught and goes to trial and gets sentenced to prison. Did auto theft cause his incarceration, or did the trial cause his incarceration? Technically, I suppose it's both, but if we follow the normal logical train of thought looking at timelines and chains of events, it is the major event that occurs first in the timeline that should be seen as primarily causal, which means that Jimmy's decision to steal a car is what should be viewed as the main cause of his incarceration (oh my, how we tend to struggle with timelines, chains of events, and causation- substantially and regularly).

To the people who have previously believed and given voice to the notion that "the Civil War wasn't about slavery", kindly note that moving forward, now that you have been made aware of the relevant historical document that directly contradicts what you've unfortunately been misled to believe, please know that any future comments along these demonstrably false lines will fall less under the "misinformed" umbrella and more under the "dishonest" umbrella or the "racist" umbrella.

Another current issue that must be viewed in historical context involves the enormously common phenomenon of white people bringing up a black person who agrees with them as evidence of a lack of racism on the white person's part.

Allen West said the same thing I did. How can it be racist if a black person says it also? Is Allen West a racist, too?

This goes all the way back to slavery, as Malcolm X famously pointed out in his "House Negro, Field Negro" speech. There existed black slaves who were pro slavery. They wore tuxedos, lived in comfortable quarters indoors, and were to a very real extent treated like part of the family of the white master (except for that whole being a slave thing). These were the house negroes, and an extremely common aspect of a house negro's mentality was their eagerness to talk shit about the field negroes, especially when white people were around.

This phenomenon manifests itself even to this day. Most people assume that this issue persists due to deep self-loathing and a longing to be accepted by or be more like white people, and I certainly do see evidence of that (I thought Michelle Obama missed a great opportunity by continuing to iron her hair- Michelle Obama is gorgeous and brilliant and inspiring- and yes, I know I am flaunting my male privilege here because we as men don't have hair-related demands hurled at us by society our entire lives, but I stand by my point and I think it would have made a tangible difference for black women, many of whom would prefer not ironing their hair but are justifiably concerned about the effects of that decision in the job market).

But even though I do continue to see what looks like evidence of disproportionate self-loathing on the part of American black people (like a handsome and in-shape black man beaming with pride at the unattractive and chunky white woman by his side, something which almost never happens the other way around), sometimes I think the true motive isn't self-loathing but a decision to play the game a certain way. After all, if you're black, there is no better way to check yourself in with many white people than to speak ill of other black people. I would be willing to bet that at least some of the "house negroes" over the years, from slavery until today, were infected neither with self-loathing nor racism toward other black people, but in fact lived the way they lived and said the things they said and wrote the things they wrote based on a strategic choice to improve their own lives within the circumstances they found themselves in that were beyond their control. So even though I consider a black person who talks down on black people collectively to be a house negro, I am not a person who thinks all house negroes shared or share the identical motivations or personality traits.

Another way in which we see our history manifest itself into modern times is the issue of the Confederate flag. For starters, it should be noted that neither I nor anyone else can definitively say what the Confederate flag means to another person, so I can't say that everyone who honors that flag is a hateful racist. However, in the context of the recent controversy in South Carolina in the aftermath of the Dylan-Roof-perpetrated massacre, we did learn that South Carolina decided to fly the Confederate flag at the state capitol in 1961 as a very, very, very non-subtle response to the Supreme Court decision to desegregate the schools and the pending Civil Rights Movement, which means that we can reasonably deduce that the people who made the decision to fly the Confederate flag over the state capitol had race on their minds and racism in their hearts. And, as no one I know has suggested that we pass a federal law prohibiting the sale or display of the Confederate flag, which would be a clear 1st Amendment violation, the only relevant issue was whether or not the flag should come down in South Carolina. And considering that it was raised in the first place as a deliberate and cruel defense of white supremacy, continuing to display the flag on South Carolina's state capitol grounds was in no way defensible, which Nikki Haley ultimately recognized through her decision to take the Confederate flag down. Ask yourself this- would you buy into the "heritage, not hate" argument coming from a German with a swastika tattoo?

As we are on the topic of the Civil War, I also feel compelled to contradict the historical biases that cause many of us to think that racism was and is exclusively a Southern problem. This line of thinking glosses over some very cool history, like my great, great, great grandfather Captain Henry Schwethelm fighting for the Union army explicitly because he was an abolitionist but despite the fact that he lived in Texas, and it also obscures some very ugly history, as historical evidence utterly discredits the idea that discrimination against black people in America somehow existed (or exists) only in the South.

To illustrate this point, please consider the following historical facts:

In the infamous Dred Scott case, Chief Justice Robert B. Taney wrote the decision that prohibited black people from becoming citizens. Justice Taney was from Maryland, which fought on the Union side in the Civil War.

In the tragic Plessy v. Ferguson case, Justice Henry Brown wrote the majority opinion that legalized segregation. Justice Brown was from Massachusetts, which fought on the side of the Union in the Civil War.

In the famous Brown v. Topeka Board of Education case, Chief Justice Fred Vinson had stalled and constructed road blocks to stop the case from even proceeding, and it wasn't until his death and Eisenhower's appointment of Earl Warren that the case was heard and decided. Justice Vinson was from Kentucky, which fought on the side of the Union in the Civil War.

President Lyndon Baines Johnson personally shepherded the entire Civil Rights agenda through the US Congress. President Johnson was from Texas, which fought on the side of the Confederacy in the Civil War.

Because of cases like John Crawford and Tamir Rice in Ohio or Eric Garner and Sean Bell in New York (along with countless others), American black people have always known that racism is a national problem, not a regional problem, and it is high time that our media and our academic elites step up and admit the same. Again, we can't solve a problem that we tend to deny or marginalize, and thinking that racism is Alabama's problem but not California's problem prevents us from even trying to arrive at a comprehensive solution rather than a series of checkeredly effective and sometimes counter-productive partial solutions.

As we have previously discussed, in addition to misunderstanding facts, a lot of people don't understand the nature of "chain of events". We generally recognize that we as a nation have a history of treating black people horrifically unfairly in our criminal justice system, and many also recognize that this unfairness, while seemingly slightly better, is not just historical, but also very much ongoing (as, again, even the Mississippi Supreme Court recognized as recently as 2007 upon examining the available facts and evidence).

This historical and ongoing glaring unfairness DIRECTLY CAUSED the #BlackLivesMatter movement. The #BlackLivesMatter movement didn't happen arbitrarily in a vacuum. It happened as a DIRECT RESULT of how some of our law enforcement officials have treated black people and **gotten away with it scot-free**. So, to insinuate that the "dangerous rhetoric" caused the recent run of police officers tragically losing their lives in gutless ambush-style attacks, and to imply that people like me have blood on our hands for speaking out against police violence, just shows, again, how much we sometimes struggle to understand the nature of "chain of events". If anything, police misconduct and the blue wall of silence that protects racist and/or criminal cops caused these tragedies, making them classic cases of the chickens coming home to roost. However, personally, I don't buy into that at all- I think the murderers who pulled the triggers are to blame, not some racist criminal cop in Staten Island, and certainly not the #BlackLivesMatter movement as a whole. Again, if you're going to claim the BLM movement spawned the violence, you need to ask what spawned the BLM movement, or you're operating 100% illogically, as chains of events don't start in the middle. They just don't.

We also see this phenomenon of people struggling with timelines and chain of events and cause and effect surrounding the debate over rap music. Let's look at a little history here- in a nutshell, to handle the migrations of American black people from the rural South to the urban North, the federal governments under Roosevelt, Truman, Eisenhower, Kennedy, and Johnson built government housing to accommodate the massive influx of poor black people into our major metropolitan areas.

At first glance, this may look altruistic, but it was actually mostly done to control the location of the black people and enforce the de-facto segregation that existed in the North (as opposed to the sanctioned segregation of the South). In a nutshell, the government built low-cost housing to keep black people confined to certain areas only, in order to be better able to "keep an eye on them" (and keep an eye on them we did!!).

Of course, when you stack poverty on top of poverty, thereby producing the most concentrated pockets of poverty in American history, the results are fairly predictable, namely that the housing projects rather quickly become an undesirable place to live.

And this is where we again get into trouble with cause and effect and timelines. The government created areas with extremely high population density and overcrowding combined with universal poverty and racial segregation. These housing projects have been around since the 1930's, yet tons of white people want to blame rap music for having a destructive influence on "urban communities", despite the fact that rap music wasn't even around until 50 years after the modern urban ghettoes were created. As such, blaming rap music for urban conditions fails to consider a very basic truth, which is that urban poverty created rap music, not the other way around.

I also have found it to be astounding how many white people, including prominent white people like Rush Limbaugh and Alex Jones, seem to blame Barack Obama for racism in America, even though racism in American preceded Barack Obama's birth by hundreds of years. This common claim makes exactly as much sense as blaming Margaret Thatcher for the Bubonic Plague.

Now, some people will qualify their initial statement after I call them out, but their amended statement usually goes something like this:

"I'm not saying Barack Obama caused racism. I'm saying he made it worse. He could have been a uniter, but instead he was a divider."

To this, I ask- worse than what? Slavery? Jim Crow? Lynchings? Exactly how is racism worse today than ever before? And to the accusation that Barack Obama was a divider, I ask- when in our history do you think we have been racially united? Were we racially united during segregation? Or during George W. Bush's handling of Hurricane Katrina?

The truth is we have never been racially united as a country, but having a black President caused a bunch of previously oblivious white people to start thinking about our racial problems, often for the first time in their lives, and it made them uncomfortable and therefore hostile to the person they feel like made race a front and center issue (for the record, many if not most of my black friends are at least somewhat disappointed in Barack Obama for not making race a central enough issue, if that opens your eyes to how wide the gulf is dividing us racially).

Politicians also struggle mightily to understand chain of events and cause-and-effect. Rahm Emanuel's "leadership" in Chicago provides an excellent case study. Under Rahmbo's "leadership", if you can call it that, Chicago has closed 50 neighborhood schools since 2013, nearly all of them schools that served at-risk black and brown children. So, we take the least advantaged kids, and we close their schools, which increases burdens on parents and children, which leads to increased truancy and decreased academic performance, thus ultimately increasing academic hopelessness, then drop outs, then joblessness.

Not to mention, Chicago has always been a VERY neighborhood-by-neighborhood kind of city, where if you ask someone "where are you from?" they might say "Oak Park" rather than "Chicago". And these neighborhoods have developed a lot of complex rivalries that have often spilled over into inter-neighborhood violence since Chicago first became a large city, long before the "gangs" getting the most attention were comprised primarily of black and brown young people. So, not only did uprooting a bunch of kids from their neighborhood schools increase hopelessness then dropouts then joblessness while decreasing academic performance, but it also dramatically increased instances of youth violence, much of which has been driven by inter-neighborhood rather than inner-neighborhood feuds.

And what is Rahm Emanuel's "solution" to the violence we see in Chicago? Will he accept cause-and-effect responsibility, recognize that his policy of school consolidation to save money helped cause this and reopen the shuttered schools to rebuild them into the community pillars they had always been? Nope. Will he develop innovative economic policies to bring jobs to neighborhoods that have been devastated by the half-century decline in American manufacturing? Nope.

Instead, he will ratchet up military-style policing while throwing a few million bucks into a little pet program to teach young black and brown kids "morality", as if that's the problem. And, he is pushing for tougher sentencing laws for possession of "illegal" firearms, when I thought the 2nd Amendment already covered this issue- seriously, how on earth is the NRA not going bananas when municipalities try to strip American citizens of their right to bear arms? It is probably the same reason the NRA didn't flip out over the Mumford Act in 1967 when Governor Reagan signed the repeal of California's open-carry laws due to Black Panthers exercising their rights by carrying rifles during their neighborhood "copwatching" patrols. Truly, it often seems to me like the people who consider themselves to be the staunchest 2nd Amendment advocates don't think the 2nd Amendment should equally apply to you if you're black, or brown, or Muslim, etc.

Basically, Rahm's plan is to arrest way more black and brown people and incarcerate them for a way longer period of time, for the "crime" of bearing arms, which is a protected right, not a crime.

But, hey, his political mentor is Bill Clinton, so I guess we shouldn't be too surprised, as Nixon started the War on Drugs, Reagan escalated it, but Clinton perfected it; and we all know the War on Drugs quickly but predictably became a War on Black People, something that should have already been abundantly clear to Clinton statistically by the time he signed his now infamous 1994 crime bill.

So, I would like to take this opportunity to thank Rahm Emanuel for reminding all of us that being a racist moron is decidedly not restricted to members of the Republican Party. Way to go!!

Moving forward, I really wish that American white people would collectively stipulate that historical prejudice has a legitimate lasting effect on modern race-based inequality, as it would go a long way toward building an America that affords equal opportunities and makes us all equally proud.

Let's say you meet a person whose father lost his life in the terrorist attacks of September 11, 2001, and you discover that he harbors resentment against radical jihadists, or even has suspicion toward Muslims broadly, based on what happened to his father. Is this understandable?

Or, you might meet a man whose friend died in the Vietnam War, only to learn that he too feels lingering hostility and resentment toward the Russians and the Vietnamese. Is this understandable?

I think in both cases, many if not most people would recognize that both men with broad feelings of suspicion toward those particular groups of people are not wholly unreasonable people. In other words, we collectively admit that a historical fact that harmed a person can have legitimate lasting effects on the friends and relatives of that person.

Yet, when it comes to race relations in America, too many people experience a total disconnect on the simple idea that when a group of people has harmed your friends and relatives, that history affects your psyche and world view regarding that group of people. In the "modern" era, no one disputes that our history as a nation has been horrendously discriminatory toward American black people, but black people are supposed to universally and instantly forgive and forget? We don't ask that of any other group of people.

Basically, when a black person has feelings of suspicion toward police officers and other individual personifications of white power structures, those feelings are not baseless. For at least the past 10 years, I've been reminding myself that white racism directed at black people has no rational or historical basis, whereas black racism directed at white people is neither irrational nor historically baseless (note that understandable and acceptable are not synonyms, and I am not at all OK with black racists).

It truly is astounding to consider how many people admit to past racism, yet so many of those same folks mostly seem convinced that this egregious prejudice stopped on a dime and halted completely in 1965. For example, we know that J. Edgar Hoover unconstitutionally harassed and threatened Martin Luther King, JR in 1964, but you would have me believe that Hoover was a staunch ally of Dr. King by 1966 because of a new package of federal laws? I suppose that I am willing to accept the possibility that a miraculous overnight change of heart did occur within some white people, as long as you are willing to accept the possibility that this miraculous overnight change of heart could not possibly have occurred universally in all white people. After all, as James Baldwin correctly noted, "People's attitudes don't change because the law changes (https://www.youtube.com/watch?v=3Wht4NSf7E4)" and you can also see that clearly in many other aspects of American life. Did the Roe vs. Wade Supreme Court decision make all pro-life Americans instantly become pro-choice? Can you think of any example where a US federal law or Supreme Court ruling immediately reversed the opinions and attitudes of the people who had opposed the change in question?

Systemic prejudice has never stopped on a dime in any society in the world in our entire human history; rather, it reduces very slowly over time, if it reduces at all. Are women totally equal in the US since they achieved suffrage? Did the allied victory in World War II permanently end anti-Semitism in Germany? Did the Emancipation Proclamation make things totally equal for black people because it abolished slavery? Has homophobia and discrimination against gay people ended completely because of the recent Supreme Court ruling on marriage equality? While we have largely stopped portraying American Indians insultingly in movies, have we stopped stealing their land and their natural resources? It's just such a historically preposterous view to admit to long-standing and egregious racism and bias over the course of the first 90% of our history but to also think that the problem has somehow magically and totally disappeared within the most recent 10% of our history.

CHAPTER 8

GROUP BLAME AND STEREOTYPES

When former Louisiana Congressman Bill Jefferson got caught with $50,000 cash in his freezer, most white people (and quite a few black people) on both the left and right made it about race.

Many liberals cried, "What has happened to the state of black leadership in this country? Oh, how I long for the days of Martin Luther King and Ralph David Abernathy!"

And many conservatives gnashed their teeth and said, "You SEE- *these people* are incapable of playing by the rules!"

When former Speaker of the House Tom Delay got caught committing a lot more than $50,000 worth of impropriety, on the other hand, people made it about politics, not race.

Most liberals gleefully gushed (and group blamed based on partisanship), "What a shocker- we told you that Republicans are under the covers with big business and this is what happens!"

And most conservatives demurred (and group blamed based on general distrust of politicians), "Typical politician. Total scumbag. Can't trust 'em."

I know what some of you are thinking- but Tom Delay's behavior had nothing to do with his race. I agree completely, but neither did Bill Jefferson's, and that's the point. Linking behavior with race is what a racist does, and it's neither fair emotionally nor logical deductively. Bill Jefferson and Tom Delay are thieving shitheads as individual human beings, and you just can't reasonably believe that Bill Jefferson stole because he is black unless you're also going to believe that Tom Delay stole because he is white.

Seriously, think about it- does anyone actually believe that political corruption is a race-based problem? Did Tom Delay, Rod Blagoyavich, Richard Nixon, and Lyndon Johnson make the politics-based criminal choices they made because they are white? I certainly don't think so, and it's equally illogical to think that Bill Jefferson's skin color dictated his criminality.

Too many white people just don't give black people a fair shake. None of the Fox News folks have ever associated any white criminal with his (or her) race. Not one time. But when a black person behaves badly, it always sounds like, "what a shame black people can't get their shit together" even though there is a neverending historical and current avalanche of information on white people behaving badly also (there is of course also a neverending avalanche of historical and current information on black and white people behaving well and doing wonderful things- but that doesn't seem to drive ratings). A person who behaves badly should be called out as a person. Race has not one damn thing to do with it. A black murderer didn't commit murder because he's black- he committed murder because he's an asshole (or a lunatic). Same with a white murderer.

It upsets and discourages me when I encounter white people who can not believe or accept this simple truth and who seem to almost believe that black people have a monopoly on bad behavior. The basic reality is that no race has a monopoly on good or bad behavior, and consequently, no individual's choices and behavior should be seen as a reflection of their race overall.

That having been said, I can still remember as a kid, maybe seven years old, the time I witnessed a black woman go nuts on a Burger King employee who screwed up her order. I've seen lots of people get inappropriately pissed off in lots of situations, yet I remember that black lady from more than 30 years ago like it was yesterday.

This can be explained by "Confirmation Bias"; IE, this was the first time I had ever encountered a black person acting like an idiot, yet that one instance stuck with me forever because that is the image I had already been trained to expect. Remember, I was already laughing at and probably even telling nigger jokes by this time, so I had already formed negative opinions of black people fueled by age-old stereotypes before I had ever encountered a black person who actually lived up to even one of the negative stereotypes that I had already been brainwashed into believing.

Additionally, I will never forget going to a small town in Texas with one of my college roommates, and attending a field party. Being a snotty city slicker, I had been making fun of "trailer park trash" country white people with the classic, stereotype-based line, "only three things to do in a small town- drink, fight, and fuck!!" for basically as long as I could remember. Well, wouldn't you know it, everyone was piss drunk and two real fist fights broke out and multiple (like at least five) couples kept disappearing into the bushes to get down and dirty. I remember sarcastically but rather gloatfully thinking to myself, "what a shocker!!", despite the fact that I had spent time in small towns at least a dozen times previously without witnessing any of the stereotypical behavior I saw that night at the field party.

Here's the truth, and this point has been repeatedly stated and will be reiterated, but we as human beings tend to remember and pay attention to experiences that reinforce stereotypes way more than we remember and pay attention to experiences that contradict stereotypes.

With this in mind, let's take a deep dive and thoughtfully examine the "big four" negative stereotypes about black people, especially black men, that white folks have widely believed since the days of slavery: Violent, Stupid, Lazy, and Sex Crazed.

Violent

We tend to view black people as being violent, so let's do a brief historical race-by-race comparison of the most violent people in known human history in order to see how well this stereotype holds up.

Black

Ugandan dictator Idi Amin tortured and killed between 300,000 and 500,000 people during his time in power.

Nigerian dictator Yakubu Gowon killed 1.1 million civilians, mostly through a blockade that led to mass starvation.

Ethiopian dictator Mengistu Haile Mariam murdered between 400,000 and 1.5 million people through his Red Terror campaign.

<u>White</u>

King Leopold of Belgium killed around 10 million civilians through his forced labor camps and mass executions in the Congo.

Jo Stalin murdered or deliberately starved to death between 6 million and 23 million Soviet civilians.

Adolph Hitler killed between 11 million and 17 million civilians.

<u>East Asian*</u>

Japanese Emperor Hirohito was responsible for around 6 million civilian deaths.

Genghis Khan murdered between 20 and 50 million people, including an astonishing 700,000 in a single day (and we thought Chicago was bad in the Summer of 2016).

Mao Zedong was responsible for the deaths of between 50 million and 70 million civilians.

*Chang Kai-Shek also killed around 10 million people, but I could not find any sort of breakdown between enemy combatant deaths versus civilian deaths.

<u>South Asian/Arab</u>

Saddam Hussein is said to have murdered around 2 million civilians, highlighted by his notorious attempt at Kurdish genocide.

Pakistani dictator Yahya Khan killed between 2 and 12 million civilians, highlighted by the genocide in Bangladesh.

Ottoman military leader Ismail Enver Pasha is largely held responsible for the Armenian genocide and other atrocities that claimed about 2.5 million lives.

<u>Latino</u>

As much as we hear about awful Caribbean and Central American and South American dictators such as Chile's Augusto Pinochet, Cuba's Fidel Castro, and so on, they seem to have killed fewer than 1 million civilians combined (as none of the Latin American dictators made any of the most bloodthirsty tyrant lists, specific data on this topic is difficult to ascertain).

I also Googled the list of history's worst serial killers to further investigate the stereotype of black people being inherently more violent than other racial groups (thereby presumably placing myself on dozens of government watch lists). Globally, we are aware of 145 serial killers with more than 10 confirmed victims. Of this group, 71 were white people of European descent, 27 were black people of African descent, 18 were East Asian, 16 were Hispanic, and 13 were South Asian or Arab.

If we look at world demographics, the world has around 750 million white people of European descent and about 970 million black people of African descent living amongst a global population of around 7.5 billion. So, while white people make up around 10% of the world's population, we account for 49% of the double-digit-victim serial killers. Black people, on the other hand, make up around 13% of the world's population, while accounting for roughly 18.5% of the double-digit-victim serial killers.

It is also noteworthy that the Aryan Brotherhood accounts for less than 1% of the prison population but commits roughly 30% of the murders that take place inside our penitentiaries. Call me crazy, but my speculation is that this ultra-violent gang of thugs is largely comprised of people who aren't black.

I know what many of you are thinking.

"YOU'RE CHERRY PICKING STATS!! THE NUMBERS DON'T LIE!! BLACK PEOPLE COMMIT WAY MORE MURDERS THAN WHITE PEOPLE!!"

Yes, it is true that according to 2015 FBI homicide statistics, black people committed 5620 murders, while white people committed 4636 murders. This means that when examined based on proportional US population, black people in America were 623% more likely to commit homicide than white people in America in 2015.

Although in many cases I dispute the methodologies and law enforcement/criminal justice practices that produce the "crime stats" (as you know from previous chapters), I don't dispute this math, especially on homicide, which is by far the hardest statistic to skew, although we do radically and chronically under-report deaths caused by police officers, some of which should have been ruled homicides but were not. However, the 623% disparity between the black and white American civilians homicide rate is true- black people do commit homicide in the US at a grossly disproportionate rate.

That having been said, it is very important to ask **why** so many white people memorize and recite the "600% more likely to commit murder" stat. Other than social lepers, human beings do not randomly cite facts without a purpose. To attempt to uncover the why, here's a sample conversation I've had 100 times with white people who bring up this stat:

PBS: Why did you just feel the need to highlight that statistic?

Random White Person: Because it's true.

PBS: Yes, it is. I agree. But many statistics are true. **WHY** did you cite this one?

RWP: Because we're talking about race.

PBS: Yes, we are. But there are so many statistics about race that you could have highlighted- **WHY** did you choose this stat?

RWP: I can cite whatever stats I want to.

PBS: No doubt. Do you think black people are more violent than white people?

RWP: Absolutely, the stats clearly show that.

PBS: OK, now we're getting somewhere. So, it's not racism, it's realism?

RWP: Damn right.

PBS: OK. So you believe that race drives individual behavior, but you don't consider yourself to be a racist?

RWP: I didn't say that.

PBS: You just said that black people are more violent than white people. You just said that.

RWP: They are!

PBS: Yes, so let me finally answer my own question of **why** you reflexively regurgitated this particular statistic. You are attempting to pull off a magical mental trick of denying racism's existence by arguing that disproportional criminality rather than racism drives disproportional incarceration, while at the same time justifying racism by asserting that black people are inherently more violent and therefore deserving of extra scrutiny from the police. Now let me ask you one more question: why would you feel the need to deny something you justify, or justify something you deny?

The white people I've engaged with on this topic have one helluva time answering my questions, instead mostly just getting angry and lashing out at me, but additionally, if we're willing to listen to and trust stats that correlate homicide with race, we should also be willing to listen to and trust the violence-related stats that I presented earlier in this chapter, as they paint a clear picture that human violence throughout history is not currently and never has been a "black" problem. Additionally, please also be willing to pay attention to the information below, as it provides valuable supplemental illumination as well as context regarding the violent crime rates in the US.

For starters, the 2008 Bureau of Justice Statistics annual report concluded that white criminals are slightly more likely to harm black victims than black criminals are likely to harm white victims. According to Table 42, Percent Distribution of Single-Offender Victimizations, by Type of Crime, Race of Victim, and Race of Offender, 15.9% of black violent crime victims were harmed by a white person, compared with 15.4% of white violent crime victims who were harmed by a black person. That gap is negligible, but it does cast serious doubt on the notion that black-on-white violence deserves as much attention as it receives while highlighting the reality that violent crime in America overwhelmingly features a victim and an offender who are the same race (https://www.bjs.gov/content/pub/pdf/cvus08.pdf).

Additionally, since the time of Aristotle, many learned people have understood that as a general rule of thumb, "poverty is the parent of crime". Literally thousands of studies globally over the last 100 years have shown a strong correlation between poverty and crime. For example, a World Bank study concluded, "Crime rates and inequality are positively correlated within countries and, particularly, between countries, and this correlation reflects causation from inequality to crime rates, even after controlling for other crime determinants."

Unfortunately and frustratingly, our government does not keep any crime stats whatsoever regarding social class status or income levels of offenders, nor do we keep stats showing any sort of relationship between race, social class, and crime. As such, we know how many white men committed a homicide, and we know how many black men committed a homicide, but we are left, for the most part, to guess about the social class or relative wealth of the offenders.

Fortunately, we do have at least some information about the pre-incarceration income of prison inmates, as the Bureau of Justice conducted a report on poverty and incarceration in 2004 (incredibly, this was apparently the last year they released this information). If you agree that Aristotle was a pretty bright guy, you won't be surprised to see a huge gap between the pre-incarceration income of inmates by race compared to the income of non-incarcerated Americans by race. Specifically, black prisoners had a pre-incarceration median income of $17,625 compared with a median income of $31,425 for non-incarcerated American black people, while white prisoners had a pre-incarceration median income of $21,975 compared with a median income of $47,505 for non-incarcerated American white people. Frustratingly, this 2004 study is the only government report I could find that looked at the relationship between race, poverty, and crime, rather than only two of the three, but it clearly shows:

A) There is a STRONG connection between poverty and crime, which means that the disproportionate rate of violent crime committed by black people should be expected, not because of race, but because of disproportionate black poverty.

B) Black poverty is invariably measurably worse and harder than white poverty, as incoming white prisoners had a 24.6% higher median pre-incarceration income than incoming black prisoners.

Also, the famous Ohio State University study that investigated this topic helps illuminate the intersection between all three factors (poverty, race, and crime). According to Krivo and Peterson (the study's authors), violent crime in poor white neighborhoods was very similar to violent crime in poor black neighborhoods in terms of incidents per 1000 residents (20/1000 in the poor white neighborhoods and 22/1000 in the poor black neighborhoods). Although 22/1000 means that even when controlling for poverty, this study found that poor black people in Columbus committed violent crime at a 10% higher rate than poor white people, 10% is of course a far cry from oft-cited 623% homicide rate disparity (the authors of the study attribute the slight difference to the fact that the poor white neighborhoods in Columbus were surrounded by middle class neighborhoods compared with the poor black neighborhoods which were more isolated and therefore less integrated in terms of social class, although they don't offer data to support this secondary theory).

We also have good data from a 2014 Bureau of Justice report that examined the relationship between poverty, crime, and race, but they only looked at crime victims by the three key factors in conjunction with each other. For some reason, they did not give us any data about criminal offenders broken down by all three factors. However, because we do know that the overwhelming majority of violent crime is intra-racial rather than inter-racial, we can reasonably assume that the vast majority of the victims portrayed below were harmed by someone of their own race. As such, while these stats aren't exactly the type of stats I was hoping to find, they are nevertheless quite informative. Key findings include:

Broken down by race, poor white people and poor black people have similar violent crime victimization rates (46.4/1000 for poor white people versus 43.4/1000 for poor black people).

Although we tend to believe that the urban poor are more dangerous than the rural poor, actual violent crime victimization rates hold fairly steady, with poor people living in urban areas coming in slightly higher than poor people living in rural areas (43.9/1000 versus 38.8/1000).

When comparing the violent crime victimization rates of poor urban black people with poor urban white people, the results again hold quite steady, with poor urban black people reporting a slightly lower rate than poor urban white people (51.3/1000 versus 56.4/1000).

This study also serves to largely confirm what Aristotle knew intuitively thousands of years ago- whether black or white, urban or rural, poor people are over-represented in violent crime and the victimization rates hold quite steady across all racial and geographic groups.

It also makes sense to delve into black poverty a little bit here as well.

For starters, according to the 2016 Henry J. Kaiser Family Foundation annual report, 24% of black people are poor, compared with 9% of white people.

We also know from the 2014 Bureau of Justice report referenced above that regardless of race, the violent crime victimization rate was more than twice as much for low-income people (39.8/1000) as for high-income people (16.9/1000).

As such, it's very logical to connect black people's disproportionate violent criminality with their disproportionate poverty, and there's very clearly a connection, as this chapter has already shown, but I want to also delve into relative poverty density as well, because I think that's an under-explored source of a lot of the problems we see in our "urban" communities of color.

To understand the phenomenon of the extraordinary levels of poverty density in urban communities of color, we need to go back in time and remember that politicians had a serious problem on their hands in the 1930's as millions of Southern black people said "enough" and decided to pack up and move to the "enlightened" North. However, the demand for housing radically outpaced the supply, as all those enlightened Yankees overwhelmingly flat refused to rent or sell housing to a nigger (the stereotype that racism is the South's problem drives me crazier; random fun fact on this topic: in 2016, San Antonio, in the heart of the "awful right wing redneck paradise" that I damn proudly call home, had the smallest black-white unemployment gap in the country, while Milwaukee, pretty much about as far away geographically from the South as a major American city could be, had the largest black-white unemployment gap in the country). Anyway, from the perspective of the politicians in the 1930's, inaction was leading to mass homelessness and squatters' camps, which was really pissing off the white people who were going to determine their political futures. However, a just action, requiring landlords and property owners to rent and sell on a non-discriminatory basis, would have integrated neighborhoods and REALLY pissed off the white people who were going to determine their political futures. As we know, their "solution" was to build high-rise public housing projects on previously vacant tracts of land, which resulted in the highest concentration of poverty that our nation had ever known.

These decisions from yesteryear, combined with the anti-black bias that has existed and continues to exist in the housing sector, have led to a fixed status of black poverty being substantially more concentrated than white poverty (according to an Economic Policy Institute review of the Annie E. Casey Foundation's 2012 "Kids Count" report, 45% of poor black children live in neighborhoods with concentrated poverty compared with 12% of poor white children).

So, we know that black people are 2.7 times more likely to live in poverty, and we know that black children are 3.75 times more likely to live in concentrated poverty than white children. Add these 2 numbers together, and you get a rough estimate of the disproportionate black-white poverty ratio of 6.45, which is remarkably similar to the disproportionate black-white homicide ratio of 6.23.

Why does poverty density matter? Ask yourself a basic question, would you feel safer if two or three desperate and dangerous poverty-stricken criminals lived within a 1000 yard radius of your front door, or if 20 or 30 desperate and dangerous poverty-stricken criminals lived within a 1000 yard radius of your front door? Does this question even need an answer? OF COURSE poverty density plays a role in crime concentration and crime stats.

So, what does all of this mean? Two main take-a-ways:

One, looking at violence perpetuated by the various racial groups from an historical perspective, we as white people should shut our hypocritical mouths because we just don't have a leg to stand on trying to criticize any other race on this topic (NOTE: in case anyone is wanting to brush aside the Hitlers and Stalins of the world because they weren't American white people, let's remember that the genocide of more than 9 million

American Indians was perpetuated by American white people, as was slavery, which was not exactly a non-violent enterprise, and our government's behavior in our more recent wars has often left a lot to be desired as well, and so on).

Two, looking at modern-day violent criminal activity in America broken down by race, we see very clearly that the numerical gap between black and white doesn't hold up once we bother to dig deeper and analyze not just race but class and poverty as well.

In other words, this idea that black people are inherently disproportionately violent compared with other races doesn't withstand scrutiny. Sadly, it is a long-standing and widely believed misperception with harmful and often severe real world consequences for American black people- this is what happens when propaganda becomes cemented as facts, because it's an unfortunate truth that perception is reality.

Stupid

In addition to violent, we view black people as being stupid, as if Pamela Anderson is a rocket scientist. Really, all you have to do is watch Jerry Springer re-runs or read the Darwin Awards and you can not help but reach the conclusion that stupidity knows no color-based restrictions (additionally, way too many white people invariably describe a highly educated and/or intelligent black person as "arrogant" rather than "intelligent" anyway, making this an especially unshakeable stereotype).

However, white people who believe that black people are intellectually inferior love to point to the fabled "achievement gap" that exists on various standardized tests between American white people and American black people. But just as was the case with the stereotype of black violence, when you look a little deeper, you find controlling for important social class indicators such as poverty, level of education attained by the child's parent(s), number of books in the home, level of transience, duration of poverty (temporary, long-term, or generational), marital status of the biological parents, and level of class isolation, the "race-based" achievement gap dissipates sharply and in some cases disappears entirely.

First, let's establish firmly by the numbers that social class affects standardized test scores by taking a look at US children's results on three of the most important standardized tests, based on 2009 numbers, as that

is the most recent information I was able to find
(http://www.epi.org/files/2013/EPI-What-do-international-tests-really-
show-about-US-student-performance.pdf):

On the PISA (Programme for International Student Assessment), here's
how American children scored, broken down by class.

Reading Section

Lowest: 442

Lower Middle: 471

Middle: 504

Upper Middle: 529

Upper: 563

Math Section

Lowest: 434

Lower Middle: 464

Middle: 491

Upper Middle: 510

Upper: 548

On the TIMMS (Trends in International Math and Science Study), here's
how American children scored broken down by class.

Math Section

Lowest Class: 461

Lower Middle Class: 482

Middle Class: 515

Upper Middle: 538

Upper: 546

Obviously, these numbers reflect an important intuitive truth: upper class children score better than lower class children on standardized tests, regardless of race. However, as was the case with violence, we should also consider the possible effects of class isolation and poverty concentration. On this topic, the most recent National Center for Education Statistics report indicated that 45% of black children attend poor schools, compared with 8% of white children who attend poor schools, whereas 29% of white children attend affluent schools, compared with 7% of black children who attend affluent schools (https://nces.ed.gov/programs/coe/indicator_clb.asp).

Now that we have established that upper-class children do better on standardized tests than lower-class children, and that lower-class black children are more likely to be surrounded by other lower-class children at school, we need to conduct a brief history lesson on the education of American black people.

Black people, of course, started way behind educationally. In fact, by 1800, approximately 90% of white Americans could read, compared with about 10% of black slaves, who had achieved some level of education despite laws against teaching slaves to read. As this number ticked upward, a series of slave revolts led by educated black people caused the Southern aristocracy to enact a system of even more oppressive laws designed to prevent black people from learning to read and write, which means that black people entered the post-Civil-War era having made 0 net progress since 1800 with a literacy rate holding steady at 10%.

By 1870, however, Reconstruction laws passed under the political coalition of Southern "scalawags" (white Southerners who cooperated with Reconstruction) and freed black slaves had established taxpayer-funded public schools in every Southern state. Between around 1870 and 1900, Southern states spent roughly the same on each child's education, regardless of the child's race. During this 30 year period, the literacy rate of Southern black people skyrocketed from 10% to 50%, which includes all Southern black people, not just Southern black school children, for whom the literacy rate almost exactly matched the school attendance rate

(64% of school-aged black children could read, 65% of school-aged black children attended school).

However, as Southern white people with Confederacy sympathies regained political control of the Southern states in the late 1800's through the end of Reconstruction and the ensuing black disenfranchisement, equal funding for public schools collapsed. For example, in 1916, Georgia had 122 public four-year high schools for white children and 0 for black children. Mississippi, South Carolina, North Carolina, and Louisiana also provided 0 public high schools for black children, while Florida had exactly one. Additionally, by 1930, state funds in Alabama allocated for black school children was 11% of total state education expenditures, despite the fact that black school children accounted for 44% of all school children in the state. Meanwhile, over in Mississippi, black children accounted for 60% of total Mississippi school children in 1940, but received just 20% of state educational funds (https://www.unc.edu/courses/2006fall/educ/645/001/Anderson%20on%20Test%20Gap.pdf).

The gross inequality and horrid conditions of the public education available to black people (especially in the South) led eventually to the landmark Brown v. Topeka Board of Education case in 1954. This legendary Supreme Court decision did not by any means immediately make things fair or equal, but by the Civil Rights legislation of the mid 1960's, we were on the right track toward providing all American children (relatively) fair access to public education. Things still weren't really all that close to "equal" by 1965, but for the purpose of being able to draw a clean conclusion, let's assume that they were. So, assuming things were equal by the 1960's, this means that for more than 60 years (1900-1964), black children had been deliberately and systematically cheated out of equal funding and equal opportunities, resulting in white people having a 60+ year educational head start.

Now, let's look at the achievement gap.

NAEP Math Scores, Nine Year-Old's, 1973-2012

In 1973, nine year-old white children had a median score of 225 on the NAEP math section. In 2012, nine year-old white children had a median score of 252. This means that nine year-old white children showed a 12% improvement during the first 30 years of the NAEP. It also means that assuming the same projected 12% improvement rate, the next 30 years will see the score of white nine year-olds rise to a 282 on the NAEP math section by the year 2042.

In 1973, nine year-old black children had a median score of 190 on the NAEP math section. In 2012, nine year-old black children had a median score of 226. This means that nine year-old black children showed a 19% improvement during the first 30 years of the NAEP. It also means that assuming the same projected 19% improvement rate, the next 30 years will see the score of black nine year-olds rise to a 269 on the NAEP math section by the year 2042, which is only 4.6% lower than the projected score for white nine year-olds.

NAEP Math Section, 13 Year-Old's, 1973-2012

In 1973, 13 year-old white children had a median score of 274 on the NAEP math section. In 2012, 13 year-old white children had a median score of 293. This means that 13 year-old white children showed a 7% improvement during the first 30 years of the NAEP. It also means that assuming the same projected 7% improvement rate, the next 30 years will see the score of white 13 year-olds rise to a 314 on the NAEP math section by the year 2042.

In 1973, 13 year-old black children had a median score of 228 on the NAEP math section. In 2012, 13 year-old black children had a median score of 264. This means that 13 year-old black children showed a 16% improvement during the first 30 years of the NAEP. It also means that assuming the same projected 16% improvement rate, the next 30 years will see the score of black 13 year-olds rise to a 306 on the NAEP math section by the year 2042, which is only 2.5% lower than the projected score for white 13 year-olds.

NAEP Math Section, 17 Year-Old's, 1973-2012

In 1973, 17 year-old white children had a median score of 310 on the NAEP math section. In 2012, 17 year-old white children had a median score of 314. This means that 17 year-old white children showed a 1.3% improvement during the first 30 years of the NAEP. It also means that assuming the same projected 1.3% improvement rate, the next 30 years will see the score of white 17 year-olds rise to a 318 on the NAEP math section by the year 2042.

In 1973, 17 year-old black children had a median score of 270 on the NAEP math section. In 2012, 17 year-old black children had a median score of 288. This means that 17 year-old black children showed a 6.7% improvement during the first 30 years of the NAEP. It also means that assuming the same projected 6.7% improvement rate, the next 30 years will see the score of black 17 year-olds rise to a 307 on the NAEP math section by the year 2042, which is only 3.5% lower than the projected score for white 17 year-olds.

NAEP Reading Section, nine year-olds, 1971-2012

In 1971 (the NAEP reading section began two years before the NAEP math section), nine year-old white children had a median score of 214 on the NAEP reading section. In 2012, nine year-old white children had a median score of 229. This means that nine year-old white children showed a 7% improvement during the first 30 years of the NAEP. It also means that assuming the same projected 7% improvement rate, the next 30 years will see the score of white nine year-olds rise to a 245 on the NAEP reading section by the year 2042.

In 1971, nine year-old black children had a median score of 170 on the NAEP reading section. In 2012, nine year-old black children had a median score of 206. This means that nine year-old black children showed a 21% improvement during the first 30 years of the NAEP. It also means that assuming the same projected 21% improvement rate, the next 30 years will see the score of black nine year-olds rise to a 249 on the NAEP reading section by the year 2042, which is actually 1.6% **higher** than the projected score for white nine year-olds.

NAEP Reading Section, 13 Year-Olds, 1971-2012

In 1971, 13 year-old white children had a median score of 261 on the NAEP reading section. In 2012, 13 year-old white children had a median score of 270. This means that 13 year-old white children showed a 3.4% improvement during the first 30 years of the NAEP. It also means that assuming the same projected 3.4% improvement rate, the next 30 years will see the score of white 13 year-olds rise to a 279 on the NAEP reading section by the year 2042.

In 1971, 13 year-old black children had a median score of 222 on the NAEP reading section. In 2012, 13 year-old black children had a median score of 247. This means that 13 year-old black children showed a 11.3%

improvement during the first 30 years of the NAEP. It also means that assuming the same projected 11.3% improvement rate, the next 30 years will see the score of black 13 year-olds rise to a 275 on the NAEP reading section by the year 2042, which is only 1.4% lower than the projected score for white 13 year-olds.

NAEP Reading Section, 17 Year-Olds, 1971-2012

In 1971, 17 year-old white children had a median score of 291 on the NAEP reading section. In 2012, 17 year-old white children had a median score of 295. This means that 17 year-old white children showed a 1.4% improvement during the first 30 years of the NAEP. It also means that assuming the same projected 1.4% improvement rate, the next 30 years will see the score of white 17 year-olds rise to a 299 on the NAEP reading section by the year 2042.

In 1971, 17 year-old black children had a median score of 239 on the NAEP reading section. In 2012, 17 year-old black children had a median score of 269. This means that 17 year-old black children showed a 12.6% improvement during the first 30 years of the NAEP. It also means that assuming the same projected 12.6% improvement rate, the next 30 years will see the score of black 17 year-olds rise to a 303 on the NAEP reading section by the year 2042, which is actually 1.3% **higher** than the projected score for white 17 year-olds.

So, we know that white people had a 60 year head start educationally (really, it was much more than 60 years, but focusing on more recent history makes more sense because we have much better education data for the last 40 years than we have for the 40 years before that). However, as is the case with many other race-related topics, we struggle to connect history.

For example, there were so few public high schools in the 1950's that would accept black students that 2/3 of high-school-aged black adolescents did not even attend high school, much less graduate from high school. What this means, obviously, is that black school children in the 1960's and 1970's grew up in households with overwhelmingly uneducated parents.

Does anyone really think that a child's parents' level of education plays no role whatsoever in how that child enters and fares in the academic world? Come on, really?

The statistics also show that from the early 1970's to 2012, black children progressed on the six measured tests by an average rate of 14.4%, while white children progressed on the six measured tests by an average rate of 5.48%. So, if black children are stupid, why have they made so much more progress on the NAEP than white children? Yes, I am well aware that progress in any field gets exponentially harder each step you take: terrible to bad is easy, bad to below average is still relatively easy, below average to average is harder but readily attainable, average to above average is harder still, above average to good is damn hard, good to great is so hard that it's largely unattainable, and great to elite is almost impossible. As such, it makes total sense that black children would be making more progress based on their collective comparative starting point. However, all that having been said, if black children are stupid, how is it possible that they made any progress at all, not to mention nearly triple the progress of white children?

Speaking of progress, I want to again call your attention to the relative educational starting points for white children and black children. White people began properly funded primary and secondary public education en masse around 1870, but we'll call it 1900 since black people also had equally funded access to primary public schools from around 1870-1900 (as we've already discussed). Black people, on the other hand, were not permitted access to even remotely equal primary education or to any secondary education at all until 1960.

Now, I want to take a look at the test scores based on when each racial group was allowed to begin participating in American public education on a somewhat equal basis.

By the early 1970's, white people had been receiving quality and free public primary and secondary education for at least 70 years (1900-1970's). In 2012, black people had been receiving quality and free public primary and secondary education for about 50 years (1960-2012). So, let's take a look at the data on that basis.

After 70 years of educational access, white nine year-olds had a median NAEP math score of 225.

After 50 years of educational access, black nine year-olds had a median NAEP math score of 226, and I would like to point out that 226 is **higher** than 225.

After 70 years of educational access, white nine year-olds had a median NAEP reading score of 214.

After 50 years of educational access, black nine year-olds had a median NAEP reading score of 206, which means that the black score after 50 years was only 3.4% lower than the white score after 70 years.

After 70 years of educational access, white 13 year-olds had a median NAEP math score of 279.

After 50 years of educational access, black 13 year-olds had a median NAEP math score of 264, which means that the black score after 50 years was only 5.4% lower than the white score after 70 years.

After 70 years of educational access, white 13 year-olds had a median NAEP reading score of 261.

After 50 years of educational access, black 13 year-olds had a median NAEP reading score of 247, which means that the black score after 50 years was only 5.4% lower than the white score after 70 years.

After 70 years of educational access, white 17 year-olds had a median NAEP math score of 310.

After 50 years of educational access, black 17 year-olds had a median NAEP math score of 288, which means that the black score after 50 years was only 7% lower than the white score after 70 years.

After 70 years of educational access, white 17 year-olds had a median NAEP reading score of 291.

After 50 years of educational access, black 17 year-olds had a median NAEP reading score of 269, which means that the black score after 50 years was only 7.6% lower than the white score after 70 years.

Considering that we all acknowledge the deliberate educational access inequality that existed between 1900-1960, which means we recognize that white children and their families had a 60+ year educational head start, why, other than racism, would we assume that the current achievement gap is based on racial inferiority rather than a residual effect of the blatant unfairness that we all admit occurred? Now that we've seen clearly that there essentially is no achievement gap once we account for the relative educational access starting points for each race, I hope that we will collectively quit over-citing the achievement gap as a reason to deride black people, and I also hope we quit over-citing the achievement gap to drive education policy, because poor children (really all children) need and deserve a student-centered rather than a test-centered approach (but that is a topic for another book).

Lazy

We also view black people as lazy, which is richly ironic in America, considering our history on this subject. I mean, come on- are we really to believe that slaves were lazier than slave owners? Remember, it was common practice for affluent white mothers to be too "pre-occupied" to even bother to nurse their own children, instead preferring for their black slaves (and later nannies) to nurse the white children, but we are to believe that the black female slave (and later nanny) was the lazy one? I know, I know, the practice of black servants nursing white children is largely a thing of the past in America, however, this protestation misses the point entirely. You see, American white people derided black people for being lazy even during the era of slavery, and we as American white people continue to do so to this day, with no break between. Let that sink in for a moment, American white people. When you state or imply that black people are lazy, your comments mirror the comments of a slave owner. Literally. So it is way past time that we as American white people knock that shit off.

We're a little more subtle today than we were in the days of slavery. We no longer come right out and say, "niggers are lazy" like the "good ole days". However, what comes up time and again when I have a conversation about race with a financially stable white person is something along the lines of, "I worked hard for everything I have. No one gave me a damn thing!" which is an intensely clear implication that the "real" problem causing black inequality is a collective lack of work ethic in "the black community" (God, I hate that phrase). In other words, what you're *really* saying is, "niggers are lazy", because that's what you believe, because that's what you've been trained to believe. But it is still way past time that we as American white people knock that shit off.

I am tempted to move on to the next point, as something as blatantly racist as the "black people are lazy" narrative should not require any rebuttal. However, here is some data to consider on this absurd topic, simply because absurd people might be reading this.

For starters, based on an Economic Policy Institute study, when looking at the bottom 1/5 of wage earners broken down by race, the bottom 1/5 of black workers averages 1524 hours of work per year, compared with the bottom 1/5 of white workers, who averages 1445 hours of work per year. If poverty is caused by laziness, and being black causes laziness, how could it be possible that the poorest black people outwork the poorest white people by nearly 80 hours per year?

Furthermore, the same EPI study showed that black workers in the bottom 1/5, aka the poorest and therefore presumably the "laziest" people in America, increased their weekly hours by 2.3% between 1979 and 2015, compared with white workers in the bottom 1/5, who decreased their weekly hours by 2.1% over the same period.

Additionally, according to a 2012 report from the Center of Economic and Policy Research, 71% of long-term unemployed black men continued to look for work, compared with 61% of long-term unemployed white men. I'm not sure how anyone can mentally reconcile this data with the notion that black people collectively are lazier than white people.

The survey referenced above also renders ridiculous the common notion that the cause of disproportionate black unemployment (and poverty) is black laziness, as the stat clearly demonstrates that unemployed black people are in fact more willing than unemployed white people to put in the work to continue looking for a job even after enduring the despair of being a member of the long-term jobless community. The truth is not that black people are too lazy to seek employment, but rather that employers are disproportionately and racistly unwilling to hire black people.

Maybe that sounds harsh, but we all know about the infamous 2004 MIT study that sent out 2500 resumes for candidates with first names like John and Sally and 2500 resumes for identically qualified candidates with first names like Jerome and LaToya. The predictable results showed a horrendous bias against the Jeromes and LaToyas of the world when it came to receiving replies, call backs, and interviews.

Some have argued that the 2004 MIT results don't prove racism, but rather may prove classism, as a person with a stereotypically "ghetto" name did tend to grow up "in the ghetto" or at least have parents who grew up "in the ghetto". For the time being, let's accept that point of view (the whole "there are black people and there are niggers" thing, which is sadly all too commonly echoed by some American black people as well). Doesn't this theory totally debunk the idea that black people are inherently more lazy than white people? After all, the white-black unemployment gap is driven almost entirely by "ghetto" black people, and we just accepted that our society (including of course employers) discriminates against "ghetto" black people. So, if we admit that employers and the rest of us (of all colors) look down on black people from "the hood", thereby recognizing the strong likelihood that discrimination against "ghetto" black people plays at least some role in the difficulty this subset of American black people faces in the work force, why attribute the higher rate of black unemployment strictly to black laziness? We just stipulated that anti-ghetto bias likely plays a role in the high unemployment numbers in "urban" black neighborhoods, so there is no logical reason to then immediately turn around and ignore anti-ghetto bias as a factor in disproportional black unemployment in favor of scapegoating and categorizing and group blaming black people collectively as "lazy".

The bottom line is that we chastised black people for being lazy even when they were being forced at gunpoint to work for free, and we continue to chastise black people for being lazy, even though poor black people work longer hours for less money than poor white people, all of which collectively means that we as American white people really need to knock this shit off.

Sex Crazed

We view black people as being sexually depraved, despite the fact that American white people are on average over 98% European, whereas American black people are on average under 75% African. Given this number, it is quite clear that black women have substantially more justification to fear white men than the other way around, as contrary to popular fantasy, Thomas Jefferson didn't "wine and dine" Sally Hemmings.

As is the case with the laziness accusation, the sex-crazed allegation has been around since slavery, and is just as preposterously hypocritical, considering that in the slavery era, white men were chronically raping black women so often that 58% of present-day American black people have at least 12.5% European ancestry (https://en.wikipedia.org/wiki/African_Americans) compared with only 3.5% of present day American white people who have any traceable African ancestry whatsoever. Given this data, a white person deriding black people for sexual violence makes about as much sense as a homeless person deriding Bill Gates for being poor.

Additionally, it is also worth mentioning that rape has been used as an instrument of war since human beings began recording history, further evidence that sexual violence is by no means the sole prerogative of black people. Of course, most people can point to the horrific gang rapes in the most recent Rwandan Civil War, but very few people are aware of the massive amount of German women who were raped by the overwhelmingly white Allied troops immediately after the Nazi collapse. In fact, 1.4 million German women were raped, including at least 200,000 German women who were raped by American soldiers. Additionally, Emperor Hirohito allowed his soldiers to rape more than 200,000 ethnic Chinese during World War II. And, of course, you have Ghengis Khan, the Babe Ruth of rapists, who raped so many women that some estimates have ½ of 1% of all humanity being a descendent of the Mongolian marauder.

Presumably, some percentage of the 200,000 German women raped by American soldiers were raped by black soldiers. However, as only about 1,000,000 of the 16 million Americans who were allowed to serve in a combat role in World War II were black, we can safely assume that quite a few white American soldiers did quite a lot of raping as well. Additionally, the Soviet soldiers were responsible for raping well over 1,000,000 German women- are we to believe the ranks of Soviet troops were populated with a bunch of black people? Seems pretty far-fetched to me, to say the least. Same with Emperor Hirohito- it seems substantially probable that the majority of Japanese soldiers who committed all of the mass rapes more than likely weren't black.

So we see, once again, that a prominent long-standing negative stereotype about black people either applies fairly universally to all races or doesn't apply at all. Here's the thing, though- even if you're willing to ignore all the evidence and logic contained within this book up to this point, and nothing in this book so far has budged your position that black people are inferior, it is absolutely morally disgraceful for us as white people to hurl the same exact absurd, disproven, hypocritical, and racist garbage at black people that slave masters threw at slaves. You can of course think whatever you want, but please, for the good of America, shut your malicious mouth and keep your racism to yourself. Black people aren't the problem, you are, and if your destructive words could look in a mirror, they'd be looking at a slave master's words. We as white people should not and must not be OK with this.

A Final Note on Group Blame and Stereotypes

Since we're on the subject of stereotypes, I do so very sincerely wish that we as human beings would stop conforming to stereotypes about us, because of the damage that even a single example of stereotype confirmation can cause.

A black person can go months without seeing a single white person with a Confederate flag sticker on the back window of their truck, but what is the effect of that one white racist on the psyche of the black person when they see that image?

And a white person can go months or even years without encountering a single angry black man in person, but what is the effect of that one angry black man on the psyche of the white person?

Let me answer my own questions:

The black person is likely to think to themselves, "Even in 2017, same old shit. White people are never going to give us a chance."

And the white person is likely to think to themselves, "Gosh, that guy is out of control!! So typical!! What is wrong with *these people*?"

The problem in both of these scenarios is that the behavior had NOTHING to do with PEOPLE but rather with A PERSON. There's a MASSIVE DIFFERENCE between these 2 things.

The black person who saw the Confederate flag bumper sticker should never have thought or said anything about "white people" because that 1 white racist douchebag doesn't represent anyone but himself.

And the white person who encountered the "angry black man" should never have thought or said about "these (black) people" because that 1 belligerent asshole doesn't represent anyone but himself.

Before continuing, the next chapter will deal with rejecting false equivalency, but let me again state for the record that I don't view black-on-white racism as being anywhere even remotely comparable to white-on-black racism. Furthermore, black-on-white racism exists because of the way white society has treated black people for centuries, whereas white-on-black racism was and is in no way actually caused by the behavior of black people, despite what white racists keep telling themselves.

That having been reiterated, I have no problem asserting that we all have a role to play in solving America's foundational problem, and purposefully avoiding stereotype conformity is a productive step in the right direction. I don't blame black people for white racism, and while I believe that the primary responsibility for solving racism lies with white people, I do also know black people have played and will continue to play (and should continue to play) a role in lessening and hopefully one day eradicating white racism.

It upsets me when I see a white person promoting the Confederate flag, because I know that many if not most black people are going to blame white people broadly for that one asshole's bigotry, and I believe that the selfish decision of one white person to advertise their racism hurts all white people and America itself because of our collective tendency to engage in group blame.

And it upsets me when I encounter a largely unprovoked publicly belligerent black person, because I know that many if not most white people are going to blame black people broadly for that one idiot's behavior, and I believe that the selfish decision not to exercise public self-control hurts all black people and America itself because of our collective tendency to engage in group blame.

Moving forward, I can only once again implore all of us to keep in mind Dr. King's most important request, to judge one another as an individual by character rather than skin color. If we could all honor that simple principle of basic fairness, and consistently encourage others to do the same and call them out when they fall short, I earnestly believe we could largely solve our racial problems within a single generation.

CHAPTER 9

FALSE EQUIVALENCY

So far, we have already touched on False Equivalency, and its useless little bastard of a cousin Comparative Clemency, but they're important enough concepts to merit their own relatively brief chapter.

As we have mentioned several times before, the most common, and most egregious, example of race-related False Equivalency is the insistence that white-on-black racism and black-on-white racism should receive equal attention and be viewed as equal problems.

I have already stipulated, and will do so again, that black-on-white racism is a real thing, and it's absolutely 100% not OK. Furthermore, I'm not a supporter of Affirmative Action, because it provides extra protection rather than equal protection, which is a very clear 14th Amendment violation (my stance on the 14th Amendment is rigid and consistent- it's one of the main reasons I support full equality for gay Americans; it's also the reason why I think drug testing "welfare" recipients is a clear 14th Amendment violation unless we also drug test every single other person who receives a government check, very much including the CEO and CFO and Directors who receive corporate welfare; and so on).

That having been said, way too many white people give at least equal consideration to black-on-white racism as they do to white-on-black racism, IF they can bring themselves to admit that white-on-black racism even exists. This type of "thinking" makes no sense to me, since, as we have already mentioned before, the level of harm caused by white-on-black racism has been hugely and wildly disproportionate compared with the level of harm caused by black-on-white racism. The simple truth is that racist black people don't have enough money or power for their feelings to affect or hurt white people collectively or consistently in a tangible and meaningful way. As such, why should I, or anyone, equate these 2 types of racism?

Even-handedness is fantastic, IF, and only IF, the 2 subjects at hand are in fact even, or at least remotely comparable. But in the case of black-on-white versus white-on-black racism, even-handedness frustrates me substantially because the "equal and opposite" problems are so thoroughly and completely not "equal". It's as though people are wanting equal prison sentences for a thief who steals $5000 and a thief who steals $5,000,000, simply because both fall under the umbrella of "theft".

False Equivalency can take any form, and comparing the experiences of American black people to other minority groups in America provides another good (and common) example of a different sort of False Equivalency. A regular refrain goes like this:

The plight of the Chinese in 19th California was one of forced servitude, systemic racial discrimination, being labored until death, somewhat similar to the plight of blacks at the same time. 150 years later, the situation between Chinese-Americans and African-Americans is starkly different. Please explain to me why Chinese-Americans, without the benefit of White Privilege, were able to prosper.

I have no idea why so many white people like to make the African-American to Asian-American comparison, as if slavery and Jim Crow and lynching and redlining and school segregation and whitewashing of juries were burdens that were equally shared between the two minority groups. Sadly, this comparison is an extremely common one, often made by groups of people we should all disavow.

I'd also like to address some common talking points from white people who could be described as "moderate" or "middle of the road":

Both sides are at fault. Too many people put the blame on one side or the other.

If you're trying to decide who is right, you're wrong. Both sides can do better! Black and white people can both do better! It boggles my mind that anyone could see racism in America as a one-sided affair!

I'm the guy in the middle of the road. I want everyone to be better humans and to grow. It's not black or white people. It's not just authorities. It's every one of us.

I want to make a couple of points about the people who are "middle of the road" on the topic of racism in America.

For starters, we see glaring false equivalency with the "both sides" argument regarding law enforcement officials, as this narrative just doesn't make mathematical sense. For example, in 2016, 64 police officers were killed in the line of duty (http://edition.cnn.com/2016/08/14/us/police-officers-fatal-shooting-line-duty-nationwide/index.html). Obviously, that's 64 too many. However, there were AT LEAST 400 people killed by the police that same year, and that number is perhaps way off, as I've seen reports that it's as high as 1000 (https://www.washingtonpost.com/news/post-nation/wp/2014/09/08/how-many-police-shootings-a-year-no-one-knows/). So, if police officers are killing citizens at least 625% more than citizens are killing cops, why would I, or any person who understands math, give these 2 terrible and unfortunate realities equal attention?

Also, as my old friend and University of Houston professor Christal Seahorn once explained:

If I may, being "middle of the road" on this issue is something that I have heard from many people in direct conversation, Twitter exchanges, Facebook, and all. It is important to understand that this is a simplistic, fence-sitting position that disrespects the substantive disparities at work in the issue. Mathematically and logically, it frankly does not make sense to be in the middle of the road on an issue that is so clearly a representation of injustice. I would offer that one should be able to call the situation what it is, a broken and unjust system, without being "one-sided". Very few reasonable and intelligent people calling for changes to the justice system are being one-sided. They are, in fact, calling for a balance of fair treatment, a luxury that people who prefer not to acknowledge the disparity or try to split the difference likely already enjoy. To say that both law enforcement and members of the community have faults is acceptable but not particularly productive when one segment of that solution has such a disproportionate amount of power and formal training. Calling something that is patently unfair, unfair, is not being prejudicial, cop hating, or white hating. It is being willing to take an honest look at facts and examine hard truths about civic responsibility, profiling, social structure, etc. Fence sitting, quite seriously, is a position of luxury that some simply do not have and others have enough empathy and courage not to take. I am the family member of a police officer who was recently killed in the line of duty; I know very well the risks and sacrifices they make. But valuing law enforcement should not mean the system is above reproach. Recognizing that solutions are the responsibility of all involved is one thing, one that no one argues against, but being unwilling to acknowledge that what is going on is wrong and calling out the people who do so as prejudiced or one-sided is hiding from real engagement with the issue, not being middle of the road. Identifying injustice when it is present is not acting one-sidedly, it is the right, just, fair, and humane thing to do.

I must say, however, that although I do not disagree with anything that Christal wrote, I generally try to welcome middle of the road people and fence sitters. Don't get me wrong, I definitely believe that we have way too many ARF's (American Racial Fencesitters) in this country, but my assumption is that most ARF's had overtly racist parents, and my very hopeful assumption is that their children will be allies instead of fencesitters.

As we have already discussed, racism doesn't stop on a dime. Rather, it is a learned and constantly reinforced behavior. I suppose that as a white person, it's easy to welcome an ARF, but I know that the racial "progress" we've made as a nation hasn't been with American black people; American black people have always been, on average, equally capable of excelling in any position of leadership or any job (etc, etc, etc) as any other human being. The progress, rather, has been made by American white people (at a horrendously slow pace). So, while I encourage fencesitters to hop off that fence and transition to being an ally, I welcome them because I think they generally represent slow generational progress, and because I believe that they're doing the best they can with the information they've been misled to believe. So, even though I am going to continue to do my best to empathetically prod fencesitters, I do appreciate them for being kind enough not to be hostile.

Finally, I want to again touch on Comparative Clemency, the opposite (but not normally equal) problem that so often accompanies an allegation of False Equivalency, as it also causes substantial damage by eliminating self-reflection which pretty much eliminates self-improvement.

The most egregious example of Comparative Clemency involves many if not most white people's reactions to accusations of racism.

"A racist? David Duke is a racist, not me."

As we've touched on in the chapter on scale, and will touch on again, the level of David Duke's racism has absolutely nothing to do with anyone else's personal level of racism, so, moving forward, please accept criticism receptively rather than deflectively.

CHAPTER 10

DOUBLE STANDARDS

We all know that double standards exist (vocal little boys are seen as leaders, vocal little girls are seen as bossy, etc). In this chapter, we are going to focus on double standards that negatively affect American black people, and we are going to choose examples that place two things side-by-side that actually happened, rather than to place one actual thing that happened next to a hypothetical thing that did not happen, as it is of course so much easier to refute a hypothetical double standard rather than an actual double standard.

For example, Donald Trump made the infamous pussy grabbing comment, so a liberal might say, "Can you imagine if Barack Obama made that same comment? White people would have gone crazy. NO WAY he wins the election. Such a double standard!!"

However, while I happen to agree with the above hypothetical, I do not find it to be an effective example of the double standard phenomenon because the simple truth is that Barack Obama did not make any recorded pussy grabbing comments a few weeks before he was elected President for the first time, making it incredibly easy for your audience to dispute your train of thought.

As such, a much better example to cite about Donald Trump's sexual habits is to compare him to Herman Cain. If you recall, in 2012, Herman Cain was leading the polls in the Republican primaries. He was an un-politician, operating with a fresh approach and an unusual amount of candor. He was a successful businessman. He had a unique speaking style, and he was going to clean up the mess in DC because he was an outsider with the personal wealth to resist the allure of the lobbyist/deep state folks. In other words, Herman Cain was Donald Trump before Donald Trump, until the press revealed that Herman Cain had committed serial infidelity, and then he was finished, plummeting in the polls and dropping out of the race within three weeks of the allegations first surfacing. When looking at Donald Trump and Herman Cain side-by-side, they had basically everything in common except their political fates and their race, making it hard to pretend that their race wasn't inexorably tied to their respective political fates.

Here are some other side-by-side, race-based double standards to consider:

Perhaps the most tragic example of a side-by-side double standard involves 2 children and 2 pellet guns.

When I was a boy in Houston, I regularly walked the streets of my neighborhood with my pellet gun, looking for squirrels and birds and raccoons and possums to shoot (it was difficult, but not impossible, to kill a raccoon or possum with my pellet gun). On many occasions, police cruisers and neighborhood patrol officers would drive by, and literally not one time did any of them ever stop to ask me questions. In fact, most either didn't notice me at all, or would wave as they drove by, or would playfully make their thumb and index finger into a "gun" and "shoot" at me as if we were having some sort of "cops and robbers shootout".

When Tamir Rice was a boy in Cleveland, on the other hand, he was walking the streets of Cleveland with his pellet gun one day, and a cop car rolled up on him, and a police officer sprang from the car, and shot Tamir Rice to death, less than three seconds after arriving on the scene. Tamir Rice was 12 years old. He was a boy, just as I had been, except that he was black boy, causing him to be a dead boy.

We also see a massive double standard in the handling of the crack epidemic of the 1980's and the heroine epidemic of the 2000s.

If you recall, in the 1980s, when crack was destroying New York City, most crack users and dealers were black, and America treated the crack epidemic as a criminal problem, resulting in mass incarcerations of (mostly) black people (remember that 1 gram of crack cocaine carried the identical prison sentence as 100 grams of powder cocaine, despite the fact that crack cocaine is less potent than powder cocaine).

However, if you look at the last decade, when heroine has been destroying Ohio, most heroine users and dealers are white, and America is treating the heroine epidemic as a health problem, resulting in mass treatment of (mostly) white people.

I will also never be able to forget during the aftermath of Hurricane Katrina that the media depicted white New Orleanians who were stealing stuff from Wal-Mart as "survivalists" while the same media outlets depicted black New Orleanians who were stealing stuff from Wal-Mart as "looters".

In addition to pointing out side-by-side double standards, the other effective method to point out our racial double standards is to use aggregate data that paints an egregiously unequal picture (we have already covered a lot of these types of double standards in this book).

For example, if you recall, black people are 10% more likely to use drugs than white people but black people are more than 600% more likely to be incarcerated for drug offenses.

And, we have also already mentioned, black people are more than 900% more likely to receive the death penalty for killing a white person than the other way around.

It's also pertinent to again mention (not for the first or last time) the double standard we apply when collectively fighting government infringement upon the 2nd Amendment. Democrat-controlled city councils and mayoral offices have restricted gun rights in many major cities in the Midwest and Northeast, but you do not hear a peep from the NRA (or anyone else) because it is mostly black people's gun ownership rights that are being restricted. Also, as previously noted, Ronald Reagan signed the repeal of California's open-carry laws because members of the Black Panthers were non-violently exercising their 2nd Amendment rights on the streets of Oakland as part of their anti-police-brutality program known as "Cop Watch". We don't allow the government to strip white American citizens to have their 2nd Amendment rights without a fight, which means that we should apply the same standard to black American citizens (and all American citizens, of course).

Finally, on the topic of double standards, I wish that every white person in America would go to Twitter and search the hashtags #CrimingWhileWhite and #AliveWhileBlack, as they provide a very informative amalgamation to create a broad picture regarding the double standards with which the police generally treat American white people versus how the police generally treat American black people.

The first-person accounts are incredible, and would be unbelievable to me except for the facts that I have personally been caught by the police behaving criminally without being subjected to any consequences (at least a dozen times) and I also personally have a lot of black friends who have been harassed by the police under dubious circumstances while not behaving criminally.

Basically, several years ago, some clever group of social media users started using the hashtags #CrimingWhileWhite and #AliveWhileBlack to offer first-person accounts of the aggregate difference between white and black juvenile interactions with the police.

So, please, if you haven't already, go to Twitter and search for these 2 hashtags, as even when accounting for an error rate based on people with a political agenda making things up or embellishing stories, it's still a very powerful collection of direct testimonials regarding the disparities in how law enforcement treats white people versus how they treat black people.

Consider this highly representative list of #CrimingWhilteWhite examples from Caroline, a high school friend of mine:

You grew up with enough of us to know how true this is. Once I got stopped outside a friend's parents' house, beers in hands, jumping the fence to sneak back in at the end of the night. The cops pulled up and on the loud speakers, told us to HALT. We turned around and asked them if they had lost their minds making that kind of noise at 3 am because, "OMG OUR PARENTS ARE SLEEPING MAN. YOU TRYING TO GET ME GROUNDED????" They apologized as they watched us hop the fence as we shook our heads at their poor manners.

Pulled over as a teenager with car full of booze. We blamed it on the "boys" who were "no longer with us". No breathalyzer despite the 50 beer cans floating around. Cop said he had better things to do than "babysit". We drove home.

White kid drives home drunk (not condoning this, but it happened, and I'm not going to use his name, but I'm pretty sure you know who I'm talking about). Cop followed him home where he jumped out of the car and ran inside and the cop decided he couldn't give him the DUI but he did ring the doorbell to talk to the kid's dad. Kid tries to punch cop in the face multiple times while his dad holds him back. No charges pressed and his parents decide that his hangover "will be punishment enough".

I have endless stories like this. Endless. Kids are often stupid and they don't deserve to die for it.

I have endless stories like this as well, both from personal experiences of my extensive criminality, and based on the stories of criminality from virtually all of my white friends, and I also have endless stories from my black friends describing benign non-criminal behavior that nevertheless caused the police to treat my black friends with hostility and disrespect.

P.S. We will cover most of the alleged double standards that negatively affect white people in the chapter titled "Bullshit" (HINT: I think it is total nonsense when white people embrace a culture of race-based victimhood and grievance).

CHAPTER 11

WHITE PRIVILEGE

I had never heard the phrase "White Privilege" prior to about 2015, and when I first heard it, it made me very angry because it seemed to imply that all white people live on Easy Street and don't have to work hard to achieve success. As a small business owner who has had at least as many downs as ups, I know from first hand experiences that "making it" is damn hard, no matter what color your skin is. Plus, in general, despite being white, my life has been a long way from easy. I've dealt with plenty of tragedies and disappointments and setbacks and failures in my life, so I just did not like that phrase. AT ALL.

However, I recently actually read the 1988 article that coined the term "White Privilege" and quickly realized that my angry reaction to hearing this phrase was based on me being totally ignorant regarding the intended meaning of the term.

Simply put, White Privilege involves the reality that race negatively impacts our lives a whole lot less than race negatively impacts the lives of American black people. To further elaborate, it's much easier for white people to ignore race or racism than it is for black people. Black people can't turn race off like a faucet, as there are so many things that we as white people can take for granted that black people can not and do not take for granted, such as the right to a fair trial, the ability to lawfully traverse all roads and neighborhoods in America without fear of unwarranted interactions with the police, being able to sign a lease or take out a loan without race creating partiality, and so on- we have provided and will continue to provide lots of data and additional examples throughout this book, but for now, just please be aware of and accept the general premise that the term "White Privilege" isn't meant to shit on white people.

That having been said, White Privilege really is an inaptly (and non-productively) named "brand", as it is actually much less about the unearned advantages that white people benefit from and much more about the unfair disadvantages that black people are forced to endure (ie, the problem is not a positive effect on white people but rather a negative effect on black people). I wish that the person who coined the phrase "White Privilege" had instead called it "Black Burden" or something like that, as it would make white people less defensive about and therefore hopefully more empathetic toward the real-life experiences of American black people.

Additionally, it's incredibly important to understand that the concept of "privilege" applies quite broadly, not just to white people, meaning there's even less reason for us as white people to get so lathered up when we hear this phrase. There truly exist an almost unlimited number of "privileges" that may apply to various subsets of people, as well as completely unlimited combinations of "privileges", and I'll use myself here as an example to illustrate this point.

In addition to White Privilege, I also benefit from Male Privilege, as being born a male provides me with several unearned advantages in life. For example, walking through a badly lit parking garage at night causes me absolutely no stress. However, for women, this identical experience can be harrowing at times. Again, Male Privilege isn't about my anxiety-free trips from the store to my car, but rather the previous-experience-based anxiety that women feel under similar circumstances. In other words, by acknowledging Male Privilege, we aren't hoping for a world in which men feel equally as unsafe as women but rather where women feel equally as safe as men.

In addition to being born a white man in a nation where white men control the vast majority of both the money and the power, I also enjoyed Family Wealth Privilege, as my parents were able to pay for exclusive private schools and my grandparents paid for my college, thus allowing me to receive a first-class primary and secondary education **and** graduate from college debt free. In this country, there are many thousands of people of all races who benefit from Family Wealth Privilege, but, again, recognizing this form of privilege isn't about how awesome it is to be born into affluence, it's about how difficult it is to be born into poverty.

Additionally, as an American, I benefit tremendously from Nationality Privilege, because I happen to have been born in the greatest country in the history of the world. As Americans, we truly are so very blessed. We can drink water straight from the tap, our military leaders don't conduct coups every 10 years or so, and we have more upward economic mobility than any other nation on earth, and recognizing our blessings doesn't lessen our blessings, but it should make us more appreciative of our blessings, and more aware of how much unnecessary suffering exists in so many other nations.

I also benefit from Big Privilege, as I was born big, and have stayed that way throughout my life. For starters, being big made me far less likely to be bullied by my peers. It also allowed me to be athletically useful, which increased my confidence, and largely ensured that I would always have a built-in pool of potential friends to draw from, even as I regularly changed schools. Being big has also provided me with unearned romantic opportunities, as I have found that a fairly large subset of women prefer taller/bigger men (it should be noted, of course, that acknowledging Big Privilege is not about our advantages, but rather about smaller people's disadvantages).

I would also be remiss not to mention my Hair Privilege. Not only do I have a lovely full head of hair, but it is naturally totally straight and perfectly soft, despite the fact that I use the cheapest shampoo I can find and I do not use conditioner ever and I rarely even comb my hair before leaving home. Even as an overweight 42 year-old, I STILL have random women in bars unexpectedly caress my hair several times per year, but even when I was younger (and thinner), my hair still made me far more appealing sexually than any other feature I possess, and I find myself so appreciative not to be bald, because that would probably be the nail in the coffin that would prevent me from ever getting laid again without paying for it.

I also was blessed with Parenthood Privilege, as I had parents in my life who did not beat me, did not molest me, and always provided a roof over my head and food on my plate. Being aware of my Parenthood Privilege involves the recognition of all the kids who grew up without Parenthood Privilege.

I also benefit from being born in a multicultural major city, as that upbringing has afforded me Inflection Privilege because although I am from Texas, I do not speak with much of a twang or a drawl. As such, even though educated "well to do" people from California or New York can tell I'm not a "coastal elite", I don't sound like a redneck, so they are more willing to treat me as a peer rather than as an inbred hillbilly. In the case of black people, voice inflection matters at least as much, or possibly even more, and they're kind of screwed either way, because so many white people will reject black people if they "talk black" while so many of the black people who "talk black" will reject the black people who "talk white".

Lastly, I benefit from Health Privilege, as I was born with four functional limbs and no debilitating conditions. However, as is the case with "White Privilege", the phrase really has nothing to do the "privileged" person and everything to do with the non-"privileged" person. In other words, Health Privilege as I've described here isn't about the ease with which I am able to use the restroom and take a shower, but rather the difficulty involved in performing these simple everyday tasks for people who aren't blessed with four functional limbs.

It is also worth noting that, sometimes, "privilege" affects isolated circumstances only, sometimes it is pervasive, and sometimes, privilege can even cut both ways. For example, while I benefit from Big Privilege, Small Privilege allows smaller people to ride on airplanes in a condition other than total misery, and it allows smaller people to shop for clothes and shoes that fit without a hassle, and so on.

Finally, having discussed the concept of "privilege" in general, I want to conclude this chapter with an anecdote about "White Privilege" specifically, as that is, after all, the title of this chapter.

I recently had an amusing but poignant example of White Privilege occur in my life. I was debating where to eat lunch with my old friend Stu, and I suggested the original Frenchy's Fried Chicken on Scott Street in Houston. As we both began to expound upon our mutual love of Frenchy's, I mentioned how happy I am that Frenchy's is back, maybe better than ever, after a noticeable multi-year dip in overall quality, and Stu, who is from the historically black neighborhood where the original Frenchy's resides, said, "See, that's White Privilege right there. If I tried to say that Frenchy's was ever anything other than awesome, they wouldn't let me back into my own neighborhood." He was half kidding, and we both laughed, but in thinking about it since then, he was really on to something important.

If you think about it, black people really aren't allowed to have an opinion without race coming up if the person they offer their opinion to happens to disagree, and this tends to hold particularly true if the opinion is a political one.

If a black person has an opinion a white liberal disagrees with, the white liberal will feel sorry for the black person and see them as being deeply troubled by self-loathing.

If a black person has an opinion that a white conservative disagrees with, the white conservative will think of the black person as a modern-day slave who just wants "free stuff" and suffers from a mentality of victimhood and belongs to a fatherless culture that has rejected mainstream American values and refuses to accept personal responsibility, etc.

If a black person has an opinion that a black liberal disagrees with, the black liberal will think or say "Uncle Tom" ("Uncle Ruckus").

And if a black person has an opinion that a black conservative disagrees with, the black conservative will think or say "bottom feeder" or "slave mentality".

I am so happy that I am privileged in this country as a white person to express any political opinion I feel like without my race being dragged into it, and I'm happy to have friends like Stu, who challenge me to think, even when we're just kidding around or even when their comments make me feel uncomfortable, and I wish that all Americans of all races could say the same (on both counts).

CHAPTER 12

BLACK CULTURE

Way too many American white people tend to blame the plight of American black people on "black culture". This line of "thinking" demonstrates zero empathy toward or understanding of black people, because there is absolutely, positively no such thing as "black culture". Again, as I've stated before, black people aren't monolithic- they don't think alike, or act alike, or share the same values, or raise their children alike, or do anything else alike. They just don't, and you're a racist if you think they do.

Yes, I am aware that lots of prominent black people refer to "black culture" as well, but I find the premise to be inaccurate and unhelpful, regardless of who is espousing it. However, I try not to overly concern myself with the language black people use to describe themselves, so I don't normally argue with black people who talk about "black culture", but I do think that our collective habit of grouping black people together all the time exacerbates more problems than it solves. But all that having been said, again, there is no such thing as black culture. There just isn't. At least in my view.

Want to know the sum total of shared experiences between American black people? 100% have at one point or another experienced some form of white-on-black or institution-on-black racism, and so have their parents, and their parents and grandparents before them, and their children, and their grandchildren, and so on. That's it. That's the only universal experiential commonality. And no matter how life-shaping the 1 shared experience is, or how traumatic, or how much the 1 shared experience can at times allow for a positive connection between 2 black strangers, the idea that one single shared experience can produce something as complex as a "culture" is just utter hogwash.

When I have mentioned this reality to white people upon hearing them cite "culture" as the "real reason" black people can't get ahead, many will counter with, "OK, maybe not black culture, but Hip Hop Culture or

Hood Culture", which only serves to magnify my perception of their astounding ignorance.

I will then ask them, "how much time have you spent in the hood?" or "how much do you know about Hip Hop music?"

Invariably, the answer involves a lot of indecipherable mumbling and eye-contact avoiding, but not much else.

For the record, Bed Stuy in Brooklyn has about as much in common with 5th Ward in Houston as New York does with Texas overall. The black people in these two hoods don't dress the same, talk the same, or anything else, and if they ever set foot in each other's hood, they would stick out like a sore thumb, and if they ever interacted with each other, they probably wouldn't really get along very well (at least not at first). Want to know why? Because for the most part, Texans don't like New Yorkers, and New Yorkers don't like Texans, regardless of race. But, to the extent that neighborhood cultures exist in Bed Stuy and 5th Ward, they are not the same or even necessarily similar cultures. For example, it is not uncommon to see a black man riding a horse in 5th Ward, even in 2017, whereas it has probably been 75 years since you saw a black man- or any man- riding a horse in Brooklyn (other than maybe police officers in crowd-control settings).

Furthermore, the individuals living in these two aforementioned hoods don't share any universal traits, either, any more than rich white people share universal traits or a "white culture". For example, Tucker Carlson and Chris Matthews are both enormously wealthy white men, and yet they seem to have nothing in common beyond the superficial measuring sticks of rich, white, and male. In fact, that's the main point: for the most part, excepting periods of mass hysteria, each human being thinks and acts individually rather than collectively, and this is the case with every single person of every single race in every single neighborhood in the whole history of humanity.

One of my favorite examples of this reality is my good friend Herb Baker. Herb is from The Nickel (what many 5th Ward residents refer to their neighborhood as), and in some ways, Herb seems to embody certain stereotypes about black men, particularly black men who live in "the hood".

For example, if you piss Herb off, you could wind up eating soup for six weeks (it should be noted that Herb doesn't bother anyone- he just tolerates being bothered extraordinarily poorly).

However, Herb is one of the best fathers I know, and his favorite musical group is *Tears for Fears*. Yes, that *Tears for Fears* (NOTE: in order to make sure that Herb was not offended by this passage, because I strongly prefer eating solid foods, I sent this to him for pre-approval, and he strenuously objected that *Sting* and *The Police* are his favorite musicians, not *Tears for Fears*, but he did unashamedly re-confess his three-decade affinity toward *Tears for Fears*).

As for "Hip Hop culture", it doesn't exist, either. Hip Hop artists are about as monolithic as any other genre of musicians, which is to say not at all.

For example, would it surprise you to know there are hundreds if not thousands of black Christian rappers using music to spread the Good Word?

Or, here's a tiny subset of an incredibly long list of Hip Hop songs by extremely prominent rappers that also do not fit the narrative of "Hip Hop culture is destroying the inner cities":

"Us" by Ice Cube

In this classic from Cube, he wonders aloud whether black people focus too much on white racism and not enough on black self-improvement (the "awful racist" Malcolm X also harped on this theme constantly).

"I Know I Can" by Nas

In my second favorite Nas song ever, Nas extolls the virtues of hard work and tries to instill the confidence in young black people to reach for the stars.

"A Better Land" by Heavy D

In my favorite Heavy D song ever, Heavy D implores young black people to love each other instead of harming each other.

"Self Destruction" by the Stop the Violence Movement

The Stop the Violence Movement was a collaborative effort between a large number of prominent East Coast rappers, and Self Destruction was their seminal effort, designed to encourage black people toward peaceful conflict resolutions.

"U.N.I.T.Y" by Queen Latifa

This legendary effort from The Queen was about anti-misogyny and togetherness.

"We're All in the Same Gang" by the West Coast All Stars

Similar to the Stop the Violence Movement, the West Coast All Stars was a collaboration between prominent West Coast rappers to discourage young black people from committing acts of black-on-black violence.

"Just the 2 of Us" by Will Smith

This Fresh Prince classic is a powerful ode in celebration of fatherhood.

"Pray" by MC Hammer

This popular (but in my opinion terrible) song sent a message that turning to the Lord in times of trouble is the best path (not trying to hate on Hammer, he had lots of songs I liked, just not this one).

But even if all rap music matched the negative stereotypes about rap music, blaming "rap music" for the problems in the ghetto demonstrates, once again, a severe misunderstanding of chronology. The sort of rap music that most white people object to ("Gangster Rap") does not **create** conditions in that rapper's hood, it **reflects** conditions in that rapper's hood. Jay-Z did not start out as a rapper and then start selling crack cocaine, it was the other way around. Additionally, as we have looked into in previous chapters and will look into again in this chapter, black people have been living under very difficult circumstances since they arrived here (in chains). Black musicians have always reflected their circumstances. The Blues didn't create black poverty and sadness, black poverty and sadness created the Blues. This totally logical and intuitive concept shouldn't be so hard for so many to grasp.

I also think it's important here to discuss the violence and misogyny and glorifying of substance abuse that takes place within "white" entertainment vehicles.

For example, I'm white, and two of my three favorite movies of all time (*Miller's Crossing* and *Goodfellas*) are movies about white criminals who commit almost countless murders while serially cheating on their significant others and treating women (and men) like sex objects, not to mention doing lots of drugs and drinking to great excess.

Additionally, my four favorite country music artists of all time (Johnny Cash, Willie Nelson, Merle Haggard, and Waylon Jennings) sing extensively about things like sniffing cocaine, smoking marijuana, getting into fights, drinking extremely heavily, leading a criminal life that leads to prison, murder, objectifying women, and so on (it should also be noted that, as is the case with the blues and with rap, outlaw country music reflected rather than created outlaw country behavior).

I suppose it goes without saying that this list of my favorite (white) movies and musicians that includes vast amounts of objectionable material is by no means exhaustive. The Beatles glorified drug use, the Rolling Stones glorified drug use and objectified women, Led Zeppelin excitedly discussed sodomy, *The Godfather* was jam-packed with profanity and murder and adultery, *Braveheart* was incredibly violent and sexual, *Game of Thrones* is grotesquely violent and shows absolutely appalling treatment of women, and on and on and on and on and on and on.

That having been said, since we've looked at the negative features of so-called "black culture" that white people decry (in this chapter and the chapter before), and pointed out the glaring hypocrisy and unfairness of these various white criticisms of black people, let's take a look at some positive features of "black culture" that come much closer to the truth than the garbage accusations discussed above and previously.

For example, according to a variety of Pew studies:

78% of American black people are Protestant Christians, compared with 53% of American white people.

89% of black Christians are absolutely certain in their belief in God, compared with 76% of white Christians.

84% of black Christians rated their Christian beliefs as very important to them, compared with 64% of white Christians.

54% of black Christians attend church at least once a week, compared with 45% of white Christians.

80% of black Christians pray every day, compared with 68% of white Christians.

Amongst Americans who identify themselves as atheists or agnostics, 3% are black and 82% are white.

As such, if there were such a thing as "black culture", earnestly believing in Jesus Christ as Lord and Savior would certainly be a major pillar of it.

In addition to representing a disproportionate percent of practicing Christians, black people are also disproportionately likely to serve in the American armed forces. In fact, black people make up 13% of the US population but account for 17.8% of the active duty US armed services, whereas non-Hispanic white people make up 62.6% of the US population but just 58% of the active duty US armed services. This means that while American white people are 7% under-represented in the US Armed Services, American black people are 37% over-represented.

Considering the distance between the -7% number for white people and the +37% number for black people, American black people are proportionally 44% more likely to serve our country militarily than American white people are. As such, there should be no question that *patriotism would be another major pillar of actual "black culture", if I accepted the concept (which I do not).

*If the thought reflexively ran through your mind while reading about black patriotism, "yeah, but the only reason the blacks serve is because a judge gave them a choice of prison or the Army", don't you dare ever again even start to believe or assert that you "respect the troops", as factual records that I am about to reference demonstrate the reality that MILLIONS of black people have VOLUNTEERED to serve AMERICA in the armed services, in every single war, including The American Revolution (as we are about to illuminate below in the section on "magnanimity").

I also think it's important to look at the extent to which American black people value their extended families, and I think family reunions are quite instructive on this topic. For example, would it surprise you to know that 70% of the money that American black people spend on non-business-related Summer travel relates to family reunions (http://www.csmonitor.com/2002/0821/p11s02-lifp.html)? This figure speaks volumes about priorities, as I can tell you that my family took family vacations to places like New Orleans, Mexico City, and Disney Land, and we attended exactly one family reunion, and everyone apparently hated it so much that I don't think anyone ever bothered trying to put one together again (if they did, my immediate family certainly didn't attend).

I couldn't find any data about the actual difference between white people and black people in terms of what percent of each racial group attends family reunions, but the anecdotal evidence is pretty strong. For example, it seems like 99% of all black people I encounter are wearing a family-reunion t-shirt (that's obviously an exaggeration designed to get a laugh, but I've definitely seen WAY more black people wearing family-reunion t-shirts than any other racial group). Plus, a quick search for books and movies about family reunions reveals that the authors and intended audiences are overwhelmingly black- Tyler Perry even made a Madea movie about family reunions, which is a pretty dang good indicator that family reunions are disproportionately "a black thing".

You also see non-family-reunion anecdotal evidence all over the place about the relative extent to which black people value their extended families. For example, I've met a small number of my 2nd cousins over the years, but I'm not what could be considered close to any of them (although I have never disliked any of them). Furthermore, I could probably walk right past nearly all of my 2nd cousins on the street without necessarily recognizing any of them (at least at first glance), and vice versa, and I don't think I've ever met a 3rd cousin of mine in my entire life. However, I can't even tell you how many times I've been with a black friend and been introduced to a "cousin", only to find out later that the "cousin" in question was like a 4th cousin twice removed, and I find myself thinking, "How in the fuck do you even know this person?" It seems to me (anecdotally) that we as white people just don't "culturally" value our extended families the way that black people do, on average. The black comedian Erin Jackson even (half) jokingly asked the question, "Do white people (even) have cousins?"

All of this is to say that if there is such a thing as "black culture", valuing extended family is another clear pillar of it.

Finally, I absolutely marvel at the magnanimity of American black people. In fact, to the limited extent that I accept the notion of "black culture", I would without question also place magnanimity as a defining feature of it. Simply put, black people's collective capacity for forgiveness astounds me continuously.

Perhaps no data better represents black magnanimity than the amount of black people who cared enough about America to put their lives on the line long before this country cared about them. Here's a summary of black participation in the major American wars prior to the mid-1960's (the first point at which our country finally began in earnest to give black people something at least moderately similar to a fair chance):

American Revolution: 9000

Civil War: 200,000

World War I: 1,000,000

World War II: 1,200,000

Korean War: 185,000

This means that nearly 2.6 million black people served America during times of war prior to being granted anything even remotely close to full American citizenship. That level of not just patriotism but magnanimity absolutely amazes me, because I can tell you for 100% certain that had I been black in 1942, I would have sooner burned in hell than fought for America. NO. FUCKING. WAY.

We as white people too often love to focus on anything negative that seems to be disproportionately black, but we rarely even notice all the positive things that seem to be disproportionately black. This is unfair, and inconsistent, and it must stop.

Obviously, as I think this chapter has made pretty clear, I'm totally unconvinced that "black culture" is a useful or accurate characterization because mental-shortcut artists so readily confuse (often inaccurate) "stereotypes" with "cultural norms". Additionally, I just fundamentally believe that "culture" is more of a "house-by-house" thing than a "neighborhood-by-neighborhood" or "city-by-city" or "state-by-state" or "region-by-region" or "nation-by-nation" or "race-by-race" or "social class-by-social class" thing, partly because I am in my heart and mind an individualist, and also because I'm against lumping human beings into groups due to our tendency to blame them as a group and presume things about them as a group that usually turn out to be neither fair nor accurate nor helpful (this is why I've been careful throughout this book for the most part to say "some" white people/black people or "many" black people/white people, etc, instead of simply "white/black people", because without a qualifier, there's a presumed "all" before black/white people).

But, to the extent that "black culture" is a real thing, it's actual defining features are worthy of praise, not derision, as black people are disproportionately likely to: be genuine Christians, patriotically serve our nation in the armed forces, value extended family, and display a magnanimous spirit of forgiveness.

As such, whether or not I convinced you to cease over-citing "black culture" based on my belief that there is no such thing as "black culture", I hope that if you do continue citing "black culture" moving forward, you at least also consider the highly admirable aspects of "black culture" so that your thoughts embody fairness rather than bigotry.

P.S. If I were going to add a 5th pillar of "black culture", it would be having good sense around animals. My people let their dogs kiss them all in their damn mouths, apparently without regard for how much dogs love licking their own dicks or pussies, plus other dogs' dicks/pussies/assholes, not to mention how quite a few dogs love to literally eat shit. Plus, we do stupid shit like catch rattlesnakes with our bare hands on YouTube, we wrestle alligators, we stick our fucking heads in tigers' mouths for Christ's sake. You never see black folks acting foolishly around animals, and I just wanted to point that out.

CHAPTER 13

BULLSHIT

In this chapter, we will veer away from our chosen format of mixing (hopefully comprehensible) data with a (hopefully approachable) logic-based narrative, instead listing and refuting some of the most oft-repeated bullshit I hear fall from people's lips on this topic.

In addition to departing from the format in this chapter, I'm also substantially departing from the tone. As I hope you would agree, in spite of the profanity and occasional bursts of pissed-offedness, I have tried to model a civil and respectful and empathetic tone in this book, for the most part. In this chapter, however, I'm cutting loose just a little bit, mostly because I carry collective baggage of frustration on my back from years of repetitive back-and-forths on the go-to racist talking points discussed below, so I need to unload some of that frustration for the sake of my own mental health.

Non-Partisan White Bullshit

Slavery was a long time ago!! I never enslaved anyone!! Get over it!!

Boy, am I ever sick of hearing these three tired and invalid and closely related bullshit remarks.

Yes, slavery was (sort of) a long time ago. However, systematic discrimination against American black people didn't formally end until 1965 and it has **never actually ended**. Never. As such, please believe and accept that black people aren't mad about slavery, they're mad about how this country has (at least at times) treated their grandparents, their parents, their children, and each of them personally as individuals. Remember, as of 1966, black people were ALLOWED to eat a sandwich at lunch counters in the South, but they most definitely weren't WELCOMED when eating a sandwich at lunch counters in the South. Again, this sort of shit does not stop on a dime.

And, yes, we know you never personally enslaved anyone, as you would need to be 174 years old in order to have been an adult prior to the outbreak of the Civil War, and human beings don't live that long. But what does this have to do with anything? And how do you expect us to react when you say this? Do you feel that you're entitled to some sort of congratulatory decree for not personally participating in an evil system that has been illegal for 150 years?

Finally, as we've already discussed in the chapter on empathy, the idea that black people just need to "GET OVER IT!!" rudely denies and/or discredits the very personal history and ongoing reality black people face dealing with racism in America. Additionally, as we discussed in the chapter on history, the whole "GET OVER IT!!" thing embodies an elite level of hypocrisy, as large swaths of Southern white people insist on continuing to honor a group of racist traitors who lost a civil war, but black folks are the ones who need to "GET OVER IT"? Got it.

The hypocrisy of white people demanding that black people "GET OVER IT!!" truly extends pervasively- remember, we're the ones who have never turned the page, especially regarding our racist rhetoric (violent, stupid, lazy, sex addicted)- white people have WIDELY believed those stereotypes about black people since slavery, literally, but we think black people are the ones who need to get over it?

So, yes, we know that slavery is over. Black people and white allies won that fight, so there is nothing from that bygone era for black people to "get over". Black folks aren't pissed about slavery, they're pissed about how they and their immediate family members have been treated at various times throughout their own lives, as would any group of human beings under similar circumstances.

At what point do we turn the page? Should the grandson be held responsible for the sins of the grandfather in perpetuity?

Again, we're the ones who refuse to turn the page, not black people, and I have never said and don't believe that the grandson of the murderer directly owes the grandson of the murdered one single thing. What I have said is that the grandson of the murderer telling the grandson of the murdered how he should feel about what happened to his grandfather is a non-empathetic or maybe even a despicable sentiment.

P.S. The other reason this bullshit analogy sucks is that American black people are **still being harmed**, unlike the metaphorical grandson of the metaphorical murdered grandfather.

I agree in the past the black race was treated unfairly, and I have seen in my lifetime many changes to correct this wrong. We have made a lot of progress, and we need to keep moving forward in this area, but that's hard to do when people won't let go of the past.

Even though I agree that we have made a lot of progress, and that it should probably be noted more often than it is, it's absurd to believe that any sort of lasting celebration should occur prior to the mission being completed. Honestly, we as white people must stop congratulating ourselves for all the progress we've made. If I rape a little girl every day, penetrating her daily, both vaginally and anally, but over the years I eventually quit raping and penetrating her daily, but I still pin her down and jack off all over her face once or twice a month, do I get to celebrate all the progress I've made?

Listen, the main thing is to keep the main thing the main thing, and the main thing here is that black people are STILL being actively discriminated against in virtually every facet of American life, not how proud we are of ourselves for how much less we discriminate than previous generations did.

P.S. Again, black people aren't just upset about how their ancestors were treated in the past, they're upset about how they and their parents and their grandchildren and their children have been treated and, more importantly, are being treated.

OK, I agree with you that we still have work to do, but now isn't the right time or appropriate place for this. Just be patient, and time will heal all wounds.

If we wait to fight for racial equality in America until white people are universally ready or comfortable, we will be waiting forever, and avoiding discomfort should not be a higher priority than seeking justice.

We've made so much progress, but no one ever appreciates that or even mentions that. Instead, they only complain.

To draw another less crude and less offensive analogy, if a bully punches you in the face every single day for a very long time then gradually reduces his rate of assault from daily to twice a week and starts punching you in the stomach instead of the face, are you obligated to feel and express gratitude toward the person who is still regularly punching you because they're punching you less frequently in a less damaging area than they used to?

In all seriousness, why is it that ONLY American black people are expected to be submissive and even appreciative in the face of glaring and ongoing injustice?

P.S. I think it's great to commend our progress, if and only if you also recognize how much further we have to go. In the area of full citizenship and full humanity for American black people, we are looking for realization. We are looking to finish the race, not just progress along the route.

I'm not a racist!! I have lots of black friends!!

The chances are that if you've ever been in a position to feel the need to say this, it isn't true.

I remember probably 15 years ago, I was about 27 and the first crew of high school kids I had taught had just started moving back to Houston having now graduated from college. As such, I would see some of them at the same bars that my friends and I frequented. On one particular night, a young lady I had taught about five years previously invited about half of the bar back to her parents' house (where she was still living, as she was 21 or 22 at the time). During this particular after party, she was blurting out some racist stuff, so I tried to redirect her, and her immediate go-to defense was the highly predictable, "I HAVE LOTS OF BLACK FRIENDS" to which I replied, "Name one" to which she replied, "my housekeeper".

Look, I do not deny that a strong bond of mutual love often develops between a long-term housekeeper (especially a live-in housekeeper) and the child(ren) of the housekeeper's employers, but that doesn't make your housekeeper your "friend". It is truly astounding (and a bit counter-intuitive) the extent to which a white racist will eagerly lower the standard for what constitutes a friendship in the context of defending themselves from accurate accusations of racism.

Prior to the incident recalled above, I worked at the local country club when I was in college, which at the time did not have even 1 black member, but they did have several black employees. One in particular, a gentleman named O'Dell, had seemingly worked there forever in his role as locker-room attendant and shoe-shine specialist. Oh my, how the members "loved" O'Dell, who always had a kind and (strategically?) subservient word for every club member he encountered. During my three months working there, I must have witnessed at least 10 members drunkenly throw their arms around O'Dell and describe him as their "dear, good friend" and such and such.

For the record, and this isn't something that should even need to be "cleared up", having a cordial or even a warm relationship with a person who works at an establishment that you frequent does not make that person your friend, and being nice to a person in your direct employment also does not make that person your friend.

I always wanted to ask a few basic friendship-related questions to the members of the club who shared an (in all probability imagined) intimacy with O'Dell:

Has O'Dell ever been into your home in a non-professional capacity?

Have you ever been into O'Dell's home in any capacity at all?

Did O'Dell attend your wedding or your children's wedding as a guest?

Did you attend O'Dell's wedding or his children's wedding as a guest?

Have you ever invited O'Dell as a guest to your birthday party or any other social gathering with a group of your friends?

Has O'Dell ever invited you to his birthday party or any other social gathering with a group of his friends?

Would you be excited about or comfortable with your children or grandchildren being romantically involved with O'Dell's children or grandchildren?

For probably at least 98% of the members of this particular country club, the answer to all 7 of these questions would have been a resounding "no" (if they were being honest).

In fact, if you have found yourself defensively proclaiming, "I HAVE LOTS OF BLACK FRIENDS", you should replace O'Dell's name with the name of your "friend" and see how many of these 7 questions you can truthfully answer in the affirmative. Next, you should see how many other black "friends" you are able to replace O'Dell's name with to produce "yes" answers to most or all of these 7 questions.

If you have ever said, "I HAVE LOTS OF BLACK FRIENDS" in the wake of someone accusing you of being a racist, and you're willing to honestly evaluate yourself introspectively, using a normal standard for what defines "friendship", you will likely discover that you actually have a very small number of black friends, if you have any at all, which means that you should stop regurgitating this oft-repeated, self-congratulatory, steaming pile of delusional racist bullshit.

P.S. I actually do have lots of black friends, and that reality hasn't enabled me to fully overcome being a racist, so we must stop acting like having a black friend or 2 is a magic tonic to completely and instantly and permanently cure a person's racism.

I'm not a racist, but…

If you feel the need to deny being a racist, especially when no one has even accused you of being a racist, then you almost definitely are one (thou doth protest too much!!). Furthermore, in the English language, the entire purpose of the word "but" is to attach primary significance to the sentiment that comes after the "but" at the expense of whatever came before it.

*I am not the type of person to say "I told you so" **but** I did try to warn you, didn't I?*

Um, what? You are very clearly exactly the type of person to say "I told you so", because you just did.

*I am not into disgusting jokes, **but** did you hear the one about the pedophile and the orphanage?*

Hey, buddy, you don't get to claim you don't like disgusting jokes then move directly into a joke about the most offensive and revolting and upsetting topic out there. Yes, you are into disgusting jokes, you delusional and disgusting bastard!!

I'm sorry I beat the shit out of you (again), **but** *you* *should know better than to get in my face at the end of a hard day at work!!*

No, you're not sorry. If you were actually sorry, you wouldn't be trying to spread the blame around in order to absolve yourself, now would you? That just isn't what genuinely apologetic people do, though it is what sorry people do, as in woman beaters are a bunch of sorry motherfuckers. So, I guess you are sorry, just not in the way you're claiming to be.

It truly perplexes me why so many people don't linguistically understand that in the vast majority of cases, using the word "but" basically invalidates everything said prior to using that word. So, to the people who find themselves saying, "I'm not a racist, but…" let me say:

I understand that you claim that you're not a racist, **but** each time your unrequested impromptu disclaimer is followed immediately by the word "but" and a blatantly racist comment, you aren't fooling anyone except for yourself.

How can I be racist? I don't hate anyone!!

The first part of the Merriam Webster "full" definition of racism is this:

"A belief that race is the primary determinant of human traits..."

Any time a white person encounters an intelligent Asian person and says or thinks, "Asians are super smart", that white person is being a racist.

Any time a black person encounters a rude or hostile white person and says or thinks, "white people are never going to give us a fair chance", that black person is being a racist.

Any time a white person talks about "black culture", that white person is being a racist.

Basically, any time you think about an individual person's looks, attitudes, beliefs, behaviors, words, actions, or any other trait as being attributable to or related to race, you are being a racist, and thinking that racism without hate isn't possible is what keeps many (racist) white moderates from looking introspectively and becoming white allies.

How can I be a racist when Allen West (or Herman Cain, etc) said the same thing I said? And you do know black police officers also shoot unarmed black people, right? I guess they're racists, too!!

Just because a black person speaks negatively about or writes negatively about or acts negatively toward a fellow black person in a way that you agree with and condone doesn't automatically validate your feelings.

For starters, since when have you taken a black person's opinion on race relations as the gospel truth? It truly is so unfair to universally accept a black person's comments on race if they agree with your pre-conceived notions while universally rejecting or doubting a black person's comments on race if they disagree with or try to refute your pre-conceived notions (like racists yell at Colin Kaepernick "STICK TO SPORTS!!" while eagerly Facebook sharing the comments of Charles Barkley or Ray Lewis on the exact same non-sports-related topic).

We must all remember that black people grew up in America as well, which means they have absorbed the same negative images of black people their entire lives also, which has caused a pretty sizable chunk of black people to have been brainwashed into being racist against themselves, and that includes black police officers, who are often extra scared of black suspects just like white officers often are. However, in no way, shape, or form should we allow ourselves to believe that inferiority-complex-based, black-on-black racism excuses or justifies or even mitigates superiority-complex-based, white-on-black racism.

Furthermore, as we have already discussed, many black people know that the quickest way to an average white person's heart- the very quickest and best way to show an average white person you're "one of the good ones"- is to make derogatory comments about other black people. As such, a good chunk of the comments from people like Allen West could derive from strategy rather than self-loathing.

To set the record straight, no matter how much white racists love and agree with black-on-black racism, it doesn't lessen or justify white-on-black racism, just as a black cop who practices black-on-black racism doesn't lessen or justify white cops practicing white-on-black racism.

Martin Luther King JR was a great leader!! He would be so
disappointed with all of the rioting and looting we see today!!

White people should stop invoking MLK's name as a positive example
of the "right way" to do things, because he was by no means the
universal hero to white America in his time as so many modern
revisionist historians feel compelled to believe. Remember that FBI
Director J. Edgar Hoover viewed MLK as an enemy of the state, and that
a racist white person shot him through his brain for espousing the view
that American black people deserve an equal opportunity to live the
American Dream, which is the identical main point of every single
modern civil rights group that seems to piss white people off.

Come on, how can you claim to cherish and honor Dr. King, while
detesting "race agitators" like Jesse Jackson and Al Sharpton, both of
whom marched with Dr. King because they stood for (and stand for) the
same goals that Dr. King advanced ? And you can't be pissed at Colin
Kaepernick for peacefully protesting by kneeling during the national
anthem but believe you would have been standing with Dr. King. You do
realize that Dr. King was seen as a "race agitator" in his day as well,
right? Same with Thurgood Marshall before him, and WEB DuBois
before him, and Frederick Douglas before him.

Also, as we have previously discussed, way over 99% of the
#BlackLivesMatter protests have been peaceful and lawful, so please
stop being manipulated by our sensationalist and propagandist media
into believing that the exception is the rule. Also, you should be ashamed
of yourself for being more upset about a few bad apple black people
breaking windows and stealing televisions than you are about a few bad
apple police officers killing unarmed black people.

P.S. I'm not disputing that Jesse Jackson and Al Sharpton may have less
altruistic motives that partially drive their public decisions and behavior,
nor am I saying that their histories as human beings aren't badly tainted
morally- I'm simply saying that their stated main goal is no different
than Dr. King's, and that is not disputable.

Exactly, Jesse Jackson and Al Sharpton are nothing like Dr. King!!
Jesse Jackson has like 200 children out of wedlock... actually, come to

think of it, let's talk about Dr. King's well known womanizing- King was just as sex crazed as that animal Jesse Jackson!!

People, please make up your racist minds, instead of heaping lavish praise on Dr. King in one sentence, then slandering him in the next. The simple truth is that Dr. King was a great American, and a great leader, in spite of his personal flaws as a human being.

That having been said, I'd like to take this opportunity to remind everyone that goodness isn't required for greatness, and it never has been, or there would pretty much be no such thing as "greatness". Thomas Jefferson owned slaves, and raped them. Franklin Roosevelt had a despicable track record of committing serial infidelity, as did John F. Kennedy and Lyndon Baines Johnson and Bill Clinton and Donald Trump.

So, yes, Dr. King had moral failings as a human being, just like the rest of us, so please walk outside of your glass house before you start throwing rocks, and please stop requiring a great black man to have achieved moral perfection, because we sure as hell don't require that from great white men.

Race is only a big deal because race agitators and race profiteers and race baiters and social justice warriors make it a big deal!! All of this racial talk and anger only serves to racially divide us and further perpetuate racism!! Stop playing the race card!!

This line of "thinking" once again butchers the concept of chronology, as race and racism have been foundational problems in our nation since its birth, which means that it is impossible to "make something a big deal" that has been a big deal for centuries.

Also, why on earth is the term "Social Justice Warrior" used as an insult? No one has ever been able to explain to me why fighting for justice is something that deserves to be mocked.

As for the idea that talking about race only serves to divide us, I find myself wondering when America has ever achieved harmonic racial togetherness. As such, it makes no sense to accuse modern activists of dividing us on a topic where a massive divide has always existed.

Really, this whole train of "thought" demonstrates a probably willful detachment from reality and a fundamental mean-spiritedness, and it needs to stop. Simply put, talking about racism doesn't cause racism- it might piss racists off, but pissing off a racist is a fundamentally different thing than creating a racist.

The simple mention of black or white naturally creates segregation and is a major part of the problem. Don't think it. Don't say it. Want to diminish racism? Stop talking about it!!

I have a couple of questions for the huge number of people who seem to feel this way:

Since when is ignoring a problem the best way to fix it? Will continuing to ignore my obesity produce washboard abs?

How is it logically defensible to claim that a discussion about a pre-existing problem may be responsible for exacerbating said problem? Could it be that the real reason I keep getting fatter is because I talk about being fat too much?

I just don't understand how refusing to discuss a serious long-standing problem could possibly play a role in the solution.

We need to come together as a nation!!

I just don't like the sound of this "coming together" thing, as that implies black people and white people must travel equal distances to meet in the middle. White racism is not based on 50% white bigotry and 50% black behavior/culture/morals/whatever. White racism is based on 100% white bigotry

I think as soon as white people collectively and permanently decide that systemic racism across countless segments of our society is absolutely unacceptable morally, we will be a unified society. The battle is in the minds and hearts of white racists and white racial moderates. That's the battleground. Black people and white people don't need to "come together". White people need to empathetically embrace justice.

You're so articulate and eloquent and well-spoken and impressive and polished and non-threatening. In fact, I'd have to say you're one of the good ones, and you are without a doubt a credit to your race!!

I do not believe that I have ever in my life heard a white person described as well-spoken or polished or non-threatening, and I have certainly never heard a white person described as a credit to their race. I mean, just listen to the patronizing and condescending comments white conservatives made toward Barack Obama during the run up to the 2008 election season- the only compliment they'd pay him at all is that he's "well spoken" and a "gifted orator". Um, he graduated from Columbia and Harvard law school, and he taught at the University of Chicago's law school. So, yes, he's well spoken, but I haven't heard Lindsey Graham or Rudy Giuliani call any white politicians "well spoken," have you? It's very thinly veiled (and often unintentional) racist code.

The reason this is racist is that what you're really doing is expressing surprise, because you racistly expect black people to be inarticulate. Additionally, we as white people tend to define a black person's "eloquence" by voice inflexion, not by verbal coherence or any other factor. In other words, if they "sound black", no matter how persuasive and logical their words are, we never call them articulate because we associate being articulate and being smart with sounding (being) "white".

How can I be a racist when I voted for Barack Obama twice? How can America be racist when we elected Barack Obama twice?

If you started reading this book at the beginning, you should know by now that I believe virtually all Americans of all races are racists, falling somewhere between 1-10 on the racist scale. So, it's important to keep reminding ourselves that while all Klansmen are racists, not all racists are Klansmen. Also, most white people who voted for Barack Obama would have voted for the Democratic nominee no matter who it was, meaning that white Democrats have earned and deserve zero special non-racist bonafides due to voting for Barack Obama, because their votes were mostly based on partisanship, not a burning desire for racial justice.

As for the narrative that Barack Obama's election proves that America is a post-racial society, please keep in mind that in 2008, 53% of white voters voted for John McCain, while 45% voted for Barack Obama (https://ropercenter.cornell.edu/polls/us-elections/how-groups-voted/how-groups-voted-2008/). In other words, the white majority did NOT choose Barack Obama; rather, minority voters collectively overcame the white majority's clear preference for yet another white President. As such, this narrative makes no sense on it's face, as when we describe America as a racist country, we are referring to the dominant race who pulled (and pull) the levers of every major power structure in our nation, not the minority races who also live in America. So, in order for this train of thought to make even a little bit of sense, 51% or more of American white people would have needed to have voted for Barack Obama, and that just isn't the case.

P.S. It has been fascinating to see Donald Trump supporters insist that Trump's election had nothing to do with race despite their near universal previous attribution of Barack Obama's election entirely to race.

A racist? I don't even see race!! I live in a post-racial world!!

100% of the time a white person has said this to me, the sequence has been:

White person says something objectionable about race.

White person gets called out for being a racist.

White person claims not to see race to defend themselves against the accusation of being a racist.

Basically, I am curious to know- why would a post-racial person who "doesn't see race" feel the need to comment about race in the first place? Do you see what I'm saying? It is absolute bullshit to offer up an opinion about black people while claiming not to even be aware of their blackness.

Black people are just as racist as white people!!

First off, yes, as I've already said many times, I agree that American black people are a bunch of racists, and I am 100% not OK with black-on-white racism. However, as I've also said a bunch of times, there is absolutely no comparison between the effects of white-on-black racism and the effects of black-on-white racism.

That having been said, are you 2 years old? We are talking about **your** racism right now, not some generic unknown black person's racism, so stay on topic. This bullshit truly is childlike.

Mom: "Billy, clean up your room."

Billy: "Bobby's room is dirty, too!!"

Mom: "Yes, but we aren't talking about your brother Bobby right now, we are talking about you, and the fact that his room is also dirty doesn't mean it's OK for your room to be dirty, now does it? Plus, your room is MUCH dirtier. In fact your room is so dirty it has spawned a modern Bubonic Plague and lots of people died because of how dirty your fucking room is, so shut the fuck up, Billy, and just clean up your fucking room before I tie your hands and feet and throw you off the God Damn roof!!"

Seriously, white racists, just as Bobby's room also being dirty doesn't excuse Billy, black people also being racist doesn't excuse you. Please, grow up.

The Asians and the Irish were discriminated against when they first arrived, and they're doing just fine because they've embraced American values like hard work and self-reliance!!

I can't believe I'm taking the time to refute this bullshit, but for starters, American black people WERE NOT IMMIGRANTS. They came here extremely involuntarily, clothed only in chains. Furthermore, the history of deliberate discrimination against Asian immigrants and Irish immigrants was not for the most part a continuous and multi-generational thing, and the discrimination that existed was not codified into law and repeatedly validated by the Supreme Court of the United States of America over the course of many, many, many decades. Jim Crow did not apply to Irish-Americans or Asian-Americans, nor did universities and banks almost universally discriminate against the children of Irish and Asian immigrants in the implementation of the GI Bill, which, as we have already discussed, basically created the American middle class while excluding black people from that otherwise laudable program (most people know about the internment of Japanese-Americans during World War II, but most don't consider the tens of thousands of Japanese-Americans, Chinese-Americans, Phillipino-Americans, and Korean-Americans who fought bravely for our country against the Axis of Evil). .

Additionally, in the last 50 years, I can point to thousands of successful lawsuits filed by American black people based on blatant racial discrimination in housing, banking, law enforcement/criminal justice, employment, and just about any other field you want to discuss. Also, I can point to hundreds of federal investigations and countless academic studies in the last 50 years that firmly establish the widespread presence of ongoing racial prejudice against American black people. And, in the last 50 years, I can point to thousands of **unarmed** American black people who lost their lives at the hands of the police under dubious circumstances.

So, here's what I'll finish with on this topic. Off the top of your head, in the last 50 years, can you point to even one successful discrimination-related lawsuit filed by an Asian-American or an Irish-American, or even one federal investigation or academic study that proves ongoing severe prejudice against Asian-Americans or Irish-Americans, or even one unarmed Asian-American or unarmed Irish-American who was unjustifiably killed by the police?

If you can answer "yes" to any of those questions, I will suck out your unwiped asshole on live television. Until then, please lay off making this bullshit comparison (that only racists make).

White privilege, my ass!! You have no idea how or where I grew up!! I WORK HARD FOR EVERYTHING I GET!!

As you should already know from chapter titled *White Privilege*, the notion of "privilege" has precisely nothing to do with money or work ethic or social status or upbringing, and "privilege" comes in an almost unlimited number of forms (not just white privilege), so this common reflexive refrain mostly just serves to paint the speaker as exhibiting total ignorance on this topic.

You know what your problem is? You need to get over your white guilt!!

I hear a lot about "white guilt" when I engage white people about race. To me, this concept makes no sense on its face.

For example, if I participate in the March of Dimes despite not personally being a woman or a newborn baby, do I have "Male Guilt" or "Adult Guilt"? If I ride my bike in an MS 150 despite not personally suffering from Multiple Sclerosis, do I have "Health Guilt"? If I'm straight but value and support total equality for gay people, do I have "Heterosexual Guilt"?

In all four cases (speaking out about injustice toward black people as a white person, marching for the health of women and children as an adult man, riding a bike to raise money to fight an awful disease as a healthy person, and supporting full citizenship for gay people), the good-hearted and well-intentioned participant acted based mostly, or at least partially, on empathy for others, and it's long past time that a wide swath of folks cease erroneously believing that empathy and guilt are somehow synonyms, when they in fact aren't even related.

I would love to see a study of the relationship between people who use the phrase "White Guilt" and narcissistic or sociopathic people who generally lack empathy as a human condition. My guess is that you would see a massive correlation!!

If you don't love it, leave it!! Go back to Africa!!

If you feel that way, you should consult with the American Indians about who has the right to stay and who should get the fuck out, and I think you would discover that European Americans would find themselves on large boats headed back to Europe, immediately, so maybe white people should shut the fuck up when we feel like spewing this sort of hostile and harmful racist garbage.

P.S. None of the black people you say this to or about were born in Africa, and neither were their parents, or their parents' parents, and most of them have never even been to Africa, so telling them to go "back" to a place they've never been to before literally doesn't make any sense at all linguistically, so stop making yourself sound like an idiot.

There are black people, and there are niggers. I have no problem with black people, but niggers are destroying this country!! Even Chris Rock said this same exact thing!!

First, again, the fact that a black person agrees with you doesn't make you right, and it is highly predictable which types comments by a black person will be instantly accepted versus which types of comments by a black person will be instantly rejected, and by whom. Not to mention, Chris Rock is a COMEDIAN, and comedians tell JOKES.

That having been said, if you respect "black people" so much, you should recognize that many of the "black people" you claim to respect don't like and therefore don't use the word "nigger", and if they don't, you shouldn't, either, especially in the context of defending your overt racism.

P.S. As of about 2015, "thug" became the new "nigger", so if you are white and you refer to black people as "thugs", please be aware that we know what you really mean and you aren't fooling anybody.

Black people call each other niggers all the time, but as soon as a white person says that word, then it's a problem.

If one were to make the case that the word "nigger" is so offensive that it shouldn't be used casually by anyone, I would find that viewpoint to be a valid one, although I personally don't worry very much about other people's self-descriptive language.

That having been said, context matters. As the brilliant former data analyst Jennifer Refro Brownson explained:

I worked in data analysis for a while, and we taught the notion of context by pointing out that in banking, collateral is used to support a loan, whereas in the intelligence world, it's a dead body.

My friend Conti Davis Rice also helped shed light on the importance of context:

As a black person, I get a totally different feeling when I hear a group of white frat boys singing about hanging niggers from trees than I get when I hear young black boys say things to each other like, "Hey, what's up, my nigga?" I'm just saying that (based on context) these two words and situations are different.

Basically, it's hard to think of a reason for a non-racist white person to be so infatuated with the word "nigger". Furthermore, the vast majority of the white people who demand to know, "How come a white person can't use that word?" DO use that word, just not in public. The simple truth is that what you're really doing by posing this bullshit question is defending your use of the word, and you wouldn't be defensive unless you felt guilty, and you wouldn't feel guilty unless you knew it was wrong.

P.S. You know how it's OK for you to hit your little brother but if someone else hit your little brother then you'd intervene on your little brother's behalf in about two seconds? Is that a "double standard" or is that just basic common sense? If a black person wants to say "nigger", they can, but that doesn't mean the rest of us should. That isn't a double standard. It's just basic common sense.

The REAL problem with black America is the absence of black fathers.

First of all, when black people initially arrived here, many slave owners deliberately broke up families out of a belief that slaves would be more obedient and therefore more productive if their status as a slave was their defining life experience rather than belonging to an actual family. Today, white-dominated American society continues to force the breakup of many black families through the outrageously unfair way our criminal justice system treats American black people. As such, throughout our history and into the present time, our nation has had policies that were developed by white people that disproportionally disrupted black families, so we as white people should really shut the fuck up when we feel the reflexive need to comment negatively about black families.

That having been said, the narrative that fatherlessness is the driving factor in the plight of American black people jumps back into our collective misunderstanding of timelines and our chronic refusal to comprehend the nature of cause-and-effect and our insistence on confusing beliefs with facts. You see, as we've already discussed in the "Accept Reality" chapter, black people's financial position has actually improved by 38% during the exact window that the black out-of-wedlock birth rate has tripled. Again, as I have already pointed out, causes don't triple in magnitude at the same time the alleged negative effects decline sharply. That just isn't the way legitimately connected cause-and-effect sequences work.

Come on, people, use your brains. Americans have been progressively eating more and more sugar for the past half century- has that led to a 38% decline in type 2 diabetes or obesity? Can you think of any logically defensible cause-and-effect sequence where the cause becomes substantially more prevalent over a multi-decade period while the effect becomes substantially reduced? I doubt you can. I know that I sure can't, because, again, that just isn't the way legitimately connected cause-and-effect sequences work.

Black on black violence is the REAL problem, but no one wants to talk about that. One fat criminal has a heart attack, and they burn and loot and close down bridges to prevent decent people who actually work for a living from getting to work. Where are all the protests about black on black violence?

First, I thought that black fatherlessness is the "real problem"?

Second, plenty of people are talking about this. For example, you are talking about it when you say no one is talking about it. And Fox News talks about it, but pretty much only in the context of distracting their viewers in the aftermath of a police officer killing an unarmed black person.

Furthermore, according to the 2015 Bureau of Justice statistics, 146,729 black people fell victim to serious violent crime. It is hard to calculate exactly how many of these victims were harmed by a fellow black person, but as we know that most violent crime is intra-racial, we can safely assume that the vast majority of these victims were harmed by an offender of their own race. As such, let's just go ahead and assume that black criminals hold responsibility for 100% of these 146,729 violent crimes against American black people.

That having been said, nearly 43,000,000 black people live in America, which means that WAY less than 1% (.34% to be exact) of American black people were seriously harmed violently via "black on black" crime (146,729 divided by 43,000,000).

Now that we've taken a quick peek at "black on black" crime, let's take a quick peek at white-on-black racism.

My experience has been, based on too many conversations with American black people to even count, that 100% of American black people have repeatedly endured negative racism-related experiences. However, as that "study" is obviously an informal one, let's instead again cite the 2014 Reuter's story in the wake of Eric Garner's death, in which 24 of the 25 black NYPD officers interviewed reported experiencing police-on-black racism when they were off duty, which is 96%, and police officers are "professionals", and they are "clean cut", and they don't "sag their pants" or "loiter" or fall under any other category that racist white people use in a despicable attempt to explain away the ongoing existence of glaring racism within our society.

So, my question is, if one commonly cited issue affects less than 1% of a given population, while another commonly cited issue affects at least 96% of that population, why should that population, or anyone else with a brain, label the issue that affects under 1% as "the real problem"?

CHICAGO, CHICAGO, CHICAGO!!

Sometimes, a death of an American black person with racial overtones becomes a national story. When this happens, lots of white people will bring up the out-of-control black-on-black violence in Chicago. However, it is hard to take their self-professed "concern" too seriously, because they only reference the violence in Chicago in the context of distracting from the specific issue of race-related violence against black people (as well as racism in general). In other words, "CHICAGO, CHICAGO, CHICAGO!!" is nothing more than a classic red herring to distract our attention from the actual issue at hand.

When a gay person gets beaten to death by a homophobic (presumably closeted homosexual) thug, if I said in the immediate aftermath of the gay person's hate-related death, "you know, the real problem in the gay community is HIV and AIDS because way more gay people die from AIDS than by hate-based murder", but I really only express "concern" about the spread of HIV and AIDS immediately after a gay person has been murdered in an act of hate, what would you think? Would you think I actually give a shit about gay people's health, or would you think my sympathies might lie more with the murderer than the murdered?

When a police officer gets murdered in cold blood, if I said in the immediate aftermath of the police officer's hate-related death, "you know, in 2016, only 12 police officers lost their lives in executions that deliberately targeted random police officers compared with 32 police officers who died in car or motorcycle crashes, but no one wants to talk about vehicle safety", but I really only express this "concern" about the vehicle-related safety of police officers immediately after a police officer has been executed in an act of hate, what would you think? Would you think I actually give a shit about vehicular safety for police officers, or would you think my sympathies might lie more with the murderer than the murdered?

In my experiences, 100% of white people who keep saying, "but what about Chicago?" don't give a shit about dead black people in Chicago, or anywhere else, and they should therefore shut the fuck up.

No one ever talks about this, but black-on-black violence isn't a new thing. In fact, did you know that Africans participated in the capturing of and selling of other Africans into slavery?

So, let's say I kidnapped my neighbor's 13 year-old daughter, and sold her to a buddy of mine, and my buddy kept her as a slave, raping her and beating her whenever the hell he felt like it.

Obviously, I behaved criminally, and deserve some of the blame for the plight of the 13 year-old girl I kidnapped.

But what about my buddy? Should we let him off the hook, because he did not participate in the original criminal act?

How would you feel if you saw my buddy on TV explaining away his crimes by saying, "You know, I really had no interest in owning my slave, or beating my slave, or raping my slave, but when Peter showed up with a slave for sale, what was I supposed to do?"

Would you think my buddy was a great guy for trying to deflect away from his crimes by pointing out my related crime, or would you think he was a low-life, excuse-making piece of shit?

It truly is difficult to conceive of the logic behind this extremely common white racist talking point.

Are you trying to say that black slave-catchers were the real bad guys? Maybe without the black slave-catchers, there would have been no white slave-owners? So, black Africans forced slavery upon the otherwise Christ-like existences of the innocent white Europeans?

Or are you trying to say that there's plenty of blame to go around? That all sides could have done better?

If that's the point, why do white racists never bring up the white Portuguese slave traders, who purchased the black slaves and brought them across the Atlantic Ocean? Also, couldn't my buddy have quit raping and beating the slave I sold him? Or set her free? Did my initial immoral act somehow compel him to continue behaving immorally indefinitely?

Invariably, this comment occurs only in the context of a discussion about white slave owners and black slaves, and is nearly always intended as a shirking of responsibility. No one would suggest that my buddy should be held less responsible for his serial raping because he didn't participate in the original act of kidnapping, yet many people seem to believe (or imply) that the black race is responsible for slavery in America.

We do love to do this with black people. Someone says white banks steal from black people, someone else says black people steal from each other. Someone says our government disproportionately kills black people, someone else brings up "black on black crime". Why can't we just allow a fair criticism to stand, and work to correct it? Why must we engage in deflective (and cowardly) whataboutism?

P.S. Part of me thinks that this common refrain (that normally tends to sound defensive) is the real "white guilt". After all, is it not true that only guilty people engage in whataboutism? If you got pulled over for speeding, and you weren't speeding, would you defend yourself by pointing out how other drivers were driving just as fast or faster? Or would you defend yourself by professing your innocence? And is bringing up black slave-catchers during a discussion about the later behavior of white slave-owners not roughly the same thing as bringing up gun manufacturers during a discussion about the later decisions of gun-owners?

I've been pulled over for speeding when I was in fact speeding, and I have fairly regularly protested via whataboutism.

"Sir, I have been in the right lane with the cruise control set and cars have been zipping by me in the left lane since I got on this highway, but you're trying to write me a ticket? What about all the other drivers who were driving way faster than I was."

In these cases, I had the cruise control set deliberately at maybe 77 in a 70, and cars legitimately were zipping by me in the left lane, and I was defensive and frustrated that I was the one being chastised while others skated free.

However, there have also been times I was pulled over for "speeding" when I was not speeding, and I have never protested via whataboutism, but rather via the truth.

"Sir, I had my cruise control set on 70 on the dot, and I truly believe that your radar is wrong, and I do not feel that this stop is warranted."

P.P.S. I am aware that I have previously stated that the first major item in a chain-of-events scenario should be viewed as primarily causal, but supply-and-demand economics sometimes proves the exception to that rule, as it is often demand that drives supply rather than supply driving demand; in other words, it was the New World's appetite for slavery that drove the kidnappings, not the other way around.

If they'd make better choices, they'd be doing a lot better. That's the REAL problem!! Look at Allen West!! He's one of the good ones!! Look at Colin Powell!! He didn't make excuses, he made it happen!! But these people spend their money like a drunken sailor. Hell, you've been to the projects- everyone's on food stamps, but they all have their brand new $200 sneakers on, don't they?

Look, modern white Americans aren't old-school Afrikaaners. Yes, hundreds of thousands of black people have been able to live their American Dreams since the Civil Rights Movement, and that's awesome. And, yes, virtually all individuals bear the majority (or at least a substantial amount) of the responsibility for how their own lives turn out, but all of that totally misses the point. Black people still aren't treated equally in housing, banking, education, criminal justice, and so on, and the fact that a decent chunk of black people have overcome these ongoing injustices doesn't mean that we should now ignore the ongoing injustices.

In other words, I'm not making the case that racism is the only possible factor to explain why an individual black person isn't doing well financially (or otherwise). I know that personal choices and individual life habits play a major role in virtually all individuals' life outcomes. That having been said, though, as we have demonstrated throughout this book, racism creates an exponential effect when a black person makes a poor choice or builds a poor habit, and racism also carries with it a sort of reverse exponential saddling effect of black people's good choices or productive habits.

Also, please let me tell you something, Mr. Caucasian Expert on the Projects, I actually worked in a hood school. And a lot of the kids had expensive sneakers (that they mostly bought with their own money that they earned working a job after school-GASP-imagine that, a black high school kid with a job!!), but some of the kids had sneakers from PayLess or WalMart that were made to look enough like the expensive sneakers so the very poorest kids could feel like they belonged-ish (but not so much like the expensive sneakers that Nike would sue the stuffing out of PayLess and WalMart). And everyone knew what was going on, but we mostly tried not to say anything. Isn't it regretful that we live in a society that makes children who were born deeply impoverished feel a sense of deep shame about a personal condition they played no role in creating?

Finally, citing individual examples of the hundreds of thousands of black people who have overcome American racism as "evidence" that "racism is no big deal" makes exactly as much sense as pointing to the hundreds of thousands of Jews who escaped the Holocaust as "evidence" that "the Holocaust was no big deal" or pointing out the hundreds of thousands of American women who have thrived in spite of sexism as "evidence" that "sexism is no big deal".

In short, I'm not sure when universality became a necessary component of injustice- maybe you think that if 100% of all children aren't universally sold into sexual slavery, then sexual slavery shouldn't be characterized as an injustice and sexual slavery should be viewed as "no big deal", but this is not a concept that I embrace or accept.

The REAL problem with the blacks is the culture of victimhood!!

Damn, there sure are a lot of different things that white people keep insisting are the singular "real" problem with black people. Question- if we're willing to admit that there could be many reasons why black people are behind, can we at least put racism on the list? Please?

And, as we touched on in the chapter "Black Culture", when white people assert that black people's collective station in the US is best attributed to "culture", they are totally self snitching You see, if black culture is "inferior", then the question must be asked, "Inferior to what?" The obvious unstated implication is that white culture must be "superior" In other words, the white folks who advance this theory are by-definition, straight-up white supremacists.

But also, a 2017 NPR poll said that 55% of American white people believe that white people are discriminated against in America (https://www.npr.org/2017/10/24/559604836/majority-of-white-americans-think-theyre-discriminated-against).

And let's not forget the 2015 Fox News poll said that 81% of white evangelical Christians believe that Christianity is under attack in America (http://www.foxnews.com/politics/2015/07/21/fox-news-poll-christians-feel-under-attack.html).

Now please tell me who's playing the victim again?

EXACTLY!! The REAL prejudice in 2017 is against heterosexual white Christian men. We made America into the greatest country on earth, and now somehow we're the enemy?? That's reverse racism!! You see, no one wants to talk about that!! Affirmative action and quotas are turning white people into 2nd class citizens!!

First, I am already on the record with my belief that Affirmative Action is a clear violation of the 14th Amendment, as **extra** protection is **unequal** protection. Additionally, while I know that Affirmative Action was well intended, I believe it has outlived its usefulness to the point of actually being counter-productive over at least the past decade. As such, I do not oppose the white people who are against Affirmative Action, though my rationale is quite a bit different (more on Affirmative Action in the chapter on reform).

That having been said, regarding the larger point, there is nothing on this earth more preposterous than white men in America playing the victim. After all, white men account for about 80% of the House, 80% of the Senate, and more than 90% of the CEO jobs in the Fortune 500, so I think that we're doing OK, even as these damn women and minorities and gay people keep crying about little things like equality.

My old friend and University of Houston college professor Christal Seahorn schooled me on a brilliantly simple truth: to the people in power, equality always feels like oppression.

We have a Black History Month and a Black Entertainment Television, but can you imagine the outcry if we demanded a White History Month or if we started a White Entertainment Television network?

Ah, more of the white victimhood bullshit. Let me counter this common complaint with a true story from my time as a college basketball coach.

In the Fall of 2008, I did a dual Halloween costume with my good friend Pershin "Moonface" Williams, where he dressed as Black History Month (a black t-shirt with the February calendar on it) and I dressed as White History MonthS (a white t-shirt with a calendar of the other 11 months). Get it? If you've ever made dumbass white victimhood comments like the ones listed above, then I doubt you do, so let me explain:

We don't need a white history month because all of the other months are by default white history months.

We don't need a white entertainment network because all of the other networks are by default white entertainment networks.

Come on, American white people- we were never collectively oppressed in this country on a large scale over multiple generations, and a few token nods of recognition that black people have contributed to this country shouldn't make us feel threatened or upset, and they certainly shouldn't cause us to portray ourselves as victims.

I'm not a racist, I'm a realist!!

First, "racist" and "realist" aren't antonyms, which means they're not mutually exclusive terms. It is certainly possible to be both a racist and a realist. That having been said, moving forward, before you spout off negative stats about black people like the homicide rate or the standardized test scores in order to justify your racism, please keep in mind what you've read in this book, especially Chapter 4, Chapter 7, Chapter 8, and Chapter 9, because the truth is that the data you cling to tells the story in a terribly incomplete and misleading way. In other words, when you spew this crap in the context of disparaging black people through selectively citing only certain data, you're being a propagandist, because you're presenting only data that matches your agenda. Needless to say, unlike racist and realist, propagandist and realist actually are antonyms, which means that virtually 100% of the people who say "I'm not a racist, I'm a realist" are, as the great George Carlin would say, STUNNINGLY full of shit.

It's heritage, not hate!!

Are you a nerdy bookworm who thinks Ken Burns is the most interesting man in the world, causing you to feel compelled to participate in Civil War re-enactments? Or are you a curator of an American history museum? Or are you an American history professor whose primary area of research is the American Civil War?

No, no, and no? Then shut the fuck up. Please and thank you.

Also, heritage and hate aren't antonyms. For example, the Armenian genocide is part of Turkish heritage. The Holocaust is part of German heritage. And white-supremacy-based slavery and the institutional racism like Jim Crow that followed are part of American heritage.

In other words, I agree that the Confederate flag is part of our heritage, but it represents a heritage of hatred (and treason), and while I agree completely that this part of our heritage must not be forgotten, it should be repudiated, not celebrated, and the racist dickweeds who celebrate it should be repudiated as well.

Stop tearing down monuments and erasing our Southern history!! Robert E. Lee was a true Southern gentleman and the greatest American general to ever live!!

When looking at monuments and the like, the "primary legacy" standard should be applied, in my opinion. Washington, Jefferson, Madison, and many others owned slaves, but they aren't honored for that; rather, they're honored for their overall otherwise tremendous contributions to our nation.

In the case of Robert E. Lee, though, the simple and irrefutable truth is that his primary "contribution", and his lasting legacy, is leading a failed traitorous uprising AGAINST the United States of America in an unsuccessful attempt to preserve and uphold evil.

Sure, he might have been a reluctant traitor, but he wasn't reluctant enough. After all, Judas was a reluctant traitor to Jesus. Judas was quite conflicted. But where are all the monuments to Judas? And where are all the monuments to Benedict Arnold? He was actually quite conflicted in some regards, also.

Honestly, how can anyone claim to love America while honoring traitors?

Also, a note on "erasing history":

Hitler has no monuments in Germany. Have we erased him from history? Have we forgotten about him? Is he not mentioned prominently in books and at museums, all over the world?

Monuments aren't about preserving history, they're about honoring history, and if the thing you're most famous for was fighting to protect slavery or orchestrating genocide, you don't deserve to be honored, especially not on public land. When examining his primary legacy, Robert E. Lee was a traitor, and a loser, and he fought on the side of evil, and I have no idea why any American who isn't a raging racist would want to honor someone who is so antithetical to core American values like patriotism, winning, freedom, and goodness.

P.S. Robert E. Lee's finest military work, by far, was during a time when he chose to renounce his American citizenship, thereby disqualifying him completely from even being remotely considered as "the greatest American general to ever live", as he was literally not an American between 1861-1865.

P.P.S. I am aware that Robert E. Lee never owned slaves, and I am aware that he wrote a letter before the Civil War even commenced that harshly criticized slavery, and I agree that in his heart and mind he was probably more fighting for Virginia than against the USA, but none of that changes that the thing he is most known for- his lasting legacy was leading a failed treasonous rebellion to uphold slavery, and that primary legacy isn't something to be honored or exalted, no matter how admirable other aspects of his life might have been.

P.P.P.S. Robert E. Lee agreed with me on this topic, I might add. He was adamantly against erecting any monuments to prominent Confederate soldiers or politicians, so how about since you claim to respect him so much, you honor his fucking wishes? How does that sound?

The Civil War wasn't even about slavery. It was about economics and states' rights!!

Saying that the Civil War was about economics rather than slavery is like saying that the flooding Houston saw in the Fall of 2017 was about weather rather than Hurricane Harvey. Yes, hurricanes are a subset of the broader term "weather", and, yes, the system of slavery could be viewed as a subset of the broader term "economics". But, we're normally allowed to discuss specific causes without unnecessarily broadening the topic, aren't we?

If I said, "the bridge collapsing killed my friend Tommy", would you say, "no, your friend's death was caused by infrastructure issues"?

Or, if I said, "my friend Jimmy passed away due to cancer", no one would argue by saying, "no, your friend's death was caused by disease".

In both examples, the second broader statement is true, but it doesn't at all refute the accuracy of the initial narrow statement.

So, if you want to make yourself feel better by obfuscating the specific cause of the Civil War by using broader language, that's fine with me, I suppose, but please stop propagandizing this issue as though using broader language nullifies specific language.

P.S. As we discussed in the chapter *History*, the "states' rights" thing doesn't hold up, either, as none of secession documents mentioned any specific states'-rights-based grievances that weren't slavery-related. In fact, only Texas mentioned any specific grievances whatsoever that weren't slavery-related (they felt that the federal government should have been doing more to help "subdue" the Comanche Indians).

Everyone living in this country is more privileged than 95% of the entire world. I think it's funny that people are arguing about who out of that 5% are more privileged. It's ridiculous. We all have it good in this country. Where else in the world do black people have it better than the USA? Nowhere!! But America is supposed to be this awful place for black people? What a joke!!

So, because most people in other countries have tougher lives than the average American black person, it is "ridiculous" to concern ourselves with race-based injustice in our own country?

Would you remind paraplegic American veterans that there are quadriplegic veterans out there in other countries, so they should feel lucky and quit complaining?

Would you lecture an American rape victim that other rape victims in other countries were gang raped or serially raped or raped by their own fathers, so she should count her blessings?

This extremely non-empathetic "logic" makes about as much sense to me as masturbating with a blender.

I am so sick of seeing successful and educated blacks belly-aching about how awful things are. Deray Mckesson went to Brandeis, for crying out loud- what is HE complaining about??

As white people, we must guard against the tendency to look at successful American black people who comment on racial inequality as if they should just shut the fuck up and show some fucking gratitude. After all, no one has ever written or said that America made John Adams and Ben Franklin prosperous so they somehow lost their right to protest slavery. All Americans have the right to protest any and all injustice, no matter what.

Consider Martin Luther King JR as an example, who was the son of a prominent Atlanta preacher. I'm actually sitting in Ebenezer Baptist Church as I write this passage. It's a nice place, and so is Dr. King's birth home. Plus, Dr. King was educated at Morehouse, the top historically black college in the world. In other words, Dr. King's family and he had carved out a pretty nice middle or maybe even upper-middle class existence (especially relative to most black folks) when he decided to risk and ultimately lose his life fighting for justice.

Hopefully, we all agree that Dr. King not only **had the right** to protest, but **was right** to protest, and that the relative financial status of his family wasn't (and isn't) relevant. Furthermore, who do we think would be most effective at presenting the cause for equal justice, an educated and successful black person like Dr. King, or Buckwheat? Or maybe you'd rather listen to the rationales behind our cause coming from obnoxious, far-left white liberals who frantically cross the street any time they come near a black person besides the two or three they became friends with as undergraduates together at Dartmouth?

We as white people allow successful Latinos to speak for Latinos, we allow successful gay people to speak for gay people, we allow successful women to speak for women, and so on, so it truly is preposterous for us as white people to resent successful American black people who bravely speak up against racism.

Fine, but what I want to know is why do black people have a need to feel racially offended by seemingly everything?

Why do they have a need to feel racially offended? I feel that people who ask this question are doing so rhetorically, but I'm going to answer it anyway, as it is an absolutely critical question.

American black people don't FEEL offended, they ARE offended, because so many white people ARE offensive, and I sincerely hope that all earnestly well intentioned American white people will at the very least open their hearts and minds enough to only ask this question non-rhetorically.

Don't want to get shot by the police? Real simple- comply with their orders instead of running your mouth or running away, and they won't shoot you!! Pull up your pants and turn the damn music down!! Problem solved!!

As we have already discussed, we need to quit over-focusing on the (at least arguably) "contributory" behavior or "aggravating" factor, like running from the police, talking back to the police, dressing in a certain manner, or whatever, because it causes us to under-focus on or even dismiss the actual physical harm or death of a human fucking being.

So, sure, Freddie Gray shouldn't have run from the police, and Eric Garner shouldn't have been selling loose cigarettes, and 12 year-old Tamir Rice shouldn't have been waving his BB gun around, but did they **deserve to die**? If so, it should be noted that we don't apply this thought process to other interactions that turn violent.

For example, let's say you're in a bar, and some drunk idiot walks up on you and says, "Fuck you!! You're a pussy!!" I think most people wouldn't object too strenuously if you punched the guy in the face, and most would say the guy got what he deserved, because he started it. But what if you punched his him in the face, and then got on top of him and proceeded to beat and stomp his skull until he fell into a coma? Did the guy still "get what he deserved"? Or, what if you pull out your gun and shoot him in the head, killing him instantly. Is that OK, simply because you were "provoked"?

Do you see what I'm saying? When consequences radically exceed the infraction, we have a problem, because proportionality must matter within discussions of justice.

If a citizen is mouthy toward a cop, and the cop decides to add additional fine to the ticket for "disturbing the peace" as retribution for the disrespect? Fine, I suppose. And if a citizen makes the poor choice to run from the police, and the police tackle him from behind and he breaks his collar bone? I'm pretty much good with that, too.

But, in a free society, people DO NOT deserve severe and lasting physical injury or death for mouthing off to a cop, or running away from a cop, or dressing a certain way, or any of the "aggravating" factors or "contributory" behavior that so many of us try to use to justify the gross (and sometimes deadly) overreactions of our law enforcement officials. A police officer is a police officer, not a prosecutor, or a judge, or a jury, or a vigilante, or an executioner. That bullshit just isn't a part of a police officer's job description in a civilized society, and it's way past time that all Americans recognize this very basic truth, and apply it equally, even when the human being who was wrongfully harmed or killed has darker skin than we do.

For the record, white people who say things like "don't run from the cops and you won't get shot" or "I just don't understand why the (dead) black person made the poor choice to run" echo white people's sentiments when Emmitt Till was beaten, tortured, and drowned in Mississippi in the 1950's.

Overt and hostile white racists said, "Leave our white women alone and this wouldn't happen. Whistle at a white woman, and that's what you get!!"

And less overt and less hostile white racists (what Dr. King would have called white moderates) said, "Why would you whistle at a white women in the South like that? This is such a tragedy, but I just don't understand why he would do that, in Mississippi of all places!!"

So, you see, we as white people haven't changed anywhere near as much as we like to give ourselves credit for, and as we've discussed throughout this book, our first focus should never be, "what could the dead person have done differently?" but rather, "what could the killer have done differently?"

Somehow I don't think it would be acceptable for a white person to say they were disappointed with the "black moderate".

I don't (and will never) understand why so many white people in America love to play this little faux double standard game.

Question:

What actions (or inactions) of black moderates have prevented white people from enjoying equal justice and equal opportunity in this country?

Answer:

None.

Therefore, stop it. For crying out loud, please, just stop it.

Black lives matter? ALL lives matter!! Blue lives matter!!

These oft-repeated comments embody the lack of racial empathy displayed by way too many white people. Almost immediately, as soon as someone says #BlackLivesMatter, many white people start up with rebukes like #AllLivesMatter, #BlueLivesMatter, #AmericanLivesMatter, and #WhiteLivesMatter. The thing is, though, no one ever disputed that all lives matter or that white lives matter or that blue lives matter. Of course, everyone's life matters. The issue many people have is that historically, black lives in this country have clearly mattered much less, and sometimes, especially considering historical context, it still feels like black lives matter less (and the studies support the feelings). So that is why the #BlackLivesMatter movement exists, and why the #BlackLivesMatter movement has importance. I'm frustrated with anyone talking about #AllLivesMatter as some sort of rebuke toward #BlackLivesMatter because no one rebukes Breast Cancer Awareness Week for not instead being called All Cancer Awareness Week- please understand and accept that the #BlackLivesMatter movement is about the idea that #BlackLivesMatterALSO, not #BlackLivesMatterMORE or #ONLYBlackLivesMatter.

I do not recall the source of this anecdote, but the best example to explain the #BlackLivesMatter movement goes something like this:

Little Billy is sitting at dinner with his family. His parents serve all of his brothers and sisters a plate of food, except for him. His parents also did the same thing at breakfast and lunch, giving everyone in the family a plate of food except for Billy, so Little Billy is understandably feeling as if he has been and is being treated unjustly. As such, he decides to speak up and say, "I need a plate of food" to which both parents and most of his siblings reply, "EVERYONE needs a plate of food" before proceeding to continue eating without discussing Billy's justifiable objection of fundamental unfairness, much less making any changes to ensure that Little Billy was treated equally moving forward, instead dismissively proceeding to eat dinner while Billy had none.

Little Billy wasn't making a frivolous request, as he was being denied equal treatment by the authorities in his life, and the #BlackLivesMatter movement's objectives aren't frivolous, either. After all, we have already shown (and proven with data) some of the many ways in which our criminal justice system fails to live up to the lofty expectation that our law enforcement and judicial systems treat all American citizens equally, as set forth by the 14th Amendment to the United States Constitution. As such, maybe it's time for all of us to get upset not about a discussion of injustice, but about injustice itself.

Policing is a dangerous job!! So, what, you think cops are driving around looking for black people to randomly murder? If you don't like it, you should sign up for the police academy and try to make an actual difference instead of just complaining!!

No one denies that policing is a dangerous and vital job. However, as we have discussed, many other professions are more dangerous and equally vital, but would we accept and be OK with a national trend of soldiers and loggers and garbage men shooting or beating the shit out of unarmed American citizens?

That having been said, I don't think any sane person believes that 100% of police officers are habitually and deliberately targeting black people, hunting them like animals, shooting on sight, and all that sort of thing. But please remember, there's a scale in play here, and a police officer doesn't need to behave like Bull Conner in order to suffer from racial bias and be accurately characterized as a racist.

Finally, I've never understood the common refrain of "since you criticize the police, you should become a police officer". Um, excuse me? Since when do we think that protestors are required to join the group they're protesting against in order for the protest to have merit?

By this standard and "logic":

Israelis must renounce both their faith and their citizenship, convert to Islam, and move to Palestine in order to have the right to object to Hamas.

Tea Party members must leave the Libertarian Party or the GOP and become a liberal Democrat in order to have the right to criticize Barack Obama.

Americans who criticize the New York Times must change careers and become a journalist working for the New York Times in order to have the right to editorialize about the NYT's coverage.

Look, I agree that actual experience in a given field should be required to participate in substantive policy development in that field. For example, it absolutely drives me crazier that we've allowed business leaders and politicians to craft and drive education policy, rather than listening to our teachers and our principals.

However, while I am not qualified to write policies in the financial sector, does the fact that I have never worked in banking or investing automatically render baseless any criticism I might proffer about Bernie Madoff? Or should it be required for me to have been employed in the energy sector prior to offering the opinion that Ken Lay is a scumbag?

This entire train of thought just does not withstand even basic logical scrutiny.

I agree that racism existed in the past, but it's not the 1800's or even the 1950's. I mean, come on, that stuff doesn't happen anymore- the blacks are just playing the victim, looking for a check, making excuses, and making things up.

Before cell phone video cameras, white racists and white fence sitters lived in a permanent state of disbelief about black people's experiences dealing with the police, but it truly speaks volumes about America that even in the face of constant video proof that verifies everything black people have been saying for decades, the racists and fence sitters STILL won't open their eyes, dismissing or justifying everything they see on all of the countless videos that have emerged.

OK, fine, SOME of those videos are disturbing, and I'm not saying the police are perfect, but these inflammatory videos are isolated incidents. Or are you saying there's absolutely zero justice EVER shown to any black person in America and all cops are racists who are out to get black people for absolutely no reason? Yeah, right!!

First, please go to YouTube and search the words "black people and the police". There are almost countless videos posted of police officers behaving in an at least arguably objectionable manner toward American black people, and while I don't exactly know mathematically when a recurring event becomes a trend, I do know that "isolated" and "countless" most definitely aren't synonyms (I think Steve Jobs's real lasting legacy is the cell-phone video camera, as nothing has done more to open the eyes, hearts, and minds of younger American white people to the idea that racial injustice is definitely not "a thing of the past").

Furthermore, in the past decade alone, Chicago and New York collectively have paid more than a BILLION dollars in settlements related to police misconduct. That total is for just 2 American cities, and only includes the past 10 years. For the sake of comparison, the Catholic Church has paid $3.9 billion in settlements for all priest-related sexual abuse, worldwide, in the entire history of the Catholic Church. Granted, many Catholic Church officials continue to swear up and down that priest pedophilia is "but an isolated incident", but perhaps we can agree that as soon as paid legal settlements hit the BILLION dollar mark, then the issue leading to the very large number of different settlements with a very large number of unique victims should be categorized as a problem we must face, not a statistical anomaly we can afford to indefinitely ignore.

As for the suggestion that I believe 100% of police officers are evil racists who are actively and intentionally hurting (if not hunting) black people, or that 100% of black people are treated unfairly by 100% of police officers 100% of the time, I think I'll let Wikipedia chime in:

A straw man is a common form of argument and is an informal fallacy based on giving the impression of refuting an opponent's argument, while in fact refuting an argument that was not advanced by that opponent in the first place.

So, while I'm not going to waste time rebutting a classic straw-man logical fallacy, I am on the record in this book and elsewhere that I do believe racism is so pervasive in America as to be borderline universal, so it would be reasonable and in fact accurate to deduce that I think virtually all American police officers suffer from at least some racial bias. After all, our police officers are Americans, just like the rest of us, so there's no reason to expect that police officers would somehow magically be immune from something that I believe nearly universally affects the rest of us- but I am also on the record in this book and elsewhere that racism has a scale, and it is crystal clear to me that only a very small fraction of police officers harbor hatred for and evil intentions toward American black people.

Simply put, I am totally convinced that virtually all Americans carry with them at least some racial bias, of course including American police officers, and I am convinced that this bias causes some cops in some cases to be disproportionately afraid of black people, and this bias-based fear causes the majority of the police shootings of unarmed black people; then, of course, white jurors tend to overwhelmingly empathize with the accused police officer being terrified of black people because most of those white jurors also find black people to be terrifying, which results in white people on juries believing that the shooter cop's fears were reasonable, because to call the cop's fear unreasonable would be to hold up a deeply discomforting mirror.

Want to know what I think? Black people are terrified, not terrifying.

Just because black people are arrested at a higher rate doesn't prove racism. There could be lots of reasons why this occurs. Is the NBA racist against whites because it doesn't have hardly any white people?

Listen, as we have already discussed, nationwide over the past decade, marijuana usage between white people and black people has been very similar. And, of course, in order to use marijuana, you must possess it. But in spite of the drug's usage being approximately equal (as a percent- as a raw number, white marijuana users outnumber black marijuana users nearly 10 fold, while as a percent, black usage is slightly higher), black people get arrested for possessing marijuana at a wildly disproportionate rate. Now, if you want to make the case that other factors besides race might partially explain this disparity, that's fine. You might be at least somewhat right, but it's deeply troubling that you seem so eager to dismiss racism as even a potential partial factor in the massive criminal-justice-related statistical disparities that exist across the board between white people and black people in America.

As for the NBA analogy, let me start by saying that we have already demonstrated the huge number of white people who are well qualified to be arrested for marijuana possession but have never actually been arrested for marijuana possession. Can you point to a huge number of white people who are well qualified to be on an NBA team but have never actually been on an NBA team?

Of course you can't, but that's because your point wasn't genuine in the first place. You don't actually believe that white people are being discriminated against by NBA teams. What you're really trying to say is that America, like the NBA, is a race-blind, true, free-market meritocracy, so the **real reason** "the blacks" struggle to get ahead is that they don't work as hard and aren't as smart and weren't raised as well as white people. Some of you are thinking "DAMN RIGHT!!" but before you cement that reflexive reaction, please keep in mind that this sentiment defines and embodies white supremacy. Are you really OK with being a white supremacist and associating yourself with white supremacy? I suppose you'll have to answer that question for yourself.

I'm not familiar with these statistics you mention. Where are they from? I need more information!!

The Racial Doubting Thomas crowd gets on my nerves with their Selective Sherlock Syndrome bullshit. For the record, I have never in my life heard a white racist doubt stats or "need more info" about any stat that seems to paint a negative picture about black people, but they ALWAYS "need more info" when they encounter statistics than run counter to their racist narrative.

Say whatever you want, but if I'm a black parent, I'm teaching my kids to respect the police, and show their hands, and not make any sudden movements, and to dress professionally, and not to run from the police. An ounce of prevention is worth a pound of cure!!

If you don't think black parents have already been having conversations with their children to discuss strategies about appeasing white people in order to avoid being injured or killed, you really need to get out more. Black parents have been having "the talk" with their children for centuries, literally. The problem here isn't that black people aren't having "the talk" but rather that they still need to have "the talk" in the first damn place.

P.S. On what planet do children and teenagers of any race universally listen to and follow the good advice that their parents shower them with? With this in mind, let me just say that if you feel the need to shame the parent of a dead child, then shame on you.

P.P.S. It's ironic when white people insist that racism exists only in the mind of black people, and if they would stop talking about it so much, then it wouldn't be such a big deal, while simultaneously asserting that if black parents would talk to their children more about how to survive in a racist country by being submissive to police, then the police would stop killing black people. So, black people are or are not supposed to talk about this stuff? Your thought patterns are confusing, mostly because you are confused.

Parents need to step up to the plate. Teach your children to respect themselves, and others, especially adults and the police. Show them what it is like to work for something, The problems begin at home, and this is something that can never be controlled by laws.

This train of thought is so ironic, because it's absolutely correct. This problem does start at home, with racist white parents actively (though usually inadvertently) participating in the brainwashing their children into themselves becoming racist white people and later parents, who teach their children the same racist bullshit, and the cycle continues, on and on and on and on. Racism truly does start at home, and I hope that white parents will pay special attention to the chapter on "Individual Solutions".

You always complain, but what solutions do you offer? Look at Colin Kaepernick, taking a knee, to what end? No solutions, just complaining, his protest is completely ineffective- that's my problem with Kaepernick!! Of course I support his right to protest, but why does he have to disrespect our country, with no tangible goals behind his little protest? He's an empty barrel, making the most noise!!

First, many "race agitators" have proposed comprehensive solutions to our race-related problems. For example, Deray McKesson and a coalition of Black Lives Matter activists have created "Campaign Zero", which is 100% devoted to proffering solutions.

However, I have a strong suspicion that virtually all white racists who patronizingly demand to discuss the "solutions" would view any proposed solutions with hostility anyway (as this book has 2 chapters on solutions, we won't have to wait too long to find out). Lord knows that MLK was all about solutions, like integration and doing away with road blocks preventing black people from voting, and white people were so impressed with his solution-oriented approach that we put a bullet in his brain.

As for Kaepernick, he isn't disrespecting our country- he's protesting injustice. That isn't the same thing, and I would argue that NOT protesting chronic injustice in America is MUCH more disrespectful to our country and our ideals than anything Colin Kaepernick has done. I don't totally agree with the sentiment so often (incorrectly as it turns out) attributed to Thomas Jefferson that "dissent is the highest form of patriotism" but I absolutely believe that dissent is patriotic.

Honestly, we can't as a society worry more about (or even as much about) the form of the protest as we do about the reason for the protest, or at least we shouldn't.

All that having been said, though, this book does devote 2 full chapters to solutions, and I hope that people of all different colors and creeds will give some of the solutions we propose consideration without condemnation.

Right Wing Bullshit

Democrats are the REAL RACISTS!! The GOP is the party of Lincoln, who freed the slaves, and the founders of the KKK and all of the segregationists who tried to block the Civil Rights Movement were a bunch of Democrats!!

I agree that it is an historical fact that the deep South voted solid blue in the 1950's, and that Southern Democrats were largely responsible for trying to block the Civil Rights Movement, but I am also aware that the deep South voted solid red in 2016.

As far as I know, only 2 possibilities exist to explain this massive geographic political switch-a-roo:

1. We've seen an unprecedented half-century two-way migration, whereby a bunch of racist white Democrats from the deep South moved to states like New York and California, coincidentally occurring simultaneously with a bunch of racially tolerant white Republicans moving from states like New York and California to the deep South.

OR

2. People in the deep South over time decided the Republican Party was closer aligned with "Southern values" and consequently made the switch from Democrat to Republican.

First, let's look at a little electoral history, courtesy of http://www.270towin.com/historical-presidential-elections/:

From 1860, the year Abraham Lincoln was elected as a Republican, until John F. Kennedy's election in 1960, the last election before The Civil Rights Movement gained national momentum, the deep South voted solidly Democrat in every election except for 1864, when Southerners of course could not vote due to their decision to take up arms against the United States, and the elections of 1868, 1872, and 1876, during which times white Southerners were largely disenfranchised due to Civil War Reconstruction, and 1948, because Strom Thurmond's 3rd party candidacy based on segregation carried four deep-South states (Eisenhower, the war hero who ran as a Republican but had no previous partisan history and was courted by both parties, won some states that fought on the side of the Confederacy in both 1952 and 1956, but did not win any of the deepest of the deep South states- the contiguous belt from South Carolina to Georgia to Alabama to Mississippi to Louisiana- in 1952 and won only Louisiana in the deepest of the deep South in 1956).

On the other hand, from 1964 until 2016, the deep South has voted solidly Republican in every election except for 1968, when George Wallace's 3rd party candidacy based on segregation carried five deep South states, and some of the years with a Southerner at the top of the ticket (Jimmy Carter swept the deep South in 1976, though he did not win Virginia, which of course fought for the Confederacy; and Bill Clinton was able to win 2 deep-South states in 1992, plus another 2 that fought for the Confederacy, and 1 deep South state in 1996, plus another three that fought for the Confederacy).

Clearly, something pretty dramatic happened between 1960 and 1964, so we again return to the question: did lots of racist white Democrats move out of the deep South, or did lots of non-racist white Republicans move into the deep South, or, over time, did lots of racist white Democrats become racist white Republicans?

Given the context of what we know happened historically between 1960 and 1964, which was the Democrat-controlled executive and legislative and judicial branches of the federal government mutually co-conspiring to force integration down the throats of white Southerners, it is probably most reasonable to deduce that white Southerners felt betrayed by the Democratic Party and consequently over time switched party allegiance to the only other viable alternative in our two-party system. Indeed, if you ask around, I can promise that you will find WAY more white Republican-voting 3rd or 4th generation Alabamans with parents and grandparents who once voted Democrat than you will find white Republican-voting 1st or 2nd generation Alabamans with parents and grandparents who moved to Alabama and had always voted Republican.

P.S. This notion that Strom Thurmond was the "only" Democrat to switch parties involves a great deal of selective fact presentation. Yes, he was the only Democrat Senator who voted against the Civil Rights Act of 1964 who later switched parties to become a Republican, but he was absolutely not the only prominent American politician who left the Democratic Party to join the GOP in the years and decades that followed the Civil Rights Movement (Ronald Reagan, Jesse Helms, John Connally, and hundreds more). The decision to switch political parties doesn't happen overnight, of course, but it's pretty obvious when looking at the history and especially the timing that the Civil Rights Movement played a pivotal role in the beginning of the gradual shift in political allegiance that has occurred in our nation's former slave-holding states.

The Democrats keep the planation mentality of dependence alive with their promises of free stuff!! That's why the blacks all vote Democrat!!

First, and this is a key point, the master was dependent on the slaves, not the other way around. The slaves would have been just fine without the master; in fact, they would have been much, much, much better off without the master, as black people have gradually been afforded the opportunity to prove since slavery ended.

Additionally, according to the 2012 US Census, 58.4% of American black people received no government assistance of any sort. So, I'm curious, if a desire for "free stuff" explains why black people overwhelmingly vote Democrat, why do the majority millions of black people who receive absolutely nothing from the government nevertheless tend to overwhelmingly vote Democrat?

To set the record straight, black people don't vote Democrat because of the "pandering". Black people are plenty smart enough to see through that stuff, although I don't think the "pandering" happens anywhere near as much as some people seem to think.

One of the main reasons black people vote Democrat is because Republican candidates can not stop publicly espousing and defending blatantly racist views, like thinking that Democrat pandering and "promises of free stuff" manipulates black people, because the crystal clear implication is that the easily manipulated group isn't very smart, and in a shocking plot twist, it appears as if calling black people stupid does not make them like you very much.

I actually think if Republicans would quit making ragingly racist comments, shutting their mouths and opening their ears (and hearts), black people would be way more split politically over time, as there are plenty of issues that plenty of black people agree with Republicans on (God, gays, and guns leap to mind, though of course many black people prefer a secular Democracy to a theocracy, many black people support marriage equality, and many black people support gun regulation- but many do not).

This is very similar to MSNBC and the left-wing talking heads constantly railing against rural white voters "voting against their own interests". Well, guess what? In an equally unpredictable turn of events, come to find out that rural white people don't like being called stupid, either, so they don't like liberal "elites", at all, in large part because liberal elites absolutely refuse to stop their uninterrupted flow of condescending and insulting comments.

Right-wing white people tend to think that black people won't give them a chance, when it is in fact very much the other way around.

And left-wing white people tend to think that rural white people won't give them a chance, when it is in fact very much the other way around.

We should all remember that you catch more flies with honey than with vinegar, and it is just flat unreasonable to demand that a group of people you habitually insult should "give you a chance". First, make genuine overtures with tolerance and understanding, and then you can complain if your dove winds up on their grill; but we can't know how our doves will be received until we send them, and we can't have peace, justice, and harmony unless we're bold enough to actually at long last legitimately give each other a fair chance.

Everyone wants to claim "RACISM" but if you look at where black people have it the worst, it's in the cities like Detroit and Baltimore and Chicago that have been destroyed by black Democrats and their liberal policies!!

For starters, let's take a quick look at the 10 cities in the US where black people are the best positioned financially (https://www.forbes.com/sites/joelkotkin/2015/01/15/the-cities-where-african-americans-are-doing-the-best-economically/#6181e0d3164f) as well as the political affiliation and race of each city's mayor:

Atlanta (Keisha Lance Bottoms, Democrat, black)

Raleigh (Nancy McFarlane, Independent but received the Democratic endorsement, white)

Washington, DC (Muriel Bowser, Democrat, black)

Baltimore (Catherine Pugh, Democrat, black)

Charlotte (Vi Lyles, Democrat, black)

Norfolk/Virginia Beach (Kenny Alexander, Democrat, black for Norfolk; Will Sessoms, Republican, white for Virginia Beach)

Orlando (Buddy Dyer, Democrat, white)

Miami (Francis Suarez, Republican, Latino)

Richmond (Levar Stoney, Democrat, black)

San Antonio (Ron Nirenberg, Independent, multi-racial)

So, out of the 11 cities where black people are financially best off, six are led by black Democrats, one is led by a white Democrat, one is led by a white Independent, one is led by a multi-racial independent, one is led by a Latino Republican, and just one out of the 11 is led by a white Republican (and that one white Republican is the mayor of Virginia Beach, which is only half of the metropolitan area that often gets grouped together as "Norfolk/Virginia Beach".

It should also be noted that many of the cities most commonly cited as "evidence" of this oft-repeated talking point (Detroit, Chicago, Cleveland, Baltimore) were devastated by the slow and sad transition from the Manufacturing Belt to the Rust Belt, and this transition self-evidently had a lot more to do with globalization and federal trade deals driving corporate policies than it did with liberalism driving local policies.

In other words, the facts just flat out do not support this bullshit right-wing talking point (at all).

Left Wing Bullshit

If you voted for Donald Trump, you either support racism, or you don't believe that racism is a disqualifier to be President!!

I swear, I must have heard 100 liberals utter this bullshit in the weeks following the 2016 Presidential election.

First, do I think Donald Trump is a racist? Yes, absolutely.

But, guess what? Hillary Clinton is a fucking racist, too, whether you're willing to admit it or not.

In 1968, Barry Goldwater led the white racist response to the Civil Rights Movement. It was called the "Law and Order" movement (it's still going on, by the way), and Hillary Clinton basically took a hairy shit in Dr. King's mouth when she stumped against the Civil Rights Movement as a "Goldwater Girl".

Then, in the 1990's, she called black males "super predators" when she was stumping to drum up support for her husband's now infamous 1994 crime bill, a series of criminal justice reforms that adversely and disproportionately affected millions of American black people and their families.

What about her behavior in the 2007 Democratic Primary? Are you really going to tell me that neither she nor her camp did anything wrong related to race, as if Bill didn't tell Teddy Kennedy that the Kennedys should be supporting Hillary because Barack would have been carrying their water 20 years ago?

And she wasn't much better in the 2015 Democratic Primary, either, when her initial reactions to the emergence of the #BlackLivesMatter movement were also enormously telling in my view- she wasn't just made uncomfortable by their presence, she was pissed, before (rather quickly) realizing how politically ruinous her reflexive initial reactions were likely to be and phonily pulling herself together.

In short, Hillary might have lots of black friends, but she is no friend to black people, and she never has been.

So, let me just say that if you voted for Hillary Clinton, you either support racism or you don't believe that racism is a disqualifier to be President.

Oh, my God!! Are you serious right now?? Hillary isn't a racist, but even if she were, total false equivalency comparing her to Donald Trump!! You just totally outed yourself as a lunatic fringe far-right wingnut by acting like WE are the problem!! Everyone knows that liberals aren't racists!!

First, a quick note on Trump's racism and the notion that pointing out Hillary's racism is engaging in "false equivalency". Yes, again, I totally agree that Trump is a racist. I'm aware that he discriminated against black people when he was a residential landlord, and I think that landlords who broadly discriminate against American black people should be tossed under the jail. However, the false equivalency is opposite of what white liberals think, as Trump's discrimination harmed no where close to as many black people as the racist Clinton-era policies that Hillary Clinton stumped for and helped to enact.

Prior to his election, Donald Trump tangibly harmed thousands of black people, while Hillary Clinton tangibly harmed millions of black people, so I do agree that comparing their racist bonafides is engaging in massive false equivalency (NOTE: I'm pretty sure that Donald Trump and Jeff Sessions will catch up to and surpass the Clintons in terms of the overall number of black people their decisions and policies have adversely affected, but at the time of the 2016 election, Hillary's record on this subject in terms of tangible negative impact on black people was far worse than Trump's, whether you want to admit it or not).

But getting back to the absurd notion that "Democrats aren't racists", if you break America into voting blocks, gay people are among the most reliable Democratic pillars of strength, normally voting Democrat at around an 80% clip. And yet, if you ask any black homosexual if they've experienced racism from white homosexuals, you will get an earful, but if you try to bring this up to a liberal white homosexual, they get highly defensive:

Why are you making everything about race? I'm just not into black guys. That isn't racist!! It's just my preference!!

Ummmm, dude, if this isn't about race, why would you possibly feel the need to label the people you are or aren't attracted to by race? And if racism isn't a big problem in gay communities, why did the city of Philadelphia feel the need to add a black and brown stripe to the rainbow flags for their local pride parade, and why did so many white homosexuals lose their damn minds in opposition to amending the flag to make it more inclusive? Come on, now, use your noggins here and admit it. After all, holding blanket beliefs about people based on race literally defines racism, and there is no question that tons and tons and tons of liberal white homosexuals have "preferences" that are utterly racist.

I have noticed for the past five years or so that when someone states (or even implies) that an American white person who identifies as being politically liberal might harbor even slight racial bias against black people, they lose their fucking minds. Sorry, white liberals, but you grew up in America also, and the idea that you've somehow magically 100% escaped any presence of racial bias, even within your subconscious, involves a massive disconnect in the fields of both human psychology and basic logic.

Essentially, as I've said throughout this book, if you are an American, you are a racist- maybe as a "woke" liberal, you fall as a "2" on the 1-10 racism scale, whereas the right wingers you hate maybe fall as an "8" on the 1-10 racism scale, but you're NOT a damn zero, which means you ARE a damn racist, and, again, we can't even begin to fix this problem until we admit the pervasiveness of this problem.

But to return to the idea that white liberals are in fact a massive part of the problem, please consider Dr. King's words in his legendary Letter from Birmingham Jail:

I must confess that over the past few years I have been gravely disappointed with the white moderate. I have almost reached the regrettable conclusion that the Negro's great stumbling block in his stride toward freedom is not the White Citizen's Counciler or the Ku Klux Klanner, but the white moderate,...shallow understanding from people of good will is more frustrating than absolute misunderstanding from people of ill will. Lukewarm acceptance is much more bewildering than outright rejection.

I know that most white liberals don't want to believe that Dr. King is posthumously scolding them, but the truth is that not since the Civil Rights Movement have white liberals prioritized specifically helping black people (Affirmative Action was ushered in by Nixon, who wasn't and isn't considered to be a liberal). If you are a white liberal, you may be seething right now, but please do an honest assessment of actual liberal political priorities and tell me when was the last time a major reform has been passed that was designed specifically to prevent the ongoing abuse of black people?

Here are most of the major white liberal political priorities of the last several decades:

Environmental Protection (1970's)

Peace in the Middle East (1970's-today)

Energy Independence (1970's-today)

Gun Control (1970's-today)

Reproductive Choice (1970's-today)

Raising Rich People's Taxes (1970's-today)

Ending Wars (1970's, 2000's)

Public Education (1970's, 2000's)

Fighting Nuclear Proliferation (1970's, 1980's)

Health Care (1990's-today)

Global Warming (2000's-today)

Gay Rights (2000's-today)

Trans Rights (2010's-today)

I am sure many white liberals are mentally protesting my thoughts here by telling themselves that most of the stuff listed above **did** help (at least some) black people, such as fighting for gun control, fighting for reproductive choice, raising taxes on the wealthy, fighting for public education, fighting for health care as a human right, and fighting for LGBTQPI rights. And I agree that all of those priorities do help (at least some) black people (at least some of the time), but that's under the JFK (and later Reagan) philosophy that "a rising tide lifts all boats"- it does not take into consideration that the boats with darker-hued hulls are saddled with an extra anchor that must be removed before we congratulate ourselves for programs that "lift all boats".

It should also be noted that while modern white liberals haven't fought to enact any meaningful programs designed specifically to help black people, Bill Clinton's two most important legislative achievements- the crime bill and the welfare reform bill- almost seemed designed specifically to harm black people.

If you're a white liberal, honestly ask yourself:

Have white liberal politicians been fighting for reparations, in any form?

Have white liberal politicians been fighting to reform our Voir'dire jury selection procedures, or for sentencing reform, bail reform, or any reform within our criminal justice system to correct the race-related issues that are consistently proven to exist through mountains of conclusive data?

Have white liberal politicians been fighting to incarcerate powerful white people who blatantly discriminate against black people in banking, real estate, law enforcement, and so on?

Have white liberal politicians been fighting to implement financial consequences (or any consequences) for police departments that allow the Blue Wall of Silence to exist and function uninhibited?

Have white liberal politicians been fighting to end (or reform) the War on Drugs?

Have white liberal politicians put their foot down and taken a stand to end profit-driven prison systems?

There was a time that white liberal politicians did make it a priority to ameliorate black people's misery, and you want to know why? Because leaders of the Civil Rights Movement eventually convinced white liberal citizens to collectively **demand** that their elected officials act. In America, white people have most of the money, and almost all of the power, which means that it falls on us to **continuously prioritize** equality and justice for all Americans, or it will never happen.

Please also keep in mind, again, that when I state my belief that virtually all Americans are racists, I mean virtually all. So when I say, "white liberals are racists", I'm also saying, "all Americans are racists", because almost none of us are a 0 on the racist scale, and, again, if you're not a 0, you're a racist, plain and simple.

Obviously, as I have hopefully made clear by now, I most definitely consider myself to be a racist as well, so I'm throwing rocks at US, not YOU. But I also most definitely want to encourage all white liberals to heed Dr. King's pleading and recognize that in at least 9 out of 10 cases, you are the moderate Dr. King is scolding.

Want to know how I know that? Because it is a given that right-wing racists aren't going to participate in a racially fair agenda, so the "moderates" Dr. King referenced couldn't possibly have been on the political right. Ask yourself, when you look around, do you see a whole bunch of racial moderates on the political right? Do you now see what I'm saying?

Obviously, if white people on the right aren't the moderates Dr. King was disappointed in, who's left (no pun intended)? Through the process of elimination, he could only have been disappointed in white liberals who weren't "all in", and the same thing could be said today, ie, the #1 problem with racism in America is that white liberals aren't **ALL IN**.

Again, we know that the political right has no interest in racial justice, so it falls to white liberals to **PRIORITIZE** black people's **EQUAL HUMANITY**, which just flat hasn't happened in the last 50 years, because on the topic of race relations in America, we have too many white moderates fooling themselves into thinking they're liberals, and no where near enough honest-to-goodness white liberal allies.

OK, fine, I agree. We as white liberals aren't doing enough. But to call us racists? That's going too far!!

Many liberals suffer from a terrible case of self-issued Comparative Clemency, the mental phenomenon of absolving yourself of sin because other people's sins are worse. Yes, again, I agree that (on average) people on the American political right exhibit more and worse racism that people on the American political left, but that shouldn't serve to excuse or deny the pervasiveness of left-wing racism and racial bias.

First, let's take a look at a little bit of history here.

Harry Truman integrated the armed forces, and he was a liberal Democrat, and he was a well documented racist.

Lyndon Johnson not only signed all of the major Civil Rights legislation, but personally browbeated key holdout Southern Senators into getting out of the way, yet he was an even better documented raging racist and white supremacist.

So, if you're a white liberal who thinks you're not a racist, ask yourself:

Have you ever done anything tangible to help American black people?

If the answer is yes, was it on a scale even remotely close to what Truman and LBJ did for American black people?

Do you see what I'm saying? If Truman and LBJ were racists, and we know for a 100% fact that they were, but they did more to specifically help black people than really just about any President we've had since Lincoln, how could you dismiss even the possibility that **you** fall somewhere between 1-10 on the racist scale, rather than insisting that **you** most definitely fall at a 0?

Simply put, racism is a national problem, not a partisan problem or a philosophical problem or a regional problem, and by refusing to own your role in this national problem, you ensure it's indefinite continuation, because, again, we can not fix a massive collective problem until we admit that we have a massive collective problem.

With the premise now having been laid out, here are some specific examples of liberal racism:

For starters, the entire underlying assumption of most liberal rhetoric about black people is the patronizing belief that black people are in need of extra help. This foundational assumption is itself fundamentally racist, as only inferior people need extra help, which means that if you think black people need extra help, you believe white people are superior.

White Savior Complex also involves a healthy dose of racism, as it not only promotes the idea that black people "need to be saved" (like savages) but also that a white person should be the one in charge of doing the saving (I may suffer from this, although in my mind this book is mostly about convincing white people, not "saving" black people, though I do recognize that honest self-evaluation may be the very most difficult human mental undertaking).

Additionally, I don't see many educated white liberals who carry on and on and on and on about diversity and inclusion moving into non-gentrified historically black neighborhoods and sending their children to historically black public schools. I know, I know, I'm being very unfair if not ridiculous. After all, there's nothing wrong with not wanting to live in a dangerous neighborhood with bad schools, right? But this goes back to the lack of self-awareness, as reflexively drawing a correlation between "black" and "dangerous/bad" makes you a racist; you just haven't ever properly considered the true meaning of the word or you're lousy at the admittedly difficult task of self--evaluation. Trust me when I tell you that purse clutching and car door locking and street crossing and refusing to enter "sketchy" parts of town (especially "after dark") are habits exhibited by many if not most white people, independent of political persuasion.

Similarly, there were massive #BlackLivesMatter protests in New York City, a city that is jam packed with white liberals, but in the videos and pictures I've seen, the protesters were overwhelmingly people of color. Want to know why? Because most white liberals are just as scared of "angry" black people as white conservatives are, which is of course completely racist, as predicting or fearing stereotypical (violent) behavior based on race defines racism.

Or what about the Bernie Bros? I for one could not help but notice how they reacted to black people overwhelmingly siding with Hillary Clinton. At first, I kept hearing the same sort of racist garbage that right-wing white people spew about black people voting Democrat:

*If we could just **educate** black voters about how much better a Bernie Presidency would be for **them**, then **they** will come around.*

Eventually, the patronizing and paternalistic comments and thought patterns turned angry, with some Bernie Bros calling black voters idiots, morons, stupid, clueless, sheep, chumps, along with many other insulting names and descriptors. In other words, a pretty good chunk of far-left white progressives are just as convinced as far-right conservatives that black people are too stupid to understand their own interests (while also racistly refusing to realize that black people as individuals have widely varied political priorities, beliefs, and interests), and this group of far-left white progressives are just as frustrated as far-right conservatives at their own inability to control and manipulate a group of people they stubbornly (and racistly) insist can be so easily controlled and manipulated.

Also, liberals often feel like black people are "self loathers" for expressing an opinion that is outside of mainstream liberal ideology. For example, think about the recent Bill Maher controversy where he said the word "nigger" on live television. Many black people believed that Bill Maher should have been fired, many black people believed that Bill Maher crossed the line and should apologize but not be fired, many black people believed that worrying about a comedian's choice of words keeps black people distracted instead of progressing, many black people believed (and believe) that black people can't use that word and then get upset when white people do the same thing, and many black people believed many things not listed here. Many liberals refuse to allow black people to hold diverse political opinions without facing either condescending fake sympathy from white liberals or being branded by black liberals as an inauthentically black "Uncle Tom" (Uncle Ruckus) or "coon". For the record, this refusal to allow black people to hold diverse opinions without being ridiculed is utterly racist, as a rarely discussed but foundational element of white supremacy is the assumption of monolithic thought in non-white people, as if only white people are capable of independent reasoning and nuanced world views.

White liberals also love to unnecessarily and irrationally "prove" to black people that they aren't racist, as if treating people differently based on race disproves rather than confirms racism. Not to mention, if you're genuinely "down for the cause" you won't have to prove it, it will just show, as black folks are a lot more perceptive than over-eager white liberals tend to understand. Also, who runs around trying to disprove a negative about themselves other than people the negative in fact applies to? This sort of thing falls under the "thou doth protest too much" category, just like all the Republican politicians who spend time running around furiously trying to prove that they're not gay by denouncing homosexuality (when they're not too busy loitering in airport restrooms or harassing their male interns looking for a cock to suck).

Finally, please consider my experiences based on an email I sent to all eight Ivy League Presidents regarding blatant discrimination against poor children within their admissions procedures. "Coincidentally", the only President who replied at all was Dr. Ruth Simmons from Brown, the only black President in the Ivy League at the time (I think there are 0 black Presidents at Ivy League schools today, as Dr. Simmons has retired):

Dear Ivy League Presidents:

I wanted to reach out to you and your counterparts at other Ivy League institutions about 2 critical and related issues that appear to have been overlooked. In addition to each Ivy League President, I have also copied each Ivy League Athletic Director.

The first issue involves the method by which Ivy League schools calculate the Academic Index (AI) to determine admissibility for potential student-athletes. Currently, the formula to determine the AI doubles the weight of the standardized test (SAT or ACT) compared with the weight given to the GPA. This system unfairly rewards the wealthy student from a New England prep school with a 2.8 GPA and an outstanding SAT score while punishing the disadvantaged valedictorian from a lousy school with a mediocre SAT score.

Certainly, I understand that a standardized test score is one predictor of an individual's ability to flourish at a rigorous academic institution and that no one wants to put a young person in a position of likely failure. As such, I recognize that a terrific student from a failing school might struggle at an Ivy League school. That having been said, if that same student had parents who could afford a private SAT tutor, he or she would have jumped from a 900 on the 2 part SAT to an 1100 and this hypothetical student would have been admitted with no problem. In other words, the SAT score can so easily be manipulated and artificially inflated simply by paying top dollar in the SAT tutoring marketplace that perhaps the SAT score isn't quite as accurate or fair as an indicator of student preparedness as some people may believe.

Additionally, and I think this is critical to understand, the policy of doubling the weight of the SAT hurts an Ivy League school's ability to increase diversity. Sadly, racial diversity seems to be the only measuring stick to which most people pay attention, but diversity is so much more than skin deep. Admitting a black student from Exeter with an affluent doctor for a father may look good in terms of racial diversity, but it won't do much good in terms of experiential or economic diversity. However, by allowing the GPA and the SAT to carry equal weight in the AI formula, your athletics programs could be a much more effective vehicle to drive an increase in true diversity on your campus.

The second issue that I believe should be addressed is the compensation package for the 3ʳᵈ assistant coach in men's and women's basketball (this may be a broader issue across your entire athletics department, but my realm of familiarity is limited to basketball). Currently, the 3ʳᵈ assistant coach is barred by Ivy League rule from receiving financial compensation. On one hand, I understand that appearances are important and that Ivy League schools need to make clear to their faculties and some alumni that academics carry priority over athletics and that low salaries (or in this case no salary) for coaches versus *professors can be an important piece of that puzzle. On the other hand, the result of this particular policy has been to exclude viable candidates based on those candidates' personal financial situation. In other words, if you don't have independent or family wealth, you can't realistically enter the coaching profession at an Ivy League school. Your current and former basketball coaches can share many stories with you about the outstanding applicants (often times minority candidates, I might add) they have had to turn down because of the untenable economic situation that accompanied the position. You're basically, albeit I believe unwittingly, telling your very own graduates and former student-athletes that you will only allow them to enter the coaching profession at their alma mater if they have independent wealth or affluent parents who are willing and able to support them financially. As such, I'd like to urge you to adjust this policy at least to allow your 3rd assistant coaches to benefit from a free place to live on campus, a campus meal plan, and perhaps a small monthly stipend and/or tuition reimbursement for graduate courses. This way, your basketball coaches could hire the best possible candidate independent of the candidate's family or personal wealth.*

In both of these policies, Ivy League schools have inadvertently provided a distinct advantage to children born into affluence, which necessarily means that these policies discriminate against children born into poverty. I can not believe that a modern-day Ivy League school would deliberately implement policies that promote elitism and result in discrimination, which is why I'm writing this letter. Now that you have this information presented to you in this light, I sincerely hope you'll consider taking steps to correct these related issues.

Thanks very much for your time. I would definitely enjoy hearing back from you if you have the time.

Peter
Peter B. Schwethelm

As I've mentioned in previous chapters, in America, classist policies are racist policies. After all, any classist policy that harms poor people is going to disproportionally harm black people, and any policy that disproportionally harms black people is a racist policy. As such, the admissions policies at the ultra-liberal Ivy League schools are blatantly racist.

What the hell is wrong with the South? They lost the Civil War, and they're still racially hostile to black people. I'm happy that I live in a more enlightened part of the country, that's for sure!!

Liberal white Northerners who espouse this narrative should remember the words of Malcolm X:

America in its entirety is segregationist and is racist. It's more camouflaged in the North, but it's the same thing... New York, which is supposed to be liberal, has more integration problems than Mississippi.

Malcolm X was right then, and he's right now, and the idea that racism is "the South's" problem allows liberal white people outside of the South to believe that racism is a Southern problem rather than a national problem, thereby washing their hands and turning a blind eye to the deaths of Philando Castile In Minnesota (NOT Alabama) and John Crawford/Tamir Rice in Ohio (NOT Mississippi) and Eric Garner in New York (NOT South Carolina), which means that black people are going to continue getting killed and the killers are going to continue to walk free.

P.S. As a friendly reminder/public service announcement, Rodney King was beaten half to death in Los Angeles, not in some redneck right-wing town in the Bible Belt, just in case any liberal Californians were wanting to pretend that the Golden State is a utopian "post-racial" society.

Race is a human construct, and there is no scientific evidence to support the idea of different races of people. Race is a myth, a lie developed by authoritarianism-inclined Europeans to justify human atrocities and exert control.

I am so tired of hearing educated liberal white people spout this "highly enlightened" bullshit, because while race may not be scientifically real, but it is most definitely actually real, as in it drastically affects people's lives in a real way, and only a white person could fail to understand that. As such, I don't find the "race isn't real" thing I see lots of people talking about on Facebook to be even remotely helpful to American black people, especially in the short term. Maybe in the long term, teaching kids the science behind the truth that the notion of different races is a human construct could lay a psychological foundation to eradicate racism, but in the short term, I don't think it's a helpful or accurate notion. Ask any American black person if they think race is real, and I'm sure they'll agree that the answer is yes, and when I hear a white liberal talk like this, I find myself thinking, "How privileged you are to be able to turn race off like a faucet!!" Here's the thing, though, black folks can't exactly do that, and talking like this diminishes the life experiences of black people, who have always been forced to know that maybe nothing is more real than being black. As such, I worry a lot that this increasingly popular "scientifically enlightened" view that "there's no such thing as race" has the potential to further obscure and marginalize our very real race-related problems. It's hard enough for black people and white allies to turn people around who believe that "race is no big deal" without people who think they're well meaning on this topic inadvertently undercutting our case by asserting that "race" as we understand it doesn't even exist.

Our inner cities are being torn apart by violence, and we must get the guns off the streets to protect black children!!

The 2nd Amendment is linked to race in many ways, as I have noticed that most pro-gun advocates don't cite the actual rationale behind the 2nd Amendment, which was to protect the people from both tyranny domestic and invasion foreign, but rather talk about the need to "protect" themselves or their families. Given this consistently stated rationale, I have long been strongly suspicious that the boogey man they're actually trying to protect themselves from is (look left, look right, then whisper) "the blacks".

In fact, it does seem like the NRA NEVER stands up (in a meaningful way) for 2nd Amendment rights when Democratic-controlled city governments in places like Chicago and New York implement local policies that (at least in my view) outrageously violate the 2nd Amendment. Then, surprise, surprise, the people being grossly disproportionately arrested and incarcerated on "illegal" gun charges wind up being black, because they're the ones being searched disproportionately, but liberals swear they care so much about the mass incarceration of black people, just obviously nowhere close to as much as they care about an actual liberal priority like gun control.

I truly don't and will never understand how a city government can overrule an Amendment. A federal law? Yes, I'm all about it, as my wild, wet political fantasy is for federal taxes and authority to reduce, with local taxes and authority filling the void.

However, it's crystal clear that Amendments are the supreme law of the land, and I'm OK with that, because the people and the states consented to the Constitution and the Bill of Rights. As such, it's total bullshit that we have locked thousands of black people in prison for the crime of carrying a gun, NOT USING A GUN, but carrying a gun, all because we have allowed liberal city governments to strip (mostly black) US citizens of their Constitutional right to bear arms.

Of course, I shouldn't be surprised by this, because, again, I have long been aware that liberals have "gun control" (and many other topics) MUCH higher on their list of actual priorities than equal justice for American black people.

I am offended that you refer to African-Americans as black. That is such a racist, dated term!!

I use the phrase "American black people" or simply "black people" throughout this book, mostly because I personally detest the phrase "African-American" unless it is used to describe an American citizen who is an immigrant from Africa. American black people aren't immigrants, and their ancestors weren't immigrants, either, so unless we as white people are going to start calling ourselves "European Americans" then calling American black people by the moniker "African-American" involves the othering of our fellow Americans, which I am not OK with.

Animals are people, too!!

No, they're not, liberal white people. I'm not saying I approve of cruelty to animals, except for bugs and rodents, although no one seems to think poisoning a bug or a rodent to death counts as cruelty to animals, even though it clearly is. But that having been said, no, animals are not people, no matter how much you love them. However, black folks are people, and it frustrates me substantially how many white liberals care more about preventing cruelty to animals than ensuring equality and justice for black people.

Non-Partisan Black Person Bullshit

You think black people are the problem with black people? You're an Uncle Tom (Uncle Ruckus)!! You're a coon!!

These days, when a black leader focuses on black self-improvement rather than white racism, many black people (especially black liberals) go nuts.

For example, Allen West once said:

The first thing that the black man has got to do is straighten out the evil conditions in the ghettos. Not only materially, but morally and spiritually. We've got to get rid of drunkenness, drug addiction, prostitution and all that. We don't want welfare programs. They create laziness. We need a program to educate ghetto people to a better sense of values. When ghetto living seems normal, you have no shame, no privacy. You don't realize that you don't have these values when you've known nothing but ghetto moral conditions.

OK, confession time. Allen West didn't say that. Malcolm X did. Want to call him an Uncle Tom (Uncle Ruckus) or a coon, too? No? Then shut the fuck up and please allow all black people to voice their diverse points of view without fear of race-based mockery and shaming. It's bad enough when white people refuse to afford black people the basic human right of forming and sharing an opinion, so I can think of no reason for black people to also participate in the shaming and the silencing of black voices.

P.S. I must confess here that I have a problem with Malcolm X's words here, and in many other instances, as he paints with too broad of a brush without clarifying that the characteristics he describes were based on economics and imposed conditions more than race.

White people this, and white people that, and white people will never _____, and fuck white people, and white people, white people, white people, and wypipo, wypipo, wypipo…

As Malcolm X said:

A blanket indictment of all white people is as wrong as when whites make blanket indictments against blacks.

As I've said before, hypocrisy is a terribly unstable foundation from which to build persuasion, and I think black people, of all people, should collectively understand the fundamental unfairness of group blame and the awful damage that group blame causes, and should therefore seek to set an example by rising above it.

P.S. Some black people will read this passage as yet another white person holding black people to an unrealistic and unfair standard that white people don't hold themselves to, and I do try to empathize with that reflexive reaction because I have seen this phenomenon occur. That having been said, though, I did devote an entire chapter to the importance of white people fighting the tendency to engage in group blame, so any criticism that I'm holding black people to a different and higher standard than white people is not valid (at least not in this case- I might be guilty of this fairly common racist practice in other areas of this book, and my life, without possessing the self-awareness to realize it).

You have to work twice as hard to go half as far…

Over the years, I have heard black parents and grandparents say this phrase (or another similar phrase) to their children or grandchildren on at least a dozen occasions. On one hand, there's nothing wrong with parents trying to instill elite work ethics in their children, but by phrasing it this way, you run the risk of spawning or exacerbating hopelessness at a very young age. I know that if my mother or grandmother had said this to me, I can easily see myself thinking, "If I have to work twice as hard just to scrape by, why bother?" To my way of looking at things, this sort of narrative, while certainly based largely in reality, does more harm than good. For example, part of me thinks that being raised by no one who experienced catastrophic and traumatizing racism played a role in Barack Obama's ascent, as family history is in many ways inherited- Barack Obama never heard anyone in his family say things that may have potentially inadvertently damaged his hopefulness (NOTE: I'm not blaming black people's self talk or family talk for white people's racism- at all-I'm simply offering a coping strategy and food for thought).

You don't understand!!

Look, I agree that neither I, nor realistically any white person, can fully or truly understand what it's like to be black in America. That having been said, I have personally heard the words "you don't understand" pretty much exclusively as a conversation ender, and I think it serves the best interests of American black people to stoke rather than extinguish our national dialogue about race, particularly during personal face-to-face discussions.

You can't understand!!

If I can't understand, then why are you wasting your time? Just leave me alone. The status quo isn't hurting me. So go ahead and shut down race-related conversations with this brusque and dismissive line, but please do realize that I'm not the one being tangibly harmed by our collective refusal to engage in honest dialogue about racism (that could hopefully lead toward meaningful reform).

Oh, you think you know every damn thing because you're white. Typical whitesplaining!!

Unless you think white people have no role to play in fixing American racism, it's patently absurd to expect us not to have opinions or ideas on this subject, and when you basically dismiss our thoughts and feelings simply because we are white, you're being a racist, and being a racist while asking other people not to be racists is a fundamentally flawed approach. Practicing what you preach is always a helpful step along the path to persuasion. If Richard Simmons weighed 600 pounds, he wouldn't be particularly successful as a weight loss specialist, just as black racists aren't particularly persuasive in their efforts to combat white racism.

That having been said, I do acknowledge that in comparison to any black person, I don't know a damn thing about being black.

Black people can't be racists.

I agree, and have said throughout this book, that the definable real world negative effects of white-on-black racism and black-on-white racism are not even remotely comparable, as the harm caused by white racists has been voluminous like an ocean, whereas the harm caused by black racists has been voluminous like a pint of beer. With this in mind, I think the narrative that "black people can't be racists" is borne out of black people's frustrations with white people engaging in raging false equivalency, trying to equate or compare black racism with white racism. However, while I do understand the sentiment behind this increasingly common statement, nowhere does it say that controlling the levers of power structures to cause tangible mass harm is a prerequisite for the existence of racism. Simply put, if you're black, and you have thoughts and feelings about white people in general, or you sometimes associate the behavior of an individual white person or small group of white people with their overall race, you are a racist, period, the end.

P.S. If political power must be present for racism to exist, does that mean that only white people are racist toward black people in America? I think that the experiences of American black people would strongly suggest otherwise, as many (if not all) of my black friends have shared stories about being treated racistly by Asian-Americans and Hispanic-Americans (and African immigrants), not just by European-Americans.

P.P.S. If political power is a pre-requisite for racism to exist, can black people be racist in cities or states or countries where black people are in charge politically? And, if political power is required for racism to exist, is a white racist no longer a racist if they happen to live in a city or country where white people do not possess political power? Or, if David Duke moved to Ethiopia, he would no longer be a racist? If Hitler had moved to Israel, he would no longer be a racist?

P.P.S. During Apartheid, white racists controlled South Africa. Since the end of Apartheid, black South Africans have had complete political power, but many of the white racists chose to remain in South Africa. So, now that the remaining white racists are no longer in power, are they no longer racists?

CHAPTER 14

INDIVIDUAL SOLUTIONS

Racism at the individual level is by far the most difficult to eradicate because private thoughts and feelings can of course not be fixed through public policy. As such, it truly does fall on each of us, as Americans, to combat racism within our own hearts and minds if we are ever going to become the country that our core ideals insist we were always intended and destined to be.

To begin with, let's do a quick review, chapter by chapter, as each chapter contains a key individual solution to combat personal racism and to promote equality.

Admit we have a problem.

Nothing more needs to be said here, other than the universal truth that no problem can be fixed until it is recognized broadly as being a problem.

Recalibrate the word "racist".

Hatred on the mind and evil in the heart are not required for racism to exist at the individual level, which means that it is absolutely possible to be both a racist and a good person, which means there is no reason for us to be so sensitive and defensive when people refer to us using the word "racist".

P.S. Here again are some suggested replacement terms for the word "racist" (depending on the situation):

REBA: Racially or Ethnically Biased American

ARF: American Racial Fencesitter

RDT: Racial Doubting Thomas

NORA: Non-Overtly Racist American

P.P.S. Also, as y'all know, I prefer using "Uncle Ruckus" instead of "Uncle Tom".

Remember that racism, like all human traits, has a scale.

A person who is only a little bit racist is still a racist, and that person must admit it in order to fix it.

Accept reality.

America treating black people unfairly continues to persist pervasively, and there is a mountain of data to support this truth, and we **must therefore accept** the reality that America remains a racist country to this very day, as denial has yet to solve a single problem in the entire history of humankind.

Fight against bias and brainwashing.

Truly, for the most part, racism isn't our fault, as very few people ever sit down and make a conscious choice to become a racist, but racism is our problem, and attempting to recognize our racial biases will go a long way toward alleviating them.

P.S. White parents in particular must be aware of societal race-related brainwashing, and must combat it as they raise their children. Racism truly is largely a matter of brain washing, and white parents need to almost implement a sort of preventative counter-brainwashing regiment in order to combat the current near inevitability of white children picking up (often subconscious) racist views and attitudes.

Strive to increase empathy.

White people need to recognize the added difficulties in life that being black entails, and try to walk, if not a mile, at least a few feet in black people's shoes, and black people need to recognize the largely involuntary nature of white racism in America.

Understand history and connect history to the present.

A nation's history impacts its present and its future, and we must learn and teach our true history, even when it's ugly or uncomfortable, and we must recognize the extent to which America's historical systematic prevention of black wealth accumulation and denial of educational opportunities has negatively affected the current collective status of black people.

Work to avoid group blame, and recognize the absurdity of stereotypes.

An individual's brain drives choices and behavior, not an individual's race, and there's not a single negative racial-stereotype-based human attribute on earth that isn't broadly shared across all races.

Reject False Equivalency (and Comparative Clemency).

Try to avoid equating subjects that have no legitimate bases for comparison, and also try to avoid deflecting criticism by absolving yourself of your sins because of someone else's even bigger sins.

Acknowledge double standards.

Try to see double standards, as recognizing their existence makes us more empathetic, and increasing empathy may be the most important step we can take as a society to increase fairness and reduce injustice.

Remember that White Privilege should probably be renamed Black Burden or something along those lines.

The concept of "privilege" is a very broad concept, and should be seen through the lens of empathetically viewing non-privileged categories of people, not tearing down privileged categories of people.

Stop over-citing "black culture".

White people use the phrase "black culture" as a catch-all scapegoat to provide an alternative theory beyond racism to explain black people's collective condition, and black people use the phrase "black culture" in a way that often seems to suggest a level of black monolithicness that essentially echoes the sentiments of white racists by denying to black people the fundamental human right of individuality.

Quit spewing bullshit.

Most of the over-used and tired race-related talking points are either misguided or misleading or hypocritical or patently false or some combination thereof, and as Americans, it's way past time to value and share truth over propaganda.

In addition to applying the action form of the chapter titles to our lives as individuals, here are several other potential solutions for all of us to win the battle against our inner racist.

Spend Energy Proportionally

The legendary Miss Z Powell taught at Yates High School in Houston for decades. She was one of those teachers who holds a school together, because it's incredibly hard for even the biggest knucklehead in the school to disrespect a teacher who taught his mother before him and his grandfather before that, and who probably literally changed his diapers.

Miss Z Powell called all males "boy", and none of us said shit, because she had a special presence to her where you knew that she meant business but also that she cared.

By the time I arrived at Yates in the Fall of 2003, Miss Z Powell was in her 90's and had therefore retired but was still working as a substitute teacher and hall monitor but mostly as a universally beloved mentor to teachers and students alike.

I will never forget her advice to me within my first 2 weeks working at Yates:

BOY, you have to quit spending 95% of your energy on the 5% of your kids who don't act right. You're cheating the 95%, and you're driving yourself crazy.

We should all heed Miss Z Powell's advice, and try not to get caught up spending 95% of our energy on the 5% who don't act right. The simple and magnificent truth is that no matter what sub-category of human beings you examine, there is way more good than bad, and our attitudes and words and belief systems should better reflect this reality.

P.S. Miss Z Powell also famously (and correctly) advised me, "BOY, always remember, the children can't give you any bullshit if they're too busy catching it" and equally (in)famously commented on my goatee, "BOY, you look like you have a pussy on your face". Suffice it to say that Miss Z Powell was an American original!!

Calm Down and Listen

When emotions run hot, irrationality is soon to follow, and there is no question that emotion and irrationality have distorted our ability to participate in discussions about race using not just our mouth, but our ears and our brains as well. Obviously, it is impossible to persuade someone unless you can convince them to hear you out, which no one will do unless you're also willing to hear them out. So, let's just chill out a little bit, and try to discuss racism in America as calmly and as reasonably as possible.

One key element of listening we must get much better at involves our tendency to hear things that weren't said and read things that weren't written and then (over)react based on our misinterpretation of what was said or written.

For example, if I say:

"We have a serious problem in our criminal justice system regarding our treatment of American black people."

Lots of people hear:

"All cops are evil racists who are deliberately hunting and executing black people."

Or, if I say:

"When the doors of opportunity swing open, black people must make sure they are not too drunk or too indifferent to walk through."

Lots of people hear:

"Racism does not exist, and the REAL PROBLEM with black people is their dependency on alcohol and drugs as well as their overall shiftiness."

But the point is that we need to hear and process the actual words that were spoken or written, rather than interpreting what our bias insists the speaker or writer "really meant", and we need to do so with a patient mind and a receptive heart.

NOTE: the quote about the importance of not allowing racial oppression to spawn hopelessness, addiction, and indifference is a Jesse Jackson quote, except that as I am not black, I changed the quote slightly by using "they" instead of "we".

Believe Things You Haven't Personally Experienced

My grandfather never talked about World War II, and my father never talks about Vietnam, but if they chose to share their experiences with me, I'd believe them, even though I have never served my country militarily during a time of war. However, based on other conversations with veterans who did choose to share their experiences with me, some of the stories are so far outside of my experiences as to sound incredible or even unbelievable, but I believe them anyway.

White people need to believe black people, even though our experiences in America are so radically different in so many ways than the experiences of black people in America, but the fact that our experiences as white people don't line up with the stories we hear black people tell makes us privileged, not them dishonest.

Qualify Our Words

We must try to qualify, "some" or "many" or "most" or "a few" before "black people" and "white people". I have tried to model this strategy throughout this book; I say the words "white people" and "black people" a lot, but I make it clear via qualifying words that I am deliberately not referring to all white people or all black people (for the most part). To me, the default way a person hears an unqualified "black people" or "white people" is with an implied "all" before the other two words, which leads to defensiveness, and there aren't many emotions that shut down listening quite like defensiveness.

Mind Our Tone

Lately, I've been approaching overtly racist white people not from the standpoint of, "YOU'RE A FUCKING RACIST PIECE OF SHIT!!" but more from the standpoint of, "I'm not judging you. I personally am a racist myself. Here are some things you may not have thought about, though........."

I've been trying to remove the question of morality from the discussion because when you essentially begin a conversation by implying, "you are an immoral person", people just shut down and get defensive.

It's working a little bit better than berating people. As I've said many times throughout this book, I think it's important that the word "racist" be a conversation starter, not a conversation ender, and I don't consider myself to be an evil person, even though I am a racist, so it is equal parts hypocritical and unfair for me to automatically judge other racists as having evil intent.

Be Conversation Starters, not Conversation Enders

To everyone who earnestly cares about creating a racially just society, we must be conversation starters, not conversation enders.

Instead of saying:

YOU'RE A RACIST!!

Try saying:

Can we dive a little bit deeper into what you just said for a few minutes?

Instead of saying:

YOU DON'T UNDERSTAND!!

or

YOU DON'T GET IT!!

Try saying:

Let me share my perspective with you.

Instead of saying:

YOU'RE PART OF THE PROBLEM!!

Try saying:

As Americans, we should discuss our common ground to build on toward solutions.

In short, keep in mind some basic rules of persuasion:

1. No one likes being berated or feeling harassed.

2. No one likes being talked down to or made to feel stupid.

3. No one likes being called unflattering names.

4. Listen to be heard.

5. Give respect to get respect.

When we lose our cool or insult people, we kill conversations.

When we sanctimoniously and self-righteously and judgmentally and patronizingly lecture people, we kill conversations.

If we earnestly care about making things right, we can't afford to kill conversations.

Recognize Progress, but Finish the Race

Obviously, each generation of American black people has had a more equal opportunity to live the American dream than the generation that preceded them, which means that black people today have a more equal opportunity to live the American dream than any previous generation. This is a good thing, and I think our progress should be more often noted, especially by American black people, because conciliatory tones often make sense on sensitive topics and because allies and pliable moderates who are earnestly trying to unlearn racism, like all people, do benefit from an encouraging word.

In my view, it is remarkable, and uniquely American, that Harry Truman, who integrated the armed services, had a mother who grew up in a slave-owning household. So it is easy to agree with the sentiment:

You can decry that fifty years ago our grandfathers couldn't sit together in a restaurant or applaud that just fifty years later we had a black President. If you look just at America, the issues seem ugly and nasty (and they are). If you look more broadly at the ugliness and sinfulness of human history, what we've accomplished in 250 years is quite wonderful.

However, while I agree that it's important to celebrate progress, and I think that the pace of progress in America has been comparatively quick (at least in some regards, especially recently), I also think that making progress doesn't mean we should put on the brakes prior to reaching the finish line. Until we treat and view American black people equally as full citizens (especially in our criminal justice system), I'm going to join anyone who decries our history on this subject because it provides valuable context to the ongoing oppression. In other words, I think you can applaud and decry at the same time, and I feel strongly that if we're going to celebrate the progress we've made regarding race relations, it needs to be a mobile celebration rather than a stationary one.

Focus Effectively

I've long said that if white people would mostly focus on the remaining institutional racism within all of our major systems, and black people would mostly focus on black self-improvement, we would put ourselves on the fast track toward fixing both the foundational flaw of America and the modern inequality in America. Too often, we focus backwardly, worrying the most about the things we can change the least, which does not promote effectiveness.

I truly do not and never will understand why any white person would focus primarily on black people's behavior rather than institutional white racism. For starters, as we have already discussed, there's no example of bad behavior by a black person that white people don't also at times embody or exceed. Also, whether it's insensitive, mean, racist, or whatever- it's also COMPLETELY non-productive. It's as though certain white folks think that all black people really need is just a good stern talking to from an educated white person. I just don't get the preoccupation with the bad behavior of some black people, which isn't anybody else's business. If white people focused their time and energy on the half of the equation we can actually do something about (white-controlled institutions and industries where racism remains systemic), it could actually make a difference.

Deliberately Raise Integrated Children

Lots of parents are raising children in largely segregated neighborhoods and schools. If this is your reality as a parent, I would suggest that you find at least 1 after-school activity for your kids to participate in where the majority of the other kids are of a different race than your children. To me, there may be no better long-term strategy to combat the "racist within" than to give small children an opportunity to interact with and form friendships across different racial groups, thereby preventing the racist within from even taking root in the first place. If I were raising white children, I'd want their black friends to spend time in our home on a fairly regular basis, and I'd want my children to spend time at their black friends' homes on a fairly regular basis, because contrary to the pessimistic popular cliché, familiarity breeds positive understanding and friendship a helluva lot more often than it breeds contempt.

Call People Out

When you hear racist language, speak up, but not selectively. In other words, as of this moment, we have millions of white folks who are quick to point out the racism of a Louis Farrakhan, but loathe to criticize or even admit the racism of a Donald Trump. Conversely, we have millions of black folks who are quick to point out the prevalence of racism within white-controlled institutions, while not criticizing or even admitting the widespread racist practices within black-controlled institutions (for example, note the lack of white people in positions of leadership inside of historically black colleges and universities, or majority black high schools, and so on).

It's also critically important to call ourselves out. When the inner racist starts arguing with us, we need to argue back.

Also, if parts of this book made you feel like I am talking directly to you, the best way to fight your racial bias is by doing a specific mental inventory every single day of all the people you encounter that day who belong to the group against whom you are biased. Over time, if you stick with this daily process, you will feel your negativity start to abate as you begin to realize that the overwhelming majority of people you're biased against don't behave the way your bias suggests they will.

My old friend "Billy" (not his real name) provides a great example of this daily racial inventory routine. Billy and I had known each other since college, and had hung out quite a bit after college. Well, after Billy got a DUI and was forced to start riding the bus to work, his (previously latent) inner racist became activated, and he suddenly started expressing racial hostility toward black people.

This really took me by surprise, not because I had never heard white friends of mine say racist things before, but because this particular white friend's racist comments had not been a lifetime habit, as had been the case with previous examples of racist friends of mine speaking racistly.

After hearing him out, I started pushing back, and said something like:

"Billy, you can't tell me that 51% or more of the black people on the bus are acting like idiots. No way, man. You're being unfair right now."

And he said something to the effect:

*"When's the last time you rode the public bus? You don't understand how **these people** are!!"*

To which I replied:

"Billy, we've been friends a long time, and I need you to do me a small favor. I need you to count every single black person you encounter this week, and I need you to also count every single black person you encounter this week who behaves in a manner that you feel deserves to be criticized. Please do that for me, and we can pick this conversation back up once we have a better sense of the actual data."

Billy agreed, in a sort of huffy but mostly arrogant way, as if he couldn't wait to report what he found to prove to me that he wasn't racist, I was naïve.

A week later, I went to his apartment to smoke a little weed and drink some cheap beer, and I asked him how his data collection had gone. He couldn't look me in the eye at first, and it seemed like he was getting emotional as he admitted that he had encountered more than 300 black people that week, and 2 had behaved objectionably, but neither case of objectionable behavior had been severely objectionable (NOTE: this story has a beautiful ending, as Billy is happily married to a black woman, and bought his first house in a predominantly black neighborhood).

Another subset of the American population that needs to call themselves and each other out is the police, as it seems like the last time a "good cop" told the truth about a "bad cop" was Frank Serpico in about 1968 (presumably, there must be more recent examples, but they sure don't seem to be too common). At some point, if a good cop protects a bad cop by not speaking up, it becomes harder and harder to continue categorizing the "good cop" as good.

Moving forward on this topic, please remember that silence causes violence, so please speak up, remembering the words of Dr. King: "He who passively accepts evil is as much involved in it as he who helps perpetrate it. He who accepts evil without reporting it is actually cooperating with it."

On the subject of race, be careful how you use the words "don't" and "understand" next to each other.

Want to know the 2 most poisonous consecutive words in the world of race relations?

"Don't Understand."

As a white person, saying, "I don't understand" should be the end of your sentence as in "help me understand" NOT at the beginning of your sentence as a passive aggressive racist judgment, like, "I don't understand why black people can't/don't/won't
_____."

And as a black person, saying, "you don't understand" may be accurate, but it isn't helpful, because the normal context is ending rather than continuing the conversation.

Go to Twitter and search the hashtags #CrimingWhileWhite and #AliveWhileBlack.

We have already discussed these highly divergent hashtags in the chapter "Double Standards", but I did want to mention it again, because reading those first-person accounts will likely open your eyes and help you to see America as it actually is, rather than prematurely seeing America as it was intended to be and should be.

Stop Grading Individuals on a Standard of Perfection

If white people would dispassionately read Malcolm X's words or Louis Farrakhan's words, many if not most white people would find themselves agreeing with the majority of the points being made by these 2 legendary Nation of Islam leaders, but the only things most white people tend to remember are the "chickens coming home to roost" or that "Hitler was a great man".

And I have noticed as a long-standing "white ally" that I can say 30 things a black person might agree with then 1 thing they disagree with, and I have felt the fisheye stare and almost heard the inner dialogue of, "Yup, now we see how this dude REALLY is."

The bottom line is that attempting to require 100% agreement only serves to drown out real, honest, and productive discussions, not to mention the universal truth that perfection is a fundamentally unreasonable expectation.

Understand Proportionality

There are several aspects of proportionality that everyone should consider.

One, as we have mentioned throughout this book, way too many Americans seem to think that white racism against black people and black racism against white people should receive equal attention. The problem with this, of course, as I've mentioned several times already, involves the fact that the effects of white racism against black people have been both massively severe and universally felt, whereas the effects of black racism against white people involve way fewer victims with way less dire consequences. In other words, black racism against white people is currently and always has been mostly non-consequential in the lives of white people, particularly when compared with the consequences of white racism in the lives of black people (NOTE: Affirmative Action is white-on-white racism, not black-on-white racism, as black people do not have and never have had enough political power to create federal laws).

It truly is tough to fathom why some people seem to want us as a society to spend equal energy on 2 topics that are totally unequal. It would be like if I ranted on and on about Bernie Madoff and the millions he stole in a ponzi scheme while failing to give equal attention to some local pyramid scheme where the victims lost a grand total of $5000. The common insistence that our outrage and our attention should be shared exactly equally between the different types of racism in America just makes no mathematical sense. White people who play the victim and want to focus on black racism against white people are trying to make a mountain out of a molehill, whereas black people are pointing out an actual mountain.

We also see a widespread failure to consider proportionality when looking at the on-the-spot, due-process-free, extra-legal punishments black people receive at the hands of the police. For example, I agree that Eric Garner shouldn't have been a serial petty (non-violent) criminal, and he should have been more compliant initially when the police approached him to see if he was committing the same petty crime they'd caught him committing on many previous occasions. However, none of that justifies a violent takedown by five police officers and the use of a banned technique (baton on throat) that (at a minimum indirectly) caused Eric Garner's death.

The police officers knew that Eric Garner was non-violent, they knew he was no threat to them and no threat to flee, especially after they had him on his stomach with five grown men on top of him including one with his forearm on Eric Garner's throat. And yet they kept the violent pressure on Eric Garner's neck and body, even as Eric Garner's gasped and cried "I CAN'T BREATHE!!" They kept the violent pressure on Eric Garner's neck and body until Eric Garner was dead (and none of the five police officers who killed Eric Garner even received an indictment).

And, yet, many white people shrugged and said, "Welp, break the law, and that's what you get." I just don't understand how any American of any race can look at the Eric Garner case and feel that way. I mean, there are countries on earth where it's acceptable for the police to execute citizens on the spot for committing petty crimes or for being "disrespectful" or for trying to flee the scene of a crime or for passively resisting or being non-compliant, but America is supposed to be and should be and must be a lot better and do a lot better than that.

To use an analogy, if a guy walked up to me and said "hey, no one gives head quite like your mom" and I slugged him in the face, I'd call that pretty fair and I'd say he pretty much got what he deserved, BUT if I keep hitting him until his skull collapses and he's a vegetable or if I stomp his teeth out while he's unconscious or if I kill him, then I deserve to go to prison, even though he did "start it" and make a poor choice prior to me (over)reacting. If you ask me, the police should be held to the same standard as the rest of us, if not a higher standard, rather than the multi-century status quo where we hold the police (and really all public officials) to the lowest standard possible, if we hold them to any standard at all.

Stop Deflecting

Here are some absolutely absurd real-life examples of deflections I hear when the subject of racism comes up:

Some days I wish we would just get rid of police officers.

Why do so many people say this? When people on the political right criticize Bowe Bergdahl, I don't say, "Some days I wish we would just get rid of soldiers." Look, criticizing bad cops isn't the same thing as criticizing all cops, but even if it were, this comment is still totally off topic and consequently totally absurd.

P.S. Only racists are so uncomfortable discussing racism that they feel compelled to constantly deflect the conversation in another direction.

Did you know that it was mostly black Africans who caught slaves to sell to the Europeans?

So, if Jimmy kidnaps a 7 year-old girl, then sells her to Billy, and Billy proceeds to rape the 7 year-old girl repeatedly, I understand that Jimmy deserves some of the blame for what Billy subsequently did to the little girl, but this deflective comment is normally in the context of suggesting that Billy somehow should not be held responsible for his serial raping because he didn't participate in the original act of kidnapping. This is, of course, a ridiculous notion. Plus, we were discussing slavery, not kidnapping, so kindly stay on topic.

Did you know that Abraham Lincoln favored colonization for freed slaves out of his belief that white people and black people would not be able to live together in harmony?

So what? What's your point?

Are you saying that if even Abe Lincoln was a racist, then it's OK for you to be a racist? I agree that Abraham Lincoln was without question a racist, and he was wrong for that, but his wrongness doesn't excuse your wrongness.

Or are you saying that since Abraham Lincoln was a racist, then Jefferson Davis and the other leaders of the Confederacy therefore couldn't have also been racists? For the record, I hope it's clear to any person with a double-digit IQ that the side fighting to continue the enslavement of black human beings was probably more racist than the side fighting to end the enslavement of black human beings (yes, I know that Lincoln was fighting to preserve the Union more than to end slavery, but as the South had seceded over the issue of slavery, everyone knew that a victory by the North would mean the end of slavery).

OK, fine, I agree, you're right, all white people are evil and terrible.

No one is saying that. However, there is no doubt that white people are responsible for establishing and maintaining a racist society, so how about we practice what we preach, stop making excuses, and own our shit, and actively and consistently work to make it better, instead of just continuing with this sort of irrelevant and irrational deflective bellyaching.

We have the best criminal justice system in the world!!

Says who? What is your basis for that view? We do lock way more people up than any other Democracy, which is infuriatingly ironic in the "Land of the Free", but I'm not sure that makes our system "the best".

The other thing that's frustrating about this deflective remark is that people tend to only say it in response to a criticism based on either a black person getting screwed by our system or a white person getting treated leniently by our system.

We as Americans must remove our red, white, and blue goggles and see our criminal justice system for what it is, instead of for what it is supposed to be. I totally get the notion of being in love with our system AS IT'S WRITTEN, because the ideas written within our system are uniquely noble and just ideas. I just wish I could convince more white people to see past the brilliance of the ideas and open their eyes to the historical and ongoing corruption within our system AS IT EXISTS.

The American system of criminal justice isn't fair to American black people, and that is so well supported mathematically as to make it as close to being an objective fact as a statement about "fairness" can possibly be. That's the point, not the comparative awesomeness of our criminal justice system in relation to other countries' criminal justice systems, so please stay on topic.

Respect Each Other's Feelings

It would be nice if we weren't collectively as a nation (and probably world) so quick to dismiss people's feelings. One thing I've learned recently is that people's feelings are ALWAYS valid. Even when I don't understand them or I think they're irrational, people's feelings are real, and other people's feelings matter, especially if we expect other people to think our feelings matter.

Fight Hypocrisy

The first step to fixing a problem is admitting the problem exists, and we as a nation display massive hypocrisy on the topic of race-relations.

The foundational element of white people's hypocrisy on the topic of race relations involves our collective repudiation of past eras like Jim Crow while blissfully allowing many similar conditions to continue to exist to this day. Of course, if we confess this overlap, then our repudiation of past eras means that we also must repudiate ourselves, which isn't something that very many human beings are willing to do. However, it is illogical and inconsistent and hypocritical to condemn racism from 1964 while defending or denying or accepting racism in 2017.

It also frustrates me substantially how hypocritical many white people are on the topic of freedom. For example, if you look at the Eric Garner case, he repeatedly broke the laws of our land by selling single cigarettes out of his pack of smokes, and because he was a chronic lawbreaker, many white people feel that "he got what he deserved". I am not sure how or why people seem to think that selling loose cigarettes should carry a penalty of death, meted out on the spot in the streets of Staten Island by local police officers with witnesses watching. However, even if we accept that the serial commission of a victimless misdemeanor should justly result in the due-process-free death of the perpetrator, we should still take a look at the law itself.

Why should it be illegal in a free-market society for a person to purchase something wholesale and sell it retail? The tobacco company and the government weren't being cheated, as they had already received their revenue when Eric Garner purchased the pack of cigarettes. Why is this law necessary? How did this law even come into being? Do you think the lobbyists for big tobacco might have collaborated with their bought-and-paid-for political representatives to criminalize behavior that is both capitalistic and victimless?

Often times, it feels like wide swaths of the American people are anti-government, anti-lobbyist, anti-regulation, pro-Capitalism, and pro-freedom, but look at Eric Garner's situation (and others like it) and say, "Fuck him. Don't break the laws!!" There's substantial hypocrisy in this outlook, and I hope that one day the guiding principles of being anti-government, anti-bureaucracy, anti-regulation, pro-Capitalism, and pro-freedom won't be so regularly obscured and rejected due to the overriding principle of being anti-nigger.

Also, as we have previously mentioned, the fact that most Confederate flag waivers belligerently insist that black people need to "GET OVER IT" is among the more richly hypocritical claims imaginable. After all, the Civil War was a long time ago, and the Confederacy lost, so it is without question way past time for racist white people to "GET OVER IT".

Additionally, please consider five common traits of street gang members:

1. They think "being disrespected" is a good reason to become violent.

2. They think they are above the law.

3. They do not cooperate with investigations into their lawlessness.

4. They observe a strict code of silence to obstruct investigations into their cohorts' lawlessness.

5. They inflict severe repercussions on the very rare occasions when their cohorts actually do speak up and cooperate with investigations.

Unfortunately, these exact same five traits are also extremely common within police departments. That comment will undoubtedly infuriate a lot of people, but I challenge anyone to go back and re-read the five traits and attempt to disprove my point of view here (the Elephant Man is famous because there weren't and aren't too many like him- same thing with Detective Serpico). Obviously, police departments should not ever behave like the criminals they're supposed to protect us from, and this level of hypocrisy begs the classic KRS One question, "You were put here to protect us, but who protects us from you?"

By the way, I understand that it's totally human not to want to snitch on your own. However, in the case of "protecting your own," it should depend on the severity of the behavior you're protecting. For example, in my world of basketball, let's say I knew about a local AAU coach who got $5000 under the table from a college coach to deliver a kid, and the kid and the parents and the high school coach weren't even informed and the AAU coach kept every single penny of the $5000- should I snitch? Maybe so, but I wouldn't, even though I think that the AAU coach behaved badly and was wrong. But what if I knew a local AAU coach who was diddling 2nd graders- should I snitch then? Damn right. I would snitch on that dude in a New York second. I hope anyone would; and that's the thing- I'm sort of fine with a cop who doesn't snitch when he knows another cop took $50K off a drug dealer and only turned in $40K. But what about a cop who doesn't tell the truth when he knows how it actually went down and the shooting wasn't justifiable and a mother lost a son?

The bottom line is that when it comes to police departments, an internal culture of no snitching is so preposterously hypocritical and so incredibly contradictory to the very mission of their existence that it just does not withstand scrutiny, especially when the illegal or immoral activity is violent and/or bigotry-based.

Finally, on the topic of hypocrisy, as I have stated throughout this book, black racists are non-sympathetic advocates against racism, so black people must fight their own racism in order to maximize the credibility of their efforts to fight white racism.

Stop Scapegoating and Place Blame Correctly

We as a nation have a long and inglorious history of invalidly scapegoating black people, with our media again playing a key role in this ongoing nonsense.

We saw a lot of this in the aftermath of the 2007 economic catastrophe, with many white people pointing the finger at shiftless, irresponsible (black) American citizens who borrowed money they couldn't pay back. I will never forget or forgive George Will for making the following comments on Meet the Press just after the 2007 crash:

Much of the crisis we're in today is because the government set out to fiddle the market. That is. We had regulation in effect, legislation that would criminalize as racism and discrimination if you didn't lend to non-productive borrowers. We had, Fannie Mae and Freddie Mac existed to, well, to rig the housing market because the market would not have put people into homes they couldn't afford.

Don't get me wrong, I agree that Economics 101 advises "don't spend more than you make". Expenses must not exceed revenues. However, it's not like ONLY black people failed to consider this basic financial tenet. Rather, it was poor people of all colors, middle class people of all colors, business owners of all colors, and, of course, the biggest culprit of this self-defeating philosophy was the American government, which ran up $6 trillion in new debt in the six years prior to the 2007 crash.

So, again, while I agree that poor people, some of whom were black, took on loans they shouldn't have, does anyone really believe that poor black people in 2007 defaulted on loans that collectively approached anywhere even close to the $6 trillion in unsustainable debt that the federal government had recently accumulated? Black people have never had financial power in this country, and you can't cause a financial collapse without possessing financial power, making the scapegoating of black people that took place in 2007 absolutely indefensible and therefore reprehensible.

Another more recent example of the absurd scapegoating of black people occurred in the wake of Donald Trummp's "grab 'em by the pussy" comment. Truly, it left me astounded how many white friends of mine reflexively mentioned "rap lyrics" in an effort to make the point that sexism is a bigger problem than just Donald Trump. Of course, I agree that sexism is a bigger problem that just Donald Trump, but please don't even remotely try to imply that black people are responsible for sexism or that "rape culture" is a "black people problem". Black people did not write the lyrics to Brown Sugar (Rolling Stones), Cocaine Blues (Johnny Cash), and Tequila Makes Her Clothes Fall Off (Joe Nichols), and rap music had not even been invented a short 40 or so years ago when it was legal in all 50 states for husbands to rape their wives. Sexism and rape culture are global problems, not just American problems- and CERTAINLY not just black problems, least of all in the context of revelations about a 70+ year old white man who is running for President.

We also saw a classic case of illogical scapegoating in the media when we first saw the video that depicted the Sigma Alpha Epsilon fraternity members at the University of Oklahoma gleefully singing:

There will never be a nigger SAE
There will never be a nigger SAE
You can hang 'em from a tree
But they'll never pledge with me
There will never be a nigger SAE

In the aftermath of this video being released, the rapper Waka Flocka Flame canceled an upcoming performance at OU, prompting "Morning Joe" co-host Mika Brezinski to offer up:

If you look at every single song, I guess you call these, it's a bunch of garbage. It's full of n-words, it's full of f-words. It's wrong. And he shouldn't be disgusted with them, he should be disgusted with himself.

Next, guest Bill Kristol chimed in:

Popular culture becomes a cesspool, a lot corporations profit off of it, and then people are surprised that some drunk 19-year-old kids repeat what they've been hearing.

And then Joe Scarborough agreed:

The kids that are buying hip hop or gangster rap, it's a white audience, and they hear this over and over again. So do they hear this at home?

Well, chances are good, no, they heard a lot of this from guys like this who are now acting shocked.

I was totally floored when I watched this exchange, in large part because I know the history of that song, and I know the history of our country. SAE's have been singing that song for well over 50 years, and if you go back and look at the US Congressional Records, you'll see thousands of entries for the word "nigger" in the 1940's, 1950's, and 1960's. The word was used exclusively by white congressmen and Senators (mostly from the South) to refer to black people, and it was not meant in a nice or complimentary way. I wonder if Waka Flocka Flame is also responsible for members of the House and Senate saying "nigger" in a derogatory way 30 years before Waka Flocka Flame was even born? The "logic" here is just beyond preposterous, and yet it's extremely common.

And who can forget the white liberal scapegoating of black people after Proposition 8 passed in California in 2008, overturning a California Supreme Court ruling that had briefly established marriage equality? The LA Times and the Washington Post both ran articles essentially condemning black people's bigotry and blaming black people for the passage of Proposition 8. Now, it is true that 70% of black voters voted in favor of Proposition 8, but the articles and the very popular white liberal narrative never bothered to mention that only 10% of the people who voted were black. In FACT, there were 36% more Latinos than black people who voted in favor of Proposition 8, and there were 441% more white people than black people who voted in favor of Proposition 8. But that didn't stop major media outlets and the majority of white liberals from racistly scapegoating black people anyway, all the while deluding themselves into believing that racism against black people is a problem that only exists on the political right (http://www.madpickles.org/California_Proposition_8.html).

Finally, way too many white people blame "Affirmative Action" and "quotas" for not getting the job they wanted, or not getting into the school they wanted, but considering the huge number of white people who did get their dream job and did get into their dream school, it's pretty doggone self-evident that whiteness is not a disqualifier in America; and way too many black people blame racism and "white privilege" for their shortcomings and failures, but if you look at the huge number of white people who are unsuccessful, it's equally self-evident that whiteness is not a magical password that grants automatic success.

Avoid the Temptation to Blame Victims

When the police kill an **unarmed** black person, if you directly ask people "did he deserve to die?", most people agree the answer is "no" (although a fairly substantial and overly vocal minority percentage of white people will callously say "don't comply, and that's what you get" which is a reprehensible thing to think or say in my view).

But many white racial moderates will say, "This is a tragedy, and he didn't deserve to die, but being a cop is a hard job, and they have to make life or death decisions in a split second, and why wasn't the dead person being more deferential or more compliant or less erratic and what about all the previous transgressions in the dead person's life and it's a shame the dead person's father wasn't around but we need to wait for all the facts to come out (and so on and so forth)."

The starting point for the white moderate shouldn't be, "was this shooting justifiable legally?" but rather, "was this shooting just and necessary?" And the starting point shouldn't be, "is the dead person at least partially to blame for the tragedy in question?" but rather, "is the police officer at least partially to blame for the tragedy in question?"

We do this same exact crap to woman who get raped or assaulted.

"Should she have worn that small skirt?"

I guess not...

"Should she have had too much to drink?"

Definitely not, though it should be noted how much I enjoy having too much to drink and how few consequences I've faced for my alcohol-related (mis)behavior...

"Should she have been at that bar in that part of town by herself?"

In light of what happened, no...

"Should she have been in a hotel room in the wee hours of the morning with a man she had just met?"

Considering the consequences, obviously not...

So, would I say that she made poor choices that contributed to the awful events that befell her?

Yes, probably so...

BUT- did she deserve to get raped?

HELL FUCK NO, just like the disproportionately large amount of UNARMED black people who keep dying at the hands of police officers don't deserve to die, even when they made one or more poor choices that contributed in some small way to their deaths. We must stop victim blaming!!

Perhaps the most absurd example of victim blaming is the common tendency of white people to blame black people for white racism.

THEY WILL NOT ASSIMILATE!! LOOK AT THEIR RIDICULOUS NAMES!! I NEVER EVEN THOUGHT ABOUT RACE UNTIL WE ELECTED BARACK HUSSEIN OBAMA!!

First of all, it's patently preposterous for white people, the deliberate architects of historical AND ONGOING race-based segregation, to criticize black people for "refusing to assimilate".

But also, for the last time, a person can not possibly be responsible for creating something that existed long before that person was even born, so please stop blaming Barack Obama (and Al Sharpton, etc) for racism in America.

A common counter-point I hear is something along the lines of:

"Fine. Those two did not invent racism, but I blame them for using, preying upon, and extending racism to their own advantage."

Here's the thing, though- that counter-point mirrors what many white people felt about MLK in his time, AKA that racism is only a big deal because race agitators make it a big deal. I could make a case that if all white people would collectively admit that racism remains a very serious problem in our country, particularly within our criminal justice system, then people like Al Sharpton would be utterly irrelevant because the media does not typically cover vigorous agreements. However, since many white people initially tried to characterize the mass murder in Charleston as an attack on Christianity and many conservatives believe that race played absolutely no role in the deaths of Trayvon Martin or Eric Garner, people like Al Sharpton will continue to have a substantial media presence.

Be an Ally, Not a Sympathizer or Moderate

I am going to let Dr. Martin Luther King, JR get us started on this topic:

I must confess that over the past few years I have been gravely disappointed with the white moderate. I have almost reached the regrettable conclusion that the Negro's great stumbling block in his stride toward freedom is not the White Citizen's Counciler or the Ku Klux Klanner, but the white moderate, who is more devoted to 'order' than to justice; who prefers a negative peace which is the absence of tension to a positive peace which is the presence of justice; who constantly says: 'I AGREE WITH YOU IN THE GOAL YOU SEEK, BUT I CANNOT AGREE WITH YOUR METHODS of direct action'; who paternalistically believes he can set the timetable for another man's freedom; who lives by a mythical concept of time and who constantly advises the Negro to wait for a 'more convenient season.' SHALLOW UNDERSTANDING FROM PEOPLE OF GOOD WILL IS MORE FRUSTRATING THAN ABSOLUTE MISUNDERSTANDING FROM PEOPLE OF ILL WILL. Lukewarm acceptance is much more bewildering than outright rejection.

I had hoped that the white moderate would see this need. Perhaps I was too optimistic; perhaps I expected too much. I suppose I should have realized that few members of the oppressor race can understand the deep groans and passionate yearnings of the oppressed race, and still fewer have the vision to see that injustice must be rooted out by strong, persistent, and determined action. I am thankful, however, that some of our white brothers in the South have grasped the meaning of this social revolution and committed themselves to it. They are still all too few in quantity, but they are big in quality. Some -such as Ralph McGill, Lillian Smith, Harry Golden, James McBride Dabbs, Ann Braden and Sarah Patton Boyle--have written about our struggle in eloquent and prophetic terms. Others have marched with us down nameless streets of the South. They have languished in filthy, roach infested jails, suffering the abuse and brutality of policemen who view them as 'dirty nigger-lovers.' Unlike so many of their moderate brothers and sisters, they have recognized the urgency of the moment and sensed the need for powerful 'action' antidotes to combat the disease of segregation.

To guard against the inevitable defense of "this speech is from the 1960's, and we have come a long way since then", let's again look at the Eric Garner case to highlight the ongoing differences between an ally and a moderate.

When white people watch the video of Eric Garner's traumatic death, 10% of us say "FUCK HIM, HE GOT WHAT HE DESERVED" and 10% of us say "EVERY SINGLE ONE OF THOSE COPS BELONGS IN JAIL" while 80% of us say, "Wow, that is really awful, but why did that man resist arrest? Why was he selling loose cigarettes illegally in the first place? And why was he animated rather than being totally deferential and submissive and compliant? And why was he so fat? If he were in better shape, he'd probably be alive. And the cops didn't choke him. The policeman's forearm was on the side of his throat in a restraining move, not on the center of his throat in a choking move, and being a police officer is a hard job, and these are split second decisions, and so on."

We as white people need to progress to the point where we almost universally watch the Eric Garner video and think to ourselves, based on passionless reason, "This was not only awful, but wrong, and criminal, and I am not OK with the fact that none of the police officers involved in this incident were even indicted, much less convicted, nor am I OK with the fact that the prosecutor predictably declined to include any lesser charges at all, instead opting to only present a charge to the grand jury of murder 2, which the video definitely doesn't prove and in fact largely refutes, rather than presenting a charge of manslaughter 1, which the video supports, or manslaughter 2, which the video pretty much proves beyond a reasonable doubt."

The bottom line is that Dr. King is STILL right: white allies "are STILL all too few in quantity", but there's no reason for us to continue proving him right forever, and there's plenty of room on this bandwagon, and everyone is invited.

Acknowledge the Good

As individuals, we must train our minds to notice and recollect and praise the good we see in each other, rather than focusing almost exclusively on the bad.

If you're white, and you've cited the disproportional black homicide rate or out-of-wedlock birth rate, but you've never cited the disproportional rate at which black people serve our nation in the military, that's a real shame, and you must do better so we can be better.

If you're black, and you criticize white racists like Donald Trump while never praising white allies like Tim Wise, that's a real shame, and you must do better so we can be better.

P.S. As someone who has tried progressively harder and harder for more than a quarter century to be an ally, an encouraging word from a black person means the world to me.

Strive for Fairness and Accuracy in Our Discussions

I hear a lot about "open season" online and on television.

According to liberals and black activists, "It's open season on black people!!"

According to conservatives and police unions, "It's open season on police officers!!"

These sorts of comments are as unhelpful as they are statistically inaccurate, and presenting an exception as if it's actually the rule is the sort of thing that Heinrich Himmler did, which means it is not the sort of thing that we should do.

Go ahead and tell the WHOLE truth.

You must tell the whole truth if you expect your side to be heard, because guess what happens when you don't? The (often unofficial) opposition research team finds out on their own, and now even people who agree with you (or at least want to agree with you) can't help but wondering "what else are they hiding?" And staunch members of the opposition LOVE IT, because now they get to paint you as caring about your agenda more than you care about the truth.

An excellent recent example of this involves a popular recent meme talking about a 15 year-old black boy who stole a pair of sneakers and was tried as an adult and received a five-year prison sentence, despite zero prior arrests or convictions. As an "ally", this meme made my blood boil, until I found out the 15 year-old black boy stole the pair of sneakers at gun point. So, memes like that don't help, because if your cause and your case are worthwhile, you should have ample evidence without resorting to distortions or omissions or any other tool of the propagandist.

Reject "Faulty Generalizations"

The "Faulty Generalization" is another classic tool of the propagandist, and we as white people must resist the temptation to believe and repeat negative propaganda about American black people.

As we have already discussed in this book:

1. If 6 out of 1000 welfare recipients receive cash assistance for a period of longer than three years, clearly the metaphorical (black) "Welfare Queen" is a helluva lot less prevalent than many people imagine her to be.

2. If 8 out of 1000+ #BlackLivesMatter protests have turned violent or destructive, then it's mathematically and morally wrong to characterize the overall movement as advocating violence and destruction.

This common tendency to imagine that a totally incomplete picture is in fact complete distorts the truth, and distorts people's realities, and we must at least be aware of the "Faulty Generalization" logical fallacy that seems to be the most prevalent logical fallacy in America today.

Finally, here are some thoughts for individual black people to consider. I don't believe that racism is black people's fault, nor do I believe that it's up to black people to fix racism. I do believe, however, that individual black people have a central role to play in overcoming racism.

Be Aware of the "Bucket Theory"

The Bucket Theory, developed by Chief Savage Dave "Nat Geo" Chisolm, simply states that we as human beings often tend to bring past experiences and stereotype-based expectations into current situations, causing us to attach a specific motive that may or may not actually be applicable by putting the behavior into a "bucket".

For example, I am from a big city, and my cousin is from a small town, and I will never forget how hurt my cousin was when I refused to set her up on a date with any of my friends in college. She threw my refusal into the "Country Cousin Bucket", assuming that the reason I refused to set her up with my friends was because I was "embarrassed" by her. She assumed this in large part because of her previous life experiences of city folks looking down their noses at country folks. As such, her suppositions about my motives weren't necessarily unreasonable, but they weren't even remotely accurate, as the real reason I refused to set her up is that birds of a feather flock together, meaning that virtually all of my college friends were either lunatics, sex addicts, alcoholics, drug abusers, or some combination thereof, so I did not find any of them to be worthy of dating my amazing cousin.

I also remember one time in Houston, maybe in 2012, when I was walking down a busy street, and I noticed a shirtless homeless man loudly talking to himself and making odd gestures about 200 yards in front of me, so I crossed the street in order to avoid interacting with him. As I was crossing, I took a quick glance, hoping that he had never noticed me in the first place, and my eyes were met by his totally disgusted and completely accusing and slightly hurt eyes, and it became obvious to me that he had lobbed my behavior straight into the "Race Bucket" by assuming that I was crossing the street because he was black. My behavior actually belonged in the "Deranged and Agitated Homeless Man with No Shirt on Bucket", but I can understand why he felt the way he felt and assumed the things he assumed.

I fairly regularly see my Facebook friends posting things like:

I was at the store today, and this person was incredibly rude to me because I am (black/white/a man/a woman/gay/etc)!!

Well, I can understand why a person would lob certain situations into the Race Bucket, or the Gender Bucket, or the Sexual Preference Bucket, but the truth is that we can't know the truth.

What if the person who treated us poorly was having a bad day?

What if the person who treated us poorly is just a rude prick?

What if the person who treated us poorly was high on drugs?

What if the person who treated us poorly suffers from migraine headaches?

What if the person who treated us poorly is shy or socially awkward or autistic, not arrogant or dismissive?

What if the person who treated us poorly is a veteran who suffers from PTSD?

Sometimes, unpleasant inter-racial interactions occur because of race, and sometimes, unpleasant inter-gender interactions occur because of gender, but sometimes, unpleasant inter-racial and inter-gender interactions occur just because, and the main point about the Bucket Theory is that even when placing someone's behavior into a Bucket is in fact accurate, it still does more harm than good, particularly to the psyche of the aggrieved party. After all, you've also (at times) been treated like shit by people who share your same gender/race/sexuality, right? As such, maybe we should just throw all of the bullshit we encounter into the Asshole Bucket, unless the asshole in question gives us a specific reason to suspect a specific motive, such as using a racist or sexist or homophobic slur during the course of the negative interaction in question. Other than that, though, my advice is to do our best not to guess about people's motives and just move on and don't give the asshole one more second of your time than you already have.

In short, familiarity with the Bucket Theory should hopefully provide a bit of a psychological safeguard against the extreme mental stress that accompanies experiencing discrimination.

Restore Mental Health

Somehow, some way, black adults must find a way to preach something to young people that too many black adults don't feel, which is optimism. This psychological damage of racism is a major reason why American black people feel on average substantially more hopeless and pessimistic than American white people, and hopelessness kills ambition, and you can't live your dream unless you have a dream. As mentioned in the chapter titled "Bullshit", in my mind, part of the reason for Barack Obama's ascent was the absence of racism-inspired generational hopelessness in the household where he was raised; I also think that this partially explains why African immigrants earn 40% more money on average than American black people who have been here for generations- IE, African immigrants left hopelessness behind in Africa, and consequently did not saddle their children with their trauma-based, multi-generational hopelessness (http://home.uchicago.edu/~arauh/Rauh2013b.pdf).

NOTE: There are many factors explaining the gaps between children of African immigrants and children of multi-generational American black people, such as the fact that immigrating via normal channels to the US from Africa involves a rigorous process, meaning that many African immigrants held advanced degrees in technical fields before they even arrived, etc. Additionally, African immigrants do not face the same level of scorn and suspicion and hostility from white racists as American descendants of slaves.

Failing non-bigotry, should you strategically make yourself more palatable to the bigot in power?

As is the case with many questions black people face, there is no right answer.

A lot of black people employ this strategy, but a lot of black people are offended to the core of their living souls that they, or anyone, should be asked, or almost required, to even consider this notion.

My good friend Marcus proposes and practices pragmatism and practicality to navigate the racist world black people find themselves living in. For example, he pre-tips waiters and waitresses well over 20% of what he expects to spend, and he says "yes, sir" and "no, sir" somewhat constantly, partly because he believes in the concept of respecting your elders, but also partly because he has discovered that a submissive word here and there endears a black person to older white men.

I know that some black people read about Marcus's strategy, and their blood boils, and some may view Marcus as an Uncle Ruckus or a sell out, and they ask, "Why should black people, who are the victims of racism, be the ones to change and make accommodations all the time in order to combat racism?" And I can't answer that question, except to say that no human being **should** be asked to change or compromise the essence of who they are, and it sucks shit that black people have been forced into a position in many ways of having to choose between short-term successes as individuals and long-term humanity as a race.

Fight to End All Oppression

I wish black people collectively would stand much more aggressively with transgender, gay, immigrant, etc, because then black people would be known as the protectors of justice rather than the protectors of self interest.

P.S. I am not at all implying that white people are less bigoted against the LGBTQPI community or against immigrants- in fact, if you look at the bathroom bills and the recent (unfairly named in my view, as it only affected four countries) "Muslim Ban" as well as the campaign pledge to "BUILD A WALL!!", it has in fact been angry white men leading us down Bigotry Boulevard. Rather, I'm only saying that non-hypocritical and selfless advocates create an air of unimpeachability that leads to an aura of higher authority on the subject at hand.

Quit Allowing Melanin Levels to Stir Intra-Racial Divides

When I moved to Atlanta, I was floored to discover a fairly large percent of lighter skinned black people looked down on darker skinned black people. One man I encountered in particular, who shall remain nameless due to being the son of an enormously prominent Civil Rights leader, said derogatory things to me about black people as if his father's identity had no genetic impact on him whatsoever, always using "they and them", rather than "we and us". It was bizarre, but it wasn't the last time I encountered a similar attitude, especially during my times living in Atlanta and New York.

Darker skinned black people, on the other hand, have fairly regularly mentioned to me that light-skinned black people aren't *really* black and/or that light-skinned black people aren't to be trusted. To me, if you've ever had negative interactions with white people based on race, you're black enough, no matter the exact hue of your skin (or the inflection of your voice).

White people aren't mean to each other based on race, but black people sure are, and y'all need to stop it. Y'all have plenty of problems without being racist assholes toward each other. Full humanity for black people unquestionably means that there isn't just one way to be "authentically" black, and, again, if you've ever even one time been treated like shit because you're black, then your blackness should never be called into question, least of all by another black person.

Recognize and embrace that life is hard for everybody.

Even rich white children have problems, often stemming from being raised by caretakers and nannies and live-in housekeepers. Being born poor and black has a ton of baked in disadvantages, but the vast majority of people I know who are black and grew up poor at least experienced a childhood during which they knew for sure that they were loved, whereas a lot of the (multi-generational) wealthiest white people I know grew up feeling unloved, because their parents were jet setting all over the world. I know the jet setting sounds nice, but growing up feeling unloved sounds anything but nice, and a lot of extremely wealthy white people have a deep and unabating pain in their souls based on feeling unloved.

Every single human being is dealing with their own shit, and I think it's hugely damaging when some black people inaccurately believe that every white person lives on Easy Street, because the more you think the odds are stacked against you, the less likely you are to keep pressing forward.

Stop being Extra Hard on Black Police Officers

I wish that so many black people didn't automatically give black cops the fisheye and treat them with added suspicion and hostility or think of them as an Uncle Ruckus, because that sort of attitude permeates, which causes untold thousands of black kids who might have been amazing cops instead to pursue another career because the thought of a their own neighborhood giving them the fisheye is too much to handle (along a similar thought pattern, I have begged coaches to treat referees more courteously, because when we treat refs like garbage, our players see that, and it greatly lessens the likelihood that they might one day give back to the game by becoming a referee, thereby self-defeatingly poisoning the potential referee hiring pool).

CHAPTER 15

GROUP (POLICY) SOLUTIONS

Some of these policy solutions apply to our federal government, some apply to our state governments, some apply to our city governments, some apply to public institutions, and some apply to private institutions. If we are ever going to get this thing right, it truly will take an all-hands-on-deck approach.

NOTE: Some of these proposals would cost money, in some cases a lot of money. However, you can't put a price on justice, and every single reform I'm recommending combined would cost less than half of what we've spent on war in the last 20 years, so this isn't a question of "can we afford to provide justice?" but rather "will we prioritize justice?"

NOTE 2: Some of these proposals are borrowed straight from other sources, such as the prominent website "Campaign Zero" authored by #BlackLivesMatter activists DeRay Mckesson, Sam Swey, and Brittany Packnett; Shaun King's important series "25 Solutions for Police Brutality"; etc.

Anti-Discrimination Reform

We need an Amendment to clarify that discrimination is not protected under the 1st Amendment. Others have also advocated for an Amendment to exclude "hate speech" from 1st Amendment protection, but that is in my view a step too far because I do not want our government policing our words (any more than they already do). Plus, discriminatory words hurt people's feelings, whereas discriminatory actions hurt people's lives.

In a nutshell, all of our anti-discrimination laws need teeth. Our federal government has written some beautiful sounding anti-discrimination legislation in the last 50 years, and all of those laws need to be updated to include substantial prison sentences for flagrant violators.

Consider the case of Bank of America. In 2011, they were ordered to pay a record $355 million dollar fine for ongoing discrimination against black people. But guess what? Bank of America profited over $6.2 billion in the 3rd quarter of 2011 alone. And guess what else? Bank of America has been forced to pay out multi-million dollar settlements multiple times since 2011, which is to say that in the grand scheme of things, the record fine from 2011 was meaningless. However, if the 2011 Bank of America CEO had received 15 years to life in prison, I feel nearly certain that the next CEO would have PRIORITIZED compliance with righteous federal anti-discrimination statutes.

The same exact concept is in play within the Fair Housing Act. The fines aren't working, and they never will. But if Donald Sterling had been sent to prison for discriminating against potential black tenants and for treating his current black tenants noticeably worse in terms of building upkeep, other wealthy landlords and slumlords would certainly take notice.

The identical concept is in play within the job market. Title VII of the 1964 Civil Rights Act (on paper) prohibits employment-related discrimination related to all terms, conditions, and privileges of employment, including hiring, firing, compensation, benefits, job assignments, promotions, and discipline. And yet we see too many cases of blatant employee-related discrimination to even count, but no business owners or CEO's have been locked in prison for a decade or longer because of discrimination, so the discrimination continues.

In my world, for at least 25 years, sneaker company executives have conspired with sneaker-company-sponsored grassroots youth programs to direct top prospects to college programs that they also sponsor. However, the FBI has recently decided that this conspiracy should be designated as a criminal conspiracy, and sneaker company executives are about to go to prison. As a result, and very unsurprisingly, the practice has been stopped cold in its tracks, because educated rich people are way more afraid of prison than uneducated poor people.

Criminal Justice Reform

Accountability for Senior Leadership

When the federal government investigates local police departments, they nearly always find rampant racial discrimination. So, to "correct" the situation, first the federal government shames the local department by releasing the results to the press. Sometimes, the federal government also threatens to withhold funds if changes aren't made. And, every now and then, the local mayor or city council will bend to public pressure and sack the police chief. And that's about it, and nothing changes, because the consequences of the federal investigation are toothless. However, as would be the case with the federal anti-discrimination laws, if we started putting police chiefs in federal prison for 15 years to life when they allowed rampant racial discrimination to exist unchecked within the departments they were supposed to be leading, you can bet your bottom dollar that the incoming police chiefs would make eliminating racial injustice a top priority.

Voir Dire

Defense attorneys should be allowed to interview potential jurors and choose three before the normal jury selection process begins for the remaining nine. As it stands right now, most prosecutors and judges are elected officials (or work for one, in the case of assistant DA's). As such, the simple truth is that high conviction rates are important if a DA or judge is planning to run for re-election, because the American electorate non-partisanly believes that "tough on crime" is a good thing. Additionally, high conviction rates benefit DA's, assistant DA's, and judges who have higher career or political ambitions.

So, given the strong personal motivations for DA's and judges to secure convictions, the jury selection process remains terribly distorted against the defendant. Dozens if not hundreds of studies have been conducted on the subject of the extent to which the race of the defendant impacts jury selection, and the results have been consistently and horrifyingly conclusive. Prosecutors successfully white washing juries with judicial acquiescence when there's a black defendant has been going on since the founding of our country, which no one disputes- but people don't or can't understand or accept that THIS SHIT STILL HAPPENS TODAY, and it happens A LOT (remember, the Mississippi State Supreme Court admitted the rampant nature of this issue, as recently as 2008).

However, if the defense team were allowed to choose three jurors without the prosecutor or judge being able to intervene in any way before the other nine people were selected through our current methods, I think we would cut the number of innocent people being sent to prison, both substantially and immediately.

P.S. Even if you don't see the moral imperative of preventing (disproportionately black) innocent people from being incarcerated, you should at least recognize that non-white Americans are out-breeding white Americans, which means that we as white people are going to lose a lot of our positions of power in the next 25-50 years. So, don't support this simple reform for the sake of justice or for the sake of black people, support it for the sake of your children and grandchildren, because if you don't think oppressed people can become oppressors when given the levers of power, take a look at what happened to the white farmers in Zimbabwe after Robert Mugabe took control. In other words, please keep in mind that this adjustment protects all Americans, not just black people, and not just right now. Think about it. The year is 2045, and your white grandson has been accused of sexually assaulting a Latina. If you don't think there's a pretty good chance that in order to increase the likelihood of getting a win that a Hispanic DA might try to pack that jury with Latinas and exclude as many white men as possible, you're crazy. But, truly, the bottom line is that our system should not be so stacked up against the defendant, and jury selection is one of the most egregious ways our criminal justice system skews itself against the accused.

P.P.S. Voir Dire procedures in federal courts could be changed with a federal law, but each state has its own Voir Dire procedures, which means that a Constitutional Amendment would likely be required in order to achieve this reform.

Public Defender's Office

The Public Defender's Office must have equal funding and equal manpower per case as the Prosecutor's Office has. This is only fair, as there are an awful lot of innocent poor people in prison (often black) who got talked into a plea bargain by a public defender who earnestly (and probably truthfully) made the case:

"I can't get you off here. The prosecutor has four people working full time on this case, and I'm all you've got. They also have the entire police department at their disposal to investigate, but the state didn't even give me money for a single private investigator to help prove your innocence. Then- and you were sitting in the court room when they did it- they systematically struck any potential juror who looked anything like you or might have any sympathy toward you. Sure, they found 'legally justifiable' reasons to strike each one of them, but that isn't the point- this jury is full of people who are probably afraid of you in the first place. If you take this plea, you'll get 15 years, out in 10 or maybe even eight with good behavior. If we go to trial, and we lose, you'll never see your family again as a free man for the rest of your life. I promise you that I will fight as hard as I can for you if you decide to take this to trial, but I'm telling you it won't matter. Based on my experiences, WE WILL LOSE."

This sort of thing happens a lot more than people realize, and if the public defender's offices were properly staffed with equal resources, it would happen a lot less. And helping to prevent innocent people from going to prison is a goal we should all share. In fact, in the Land of the Free, preventing innocent people from going to prison should be the #1 priority.

P.S. Public Defenders' offices should be funded based on the percent of cases that they work on. For example, if a Public Defender's office works on 50% of the cases and the Prosecutor's budget for the year is $1,000,000, then the Public Defender's office should have a budget of $500,000 (plus additional funding for investigators and expert witnesses based on 50% of the money a jurisdiction spends on prosecution-related man-hours of city/county/state/federal employees who provide investigatory help or expert testimony).

P.P.S. I'm not necessarily calling for more overall spending. I'm calling for the spending to be proportionally equal. So, if a jurisdiction chose to comply with this law by cutting the District Attorney's budget to reallocate the money to the Public Defender's budget rather than by appropriating additional funds for the Public Defender's budget, that's fine with me.

P.P.P.S. This basic formula should also apply to court-appointed attorneys, not just "public defenders". A court-appointed defense attorney should also have equal access to funding and to manpower, on a per-case basis. State-appointed defense attorneys recommend way too many plea bargains as well, in large part based on self-interest, as the sooner a private-sector attorney clears a court-appointed case, the sooner he can return to private practice and earn way more money. Providing equal funding per case would reduce this common occurrence substantially, and immediately, and permanently.

Empower and Fund the ACLU

We must provide public funding for the ACLU and expand the role of the ACLU in three key areas:

1. The ACLU should be authorized and funded to establish a division inside of the FBI and a division inside of the Department of Justice to investigate and, if warranted, prosecute allegations of criminal activity by law enforcement officials.

2. The local chapters of the ACLU should be the place for citizens to file complaints against police officers, which means that the ACLU will need money to hire teams of professional investigators and to set up a system (web-based, app-based, in-person, by mail, by fax, etc) to receive complaints. No group of people should be allowed to investigate allegations into their own wrongdoing. Police officers should not be an exception. This is just common sense.

3. The local ACLU chapters should have the power to vet and pre-approve (or reject) the mayor's list of candidates for Police Chief. By allowing the ACLU to play a pivotal role in the selection of candidates for Police Chief, we can ensure that newly hired Police Chiefs have a record and a passion for upholding and defending Americans' civil rights.

4. The local ACLU chapters should also direct a substantial portion of Police Academy coursework in order that all new police officers understand civil rights laws and the importance of not violating them.

Jurisdiction for Deaths Caused by Law Enforcement Officials

The ACLU division of the FBI and the ACLU division of the Department of Justice should automatically take the lead in any deaths caused by police officers. It makes no sense to allow these cases to remain under local jurisdiction, considering that prosecutors and local police are on the same team. They work closely together, they need each other, and so they protect each other, creating an indisputable conflict of interests.

The Blue Wall of Silence

A lot of people would say that cops can't protect anyone if they don't trust and protect each other first, and that may be a valid view point. However, I still think it's long past time we examine and correct the internal cultures of "no snitching" that exist in police departments across this country. After all, it is not their job to protect each other, it is their job to protect the Constitution and to protect us.

For starters, by placing the ACLU in charge of criminal investigations into police officers, more police officers would cooperate, because unlike a local prosecutor, the ACLU would file obstruction of justice charges against police officers who stonewalled investigations into their fellow officers

However, I would also like to see a federal fund established (and administered by the ACLU) to provide substantial direct cash payments to police officers who snitch on racist or sexist or bullying or violent or criminal cops, if the information provided turns out to be accurate and actionable.

The bottom line is that we must shake up the nationwide police department culture of "no snitching" if we're going to make a dent in the astoundingly hypocritical police version of the Code of Omerta. Remember when cops produced those "Start Talking" videos to combat the criminal-produced "Stop Snitching" videos? I think it's well past time for police officers to follow their own advice and "start talking".

Keep Better Data

We do an awful job keeping data related to our entire criminal justice system, as former FBI Director James Comey famously noted in a speech from May of 2017:

Not long after riots broke out in Ferguson late last summer, I asked my staff to tell me how many people shot by police were African-American in this country. I wanted to see trends. I wanted to see information. They couldn't give it to me, and it wasn't their fault. Demographic data regarding officer-involved shootings is not consistently reported to us through our Uniform Crime Reporting Program. Because reporting is voluntary, our data is incomplete and therefore, in the aggregate, unreliable.

I recently listened to a thoughtful big city police chief express his frustration with that lack of reliable data. He said he didn't know whether the Ferguson police shot one person a week, one a year, or one a century, and that in the absence of good data, "all we get are ideological thunderbolts, when what we need are ideological agnostics who use information to try to solve problems." He's right.

The first step to understanding what is really going on in our communities and in our country is to gather more and better data related to those we arrest, those we confront for breaking the law and jeopardizing public safety, and those who confront us. "Data" seems a dry and boring word but, without it, we cannot understand our world and make it better.

I think there must be a federal law requiring all aspects of our criminal justice system to be tracked by race, gender, and *poverty, including but not limited to:

Decisions to issue a ticket versus decisions to give someone a break, and what tickets (if any) were issued for what offense

Decisions to arrest versus decisions to cut someone a little slack, and what reasons (if any) were given for the arrest (or non-arrest)

Decisions to file charges versus decisions not to file charges, and the specifics of charges being considered or filed (or not filed)

Decisions related to plea bargains, as well as the specifics of each plea bargain

Decisions related to bail (how much is asked for by prosecutors, how much is mandated by judges)

Decisions by law enforcement officials to use force, including deadly force

Judicial appointments

*Trials (*in every trial, we must record and report the race, gender, and level of affluence of the defendant, defense attorney, prosecutor, judge, and jury, along with the result of the trial and the sentence or fine imposed)

Probation

Parole (hearings and administration)

Prison-related data (assault by inmate or guard, murder by inmate or guard, extortion by inmate or guard, and so on, as well as all disciplinary-related matters and additional-charge-related matters, and the ACLU should establish a path for inmates to report abuse by fellow inmates or by the guards)

I'm pretty sure that if we had been doing this as a society for the last 50 years, we would be absolutely appalled at the findings. And by doing it moving forward, many individual members of the criminal justice system will be more conscientious in their decision-making processes, which means that American citizens will receive more equal treatment within our criminal justice system.

If you think about it, on a very basic human level, if every single time a police officer pulls someone over or interacts with a citizen in a manner beyond basic casual conversation they're required to record it and **report it, smart police officers are not going to pull someone over for driving 36 in a 35. Additionally, by recording this data, they will be able to hold themselves accountable if they notice a trend of non-essential interactions disproportionately occurring with a particular race or gender (the same principle applies to prosecutors and judges as well- access to this data will make them more aware of the potential for bias-based injustice).

*I would track "poverty" by the year of the car the person was driving and the zip code of person with whom the police officer interacted, as well as whether or not a criminal defendant were represented by a public defender or court-appointed attorney.

**This self-reported data should be monitored closely for bias and all police officers should be subjected to random reviews of their body camera footage to verify their reportings.

Bail

It is absolutely abysmal that we have AMERICAN CITIZENS losing months and sometimes even years of freedom because their families can't afford a few thousand dollars in bail. I don't think an American who can not afford bail should spend even one second more time in jail than an American who can afford bail. I think the 14th Amendment demands that wealth not dictate justice in our system, least of all on a topic where our history is so ugly and the consequences so grave.

I think that we should either do away with bail completely, or set up a system of automatic federal loans to cover bail, so that every citizen has equal access to the ability to afford bail.

P.S. As for the specifics, I'd offer terms of 1% above the Fed rate (or whatever percent you needed to cover the defaults), and I'd allow the money to be paid back monthly, to the tune of about $100/month. I'm fine with however the math works- if it needs to be 2% above the Fed rate and $110/month in order to make fiscal sense, that's OK with me- but I'm not fine with American citizens losing their freedom because they are poor.

Body Cameras

I agree with the idea lots of people seem to be mentioning- all law enforcement officials (local, state, federal) should be equipped with body cameras at all times. I look at this as a way to protect our law enforcement officials against false accusations and media feeding frenzies, and also to protect our citizens from illegal policing tactics. However, I think it would only work if the cameras' footage were constantly captured by a non-government entity, like Google or Facebook- otherwise, it would be too easy for a *crooked cop to claim the camera was broken, etc. This would be hugely and maybe even prohibitively expensive- I don't know. But I do think it would make our country a safer and fairer place.

* I think the percent of crooked cops versus cops who protect and serve is less than 10% of total cops, but the raw number of crooked cops nationally makes this situation serious enough to require real change.

Parole and Probation

I think that in the case of both parole and probation, there's a totally unnecessary (and costly) amount of administration regarding these 2 programs.

In both cases, all we need to do is tell the person being paroled or being offered probation that their prison sentences are going to be severe and total if they *royally screw up again.

*In general, "royally screwing up" again should mean that the person is out there in the streets doing the same stuff that got them in trouble in the first place, or committing other crimes that involve an actual victim. For example, if a paroled armed robber gets caught smoking weed, who cares? But if a paroled armed robber gets caught committing armed robbery again or gets caught stealing a car or commits any act of violence, they should receive maximum sentences across the board for all known crimes previously committed.

DNA Reviews

All incarcerated criminals should be allowed to request a DNA review, if applicable. We have thousands of pre-2010 cases nationwide where a simple DNA test would firmly establish or refute an inmate's guilt, and because we know how many innocent people we've incarcerated and executed, judicial procedures should never stand in the way of these tests being ordered and conducted.

The Death Penalty

I'm not against the death penalty, in theory. In practice, though, I can't see how any American could be in favor of it. It's just such a long list of innocent people we've unjustly incarcerated and/or sentenced to death, and those are just the ones we know about. To me, until we implement reforms to ensure that poor people receive a fair trial based on equal funding to establish equal justice, morality demands a national moratorium on the death penalty.

Dealing with Mental Health

As a nation, we have massive mental-health-related issues, with the poorest Americans suffering the most, due in part to inadequate funding. For example, in 1960, our nation had 600,000 publicly funded beds in mental health facilities, compared with only 60,000 as of 2014. Because of this, many of the most impoverished sufferers of mental illness wind up living on the streets or with heroic relatives who are regrettably far too often unable to deal with the symptoms of their family member's mental illness. Either way, police officers get placed in the completely unfair position of regularly being asked to perform a job for which they have not been trained and should not be required to handle.

To overcome this baked-in difficulty, there needs to be a specialized office in police departments comprised of highly educated and trained mental-health professionals to deal with disturbances related to mental health, and 9-1-1 operators must ask if the emergency is mental-health related so that the right people show up to deal with it.

We have also failed spectacularly to deal with causes of non-hereditary mental illness, instead only worrying about the effects. For example, the "counselors" in our public schools have been saddled with managing student and teacher schedules, leaving almost no time to do any actual counseling. Also, while Medicaid does provide for basic mental healthcare, we need to do a much better job (in coordination with our schools) of making sure that all children receive mental evaluations and care. We truly as a society seem not to realize that one of the most terrible effects of racism is the psychological damage done to children when they experience racism personally, which happens to every single black child in America at multiple points of their childhood. Fixing institutional racism is up to white people- but healing the psychological harm inflicted on black children by racism isn't something that white-controlled power structures can fix. However, increasing access to mental-health professionals inside of our public schools could go a long way toward partially alleviating this huge and under-discussed problem.

Finally, we must also routinely test police officers for Post Traumatic Stress Disorder and other common psychological afflictions that come with the territory. Policing is a difficult and dangerous job, and the mental pounding that police officers absorb can be overwhelming, and they need and deserve universal (and mandatory) mental health care.

P.S. In the wake of mass shootings, liberals are missing a HUGE opportunity to achieve adequate (or at least more adequate) funding to deal with our massive mental-health-related problems as a country, but instead, they continue to focus on gun control only, which is essentially a non-starter with probably 95% (or more) of Republican legislators. To me, whether they're sincere or not, if Republicans are bleating the talking point that "it's not a guns issue, it's a mental health issue" then all Democrats should call them out and require them to put their money where their mouth is. The best case scenario would be making the country a better place, and the worst case scenario would be exposing

Republicans as being a bunch of disingenuous double-talking do nothings. In other words, for Democrats, it's a win no matter how Republicans choose to react.

Candidate Screening

We tend to allow pretty low standards for entry-level positions within the public-sector job marketplace. However, in the case of police officers, because we arm them and because we task them with substantially more personal power than any other civil servant, we need higher entry-level standards than we do for the receptionist at the county clerk's office.

For starters, we need to know how much racial and gender bias a potential police officer displays before they get started, and we need to mandate ongoing anti-bias training for officers who display bias.

Also, we need to know which officers like to hurt people, and we need to refer them to the Armed Services, where their passions can be pursued in a far more appropriate and beneficial setting.

In short, we need a complete psychological evaluation, similar to the FBI structure, before arming and empowering an American citizen in the way we arm and power police officers.

P.S. If the new standards lead to a shortage of viable candidates, that's better than arming and empowering someone who is psychologically unfit to perform the job without unnecessarily and unjustifiably hurting or killing their fellow citizens. However, I think we could rather easily fill the gaps through smarter recruiting and retention efforts.

Restore Constitutional Probable Cause Standards

We need to reiterate via federal law that in this country, a police officer's "instincts" or "hunches" are NOT the same thing as Probable Cause. Unfortunately, as it stands right now, the Supreme Court eroded the 4th Amendment almost completely by establishing the standard of "reasonable suspicion" on the part of a police officer as being an acceptable pretext to violate The Constitution of the United States of America. We need new laws or lawsuits to revisit this issue.

The fundamental problem with the "reasonable suspicion" standard is that our rights conferred upon us by the Founding Fathers were not meant to be and should not be subject to "interpretation" and the whims of random police officers- in fact, quite the opposite!!

For starters, "racial profiling" is racist, literally, by definition, as it involves assumptions based on race. I've been pulled over in a black neighborhood probably at least five times over the years, for no reason other than having white skin and being in a black neighborhood. You see, quite a few police officers assume that a white guy in a black neighborhood must be there to buy drugs, and because of that "hunch", some police officers think that they have the right to violate my rights (for the record, I buy my drugs mostly from white people, as well as one Salvadoran). The point is that no matter how much you agree with racial profiling, Americans enjoy protections under the 4th Amendment AND the 14th Amendment that explicitly prohibit this type of behavior; and the other point is that the personal experiences I shared in this paragraph occur when black people venture into white neighborhoods a helluva lot more than the "reverse" racial profiling I described, and that isn't OK, either.

The package of new laws should also prohibit several other common police practices that tend to devolve into racial-profiling-related disproportional applications, thereby clearly violating both the 4th and 14th Amendments to The Constitution of the United States of America:
:
Stop and Frisk ("Stop and Frisk" violates the 4th Amendment on paper and the 14th Amendment in practice)

Questioning American citizens for "acting nervously" (this is a catch all excuse that allows the police to question any American citizen they feel like questioning, and it also violates the 4th Amendment on paper, plus the 14th Amendment in practice)

Questioning American citizens for fitting a broad description of a "suspect" such as "black male, 18-30" (this common occurrence violates the 14th Amendment in practice, and this package of federal laws needs to establish the right of the American citizen to demand the specifics of the "report" that the police officer referenced to justify the intervention- as it stands right now, this is also used as a catch all to justify a stop of an American citizen, often under false pretenses)

Questioning Americans for dressing a certain way (how American citizens choose to dress is clearly protected by the 1st Amendment's

FREEDOM of expression clause, and police interventions based on this also violate the 4th Amendment on paper and the 14th Amendment in practice)

Questioning Americans for wearing their hair a certain way (how American citizens choose to wear their hair is clearly protected by the 1st Amendment's FREEDOM of expression clause, and police interventions based on this also violate the 4th Amendment on paper and the 14th Amendment in practice)

Questioning Americans for sporting visible tattoos (the choice for American citizens to get tattoos is clearly protected by the 1st Amendment's FREEDOM of expression clause, and police interventions based on this also violate the 4th Amendment on paper and the 14th Amendment in practice)

Questioning Americans for wearing "flashy" jewelry (what type of jewelry American citizens choose to wear is clearly protected by the 1st Amendment's FREEDOM of expression clause, and police interventions based on this also violate the 4th Amendment on paper and the 14th Amendment in practice)

Pulling people over because their car is a clunker (under the 14th Amendment's EQUAL protection clause, if middle class people and wealthy people have the right to drive a car, then poor people must also have an EQUAL right to drive a car without fear of being pulled over without committing any actual moving violation)

Pulling people over who are "poorly dressed" but driving an expensive car (if a wealthy person wants to dress like a "slob", their choice to do so is clearly protected by the 1st Amendment's FREEDOM of expression clause, and police interventions based on this also violate the 4th Amendment on paper and the 14th Amendment in practice)

Pulling people over due to the type of bumper sticker on their car or sticker on their bicycle (the manner in which American citizens choose to *express* themselves is clearly protected by the 1st Amendment's FREEDOM of *express*ion clause, and police interventions based on this also violate the 4th Amendment on paper and the 14th Amendment in practice)

Other than racism, it truly is hard to explain why any American would be OK with such flagrant Anti-Constitutional abuses on the part of government officials. After all, in each of the examples listed above, it isn't white American citizens who are grossly disproportionately being stripped of their Constitutional Rights. As I've said before, white people who claim to cherish The Constitution really need to universally prioritize their pro-Constitution stance over their anti-nigger stance.

The War on Drugs

The War on Drugs quickly became a War on Black People, and it must end. We should decriminalize all drugs. The illegality of drugs doesn't meaningfully drop the demand; it only creates criminality. We have seen this already with Prohibition, one of the worst public policies in American history. We pay for our own self-defeating policies in at least nine ways:

1. Money spent to catch drug users and drug dealers.

2. Money spent to prosecute drug users and drug dealers.

3. Money spent to incarcerate drug users and drug dealers.

4. Money spent to keep track of drug users and drug dealers via probation and parole.

5. Money lost via what would be a massive boom of drug-related tax revenue.

6. We cost our nation untold millions of jobs and billions in economic activity by allowing the drugs that Americans consume to be produced in and distributed by other nations.

7. We cost our nation untold billions on welfare programs that would be so much less necessary if we quit incarcerating so many fathers.

8. We cost ourselves untold billions of dollars in healthcare costs, because you self-evidently can't regulate illegal activity; if so-called "hard drugs" like cocaine and heroine were regulated, we could control potency, purity, and non-toxicity, which would mean that emergency rooms nationwide would no longer have to treat such a massive number of "bad drug" episodes or overdoses in the least cost efficient manner

possible, and being able to regulate "hard drugs" would also mean that all those kids in Ohio would be breathing air instead of not breathing dirt.

9. We also cause all sorts of unnecessary street-level violence by locking up so-called "kingpins". After all, it has been repeatedly established that when you lock a drug kingpin in jail, violence ensues, as more than one underling normally wants to be the new leader. So, either they and their supporters fight it out initially for authority, or they go their separate ways but fight it out on the streets over time in various disputes over who should control which streets/neighborhoods/etc. And the government has gotten so good at locking up kingpins that the majority of the people left in control of the local drug trades are barely even adults. Imagine how an army would behave with a 19 year old general and 16 year old colonels, and you start to understand why violence spirals out of control when the Larry Hoovers of the world get hauled away for life sentences. Basically, nearly all of the "black on black crime" we claim to worry so much about is related to selling illegal drugs, and making drugs legal would of course curb drug-related violence almost overnight.

The War on Drugs is ineffective, unequally applied (and therefore Un-Constitutional), prohibitively expensive, anti-free market, and anti-liberty. It is a failed policy, and an immoral policy, and it must end.

Sentencing

Is America really the "land of the free" when we lead the developed world in incarcerating our own citizens? Extended prison sentences ruin people's lives, and in my opinion, our society should not ruin a person's life unless that person ruined someone else's life. If you engage in severe unjustifiable violence (of course including sexual violence) or if you engage in life-altering fraud or theft, then you deserve an extended prison sentence. Programs like "mandatory minimums" and "three strikes and you're out" regularly defy basic human justice as it has been understood from the time of Abraham.

Require Police Officers to Have Personal Insurance Against Claims of Police Brutality or Sexual Misconduct or any other Violent or Criminal Behavior

Insurance companies are ruthless, and we should deploy them here. In a scenario such as this, the monthly premium isn't going to be very much for the vast majority of the "good cops". I'd bet the monthly premium for police officers without police brutality claims or sexual harassment claims would be less than \$30/month, and I would gladly support a federal tax credit to offset this baseline cost.

However, for the police officers with repeated claims of brutality and/or sexual assault, their monthly premium would pretty quickly be more than their monthly take-home pay. In other words, they would need to find another line of work, unless the police unions wanted to put their money where their mouth is and pay for the required insurance to keep racist and/or criminal and/or bully cops employed as police officers.

Basically, implementing this policy would most likely serve as an efficient way to weed out the bad cops, but even if it didn't meet that primary objective, it would alleviate citizen taxpayers from having to foot the bill for police misconduct settlements (in 2015, the 10 cities with the largest police departments paid out more than \$248,000,000 in police misconduct cases (https://www.wsj.com/articles/cost-of-police-misconduct-cases-soars-in-big-u-s-cities-1437013834).

P.S. Has anyone else noticed the irony that American liberals mostly defend teachers' unions, while American conservatives mostly defend police officers' unions, when both have the identical mission and (perceived) flaw? Namely, protecting their members, even if it comes at the expense of causing real harm to American citizens? In the case of both unions, of course, there's substantial overlap between the interests of the union and the interests of the citizenry; it's just that on the occasions the union membership interests and the citizenry interests aren't aligned, both the teachers' unions and the police officers' unions are going to side with their membership's interests. Every time. And I'm not even necessarily saying that's a bad thing. If you think about it, as an employee union, that's what you're supposed to do. You're supposed to prioritize your membership's interests over the interests of the general public. I'm simply saying that it's inconsistent and therefore absurd to be angry with teachers' unions but supportive of the police officers' unions, or vice versa.

Better Training

Everyone seems to agree that police officers need "better training", but what does that mean?

For starters, as I've already mentioned, the ACLU should play a central role in the curriculum at police academies, in order to make sure that police work focuses on protecting The Constitution and protecting the citizens' rights guaranteed within. That should be the first focus.

In my view, the second focus of police academy training should be non-violent conflict resolution. Force should be the 2nd to last resort, with deadly force being the absolute last resort.

Additionally, as I've also already mentioned, incoming police officers should be tested for racial and gender bias and given access to mandatory anti-bias training, depending on the results of the bias tests.

We also need automatic extra training regiments for any officer who receives a complaint.

Finally, perhaps the most important element of the extra training is that it must be about improvement, not punishment, and it should be crafted as to make police officers better, not bitter.

P.S. It is also important that we avoid partnering young cops with veteran cops who have shoddy records, so we can avoid all of the off-the-books "training" that can occur when the wrong cop is placed in the role of mentor.

Police Officer Education

All new police recruits must have a college degree in order to become Police Officers. Without a degree, new recruits would be categorized as Police Interns, with the main difference being that Police Interns would carry guns with rubber bullets rather than actual bullets.

All current Police Officers as well as the incoming Police Interns should have a period of seven years to complete a four-year college degree, and the taxpayers should fully fund this program.

Traffic Stops

We need to look at our procedures for traffic stops and make some adjustments. For starters, it seems dangerous to conduct the interaction on the driver's side window of the car. First, this is closest to passing traffic, which puts the officer's life in danger. As such, on highways, the driver should exit and then pull over on the feeder road; and on city streets, the driver should find the nearest parking lot, and then pull over. Second, the cop can't see the person's hands until it would be too late, if the person had a gun and evil intentions. Frankly, were I a police officer, I'd be scared shitless at every single traffic stop, and we all know that jumpy trigger fingers are largely fear based.

If the driver and the police officer both exited the cars and met in the middle, the police officer could see the hands of the driver, thereby reducing potential confusion about the threat a driver might pose to the officer. Also, by meeting in the middle of the two cars, the police officer's dashboard camera and body camera would give us a much clearer picture in the event that something went wrong.

P.S. If a driver puts their hazards on, that is a libertarian's way to opt out of the interaction, in which case the police officer would simply look at the license plate as they already do, and issue a ticket using their car computer or an app, then once the police officer turns off his flashing lights and starts to drive away, the driver is free to go.

Diversify Police Forces

For a little over a year, I attended Lamar High School in Houston. At that time, and maybe still today, Lamar roughly mirrored the overall city demographically (loosely 1/3 black, 1/3 Latino, and 1/3 white- and 1/2 female), and I remember that it worked *magnificently well. In my opinion, if police departments had as a long-term goal to approximately demographically mirror the people they're policing (racially, ethnically, and in terms of gender), it would go a long way toward making things better, and I would tie federal funds to this long-term goal to motivate the departments to move in this direction.

*It worked "magnificently well" except for the one time a small group of idiotic white kids decided to wear Confederate flag t-shirts to school and got sent home after the football coaches told the principal what was going to happen to those kids after school.

Increase Community Policing

When I lived in Dallas, I worked at Skyline High School, and *two kids I coached are now serving as police officers in their hometown. As you may or may not know, Dallas is on the forefront of the "Community

Policing" movement. Clifton Wright and Lamar Glass both police the same neighborhoods where they grew up, which of course means that they have lifetime trusted relationships with many of the people they've been assigned to protect. Consequently, with trust pre-established between Lamar and the community he's policing, you increase cooperation to catch violent bad apples, and you decrease fear, which decreases unnecessary deaths. If we were able to recruit and train outstanding young people who hailed from the high-crime neighborhoods they'd be asked to police, it would go a long way toward creating more equality (and better results) in our law enforcement systems, and I would also love to see federal money tied to participation in this movement.

*Technically, I didn't coach Lamar Glass. However, I stayed in touch with the Skyline Raiders program because of my affection for the kids and also for the long-time legendary coach, JD Mayo, so I knew Lamar but did not "coach" him.

Drug Testing

Police officers must be randomly screened for steroids and other drugs that supply unnatural adrenaline rushes (amphetamines mostly). In most of the videos showing police misconduct, the police officers display not just emotion, but anger or even rage, and trained professionals should almost never exhibit rage, and the fact that we so regularly see anger or rage from police officers makes me suspect that steroid abuse is an active trend within certain segments of police departments (aka, the "weight room" crowd).

Cops in Schools

Police departments should specifically recruit and train police officers to work inside of schools who have uniquely empathetic hearts toward poor children. We need police officers who meet angry teenage words with open ears and non-threatening tones rather than equally angry words or violence. One problem police officers face in "the hood" is that the community (rightly) doesn't trust police officers, and as long as that perception exists, policing in majority-black "inner city" neighborhoods will continue to be harder than it needs to be. If, on the other hand, the children come to see police officers as friends and confidants and people you go to and can trust when you need help, it would foundationally help this situation immeasurably and in innumerable ways.

Form Charitable Wings for Direct Action

Along the same lines of changing perceptions, every police department should also have a fundraising arm that exists solely to directly help citizens in need. I have noticed that most wealthy white people speak glowingly about police officers, so I would think they would be eager to support police-directed charitable work. Even if the fundraising only led to $50/week in petty cash for officers working in high-poverty zip codes to distribute as they saw fit, the collective effect over time of these small kindnesses would add up and create a two-way emotional shift away from dehumanization.

Other Recommendations for Reform

Reparations

The subject of reparations has been infuriating a whole lot of white people since 1865. Here's a political poster from that era:

The Freedmen's Bureau referenced in the above poster was a Lincoln program that was supposed to carry out the 40 Acres and a Mule promise, but subsequent Presidents never deployed the Freedmen's Bureau as Lincoln intended (Andrew Johnson vetoed two Freedmen's Bureau renewal bills, and Grant disbanded it completely and permanently in 1872).

So, as it is a matter of historical record that America made promises to freed slaves that we didn't even come remotely close to keeping, the morality of reparations really isn't up for debate, unless you think promise breaking and/or slavery are morally reputable. What is up for debate, though, is how we should go about finally stepping up to the plate and accepting this enormous and unprecedented undertaking.

For starters, I ran some basic numbers and to actually return the total dollars of the plunder of black people since 1700 would run into the trillions (the quick math I ran was already over 4 trillion, and I have no doubt the actual number is much higher, and my calculations didn't include any interest at all). As such, we quite literally can't afford true or proper "reparations" without creating money out of thin air, which would collapse our currency and cause inflation, and inflation is of course the most regressive tax known to man, which means we'd wind up disproportionally hurting the very people we were trying to help (to give you an idea of the scale of what we owe black people in terms of broken promises and back wages, if the USA gave every single acre of land currently owned by the federal government to American black people, it would amount to 17 acres per black person, well less than half of the 40 acres that freed slaves were initially promised).

However, being unable to immediately afford full reparations shouldn't be used as an excuse to avoid discussing creative ways to at least begin addressing this egregious historical wrong that has continued to produce incalculable negative consequences for black people.

Here are some realistic and affordable ideas to get the ball rolling toward making things right with American black people:

1. We should determine the approximate discrepancy per pupil and the number of years the discrepancy existed between the white schools and the black schools during state-funded but segregated public education and we should provide that ratio in reverse for the exact same number of years to historically black high schools in historically black areas or any other high school in a high poverty majority black area (note, I'm not talking about and wouldn't support decreasing other schools' budgets to fund this but would rather prefer it to be a separate federal appropriation).

2. If you are black and you have served in the military or one of your parents or grandparents has served in the military, the federal government should lend you money using the Federal Fund Rate to purchase a home (we screwed black veterans out of many of the GI Bill's benefits on a disgustingly regular basis, including the path to home ownership, and that is a recent event that had a huge and tangible impact on the current levels of average individual black wealth comparatively).

3. We should allow American black people to refinance existing high-interest debt using federal money and the Federal Funds Rate.

4. We should allow American black people to receive federal loans using the Federal Funds Rate to start or grow a business.

I think these four programs would, over time, go a long way toward eradicating disproportional black poverty, which isn't necessarily or optimally the government's role in normal circumstances. But, if you broke it, you bought it, and no sane, literate person can deny that policies and practices in this country's history have been horribly unfair financially to black people; and that isn't right, nor is it OK, nor is it irrelevant (people come with "that was a long time ago" on this topic a lot, as if the sanctioned denial of wealth accumulation somehow does not impact inheritance).

To me, these four policies would help make things right (or at least more right), and I have no doubt we can easily afford to take these steps, as loans obviously involve way less stress to the budget than outright grants. I know the idea of establishing a reparations program isn't popular with most white people, but if our government can fix something that they broke in a limited, justifiable, and affordable way, we should, especially when doing so would finally keep the promises we made in the past. Given our history of paying reparations to Japanese Americans and the universally acknowledged historical plunder of American black people, I'm not sure why this is such a controversial topic- we can disagree on the how or the what or even the when, but there's absolutely no morally justifiable reason to disagree on the why.

Black people are collectively in a hole. They're in a hole because we put them in a hole. They want to climb out, and they will, but we should put a ladder in the hole, or at least toss down the materials to build their own ladder. We as white people largely caused this collective predicament, so basic common sense and decency demand that we participate fully in correcting it.

P.S. Reparations should only apply to Americans who can trace their family roots back to slavery in America (IE, black people who immigrated to America in the 20th century would not be eligible, even if they came from the Caribbean area and descended from slaves, as that slavery existed under an authority other than America, and the same would apply to black people who currently live in American territories and can trace their family roots back to slavery, unless America had a controlling interest in said territory prior to the end of slavery).

P.P.S. During the formation of the Euro Zone, French President Mitterand famously remarked, "If we continue to focus on issues which took place more than 25 years into our past, we will never come together and be able to move forward." To address this fairly common sentiment on this topic, let me just say that unlike the French and Germans, where both sides have legitimate historical grievances, there is no "both sides" argument to be made here. Black people got screwed, and white people did the screwing, period. Also, promises don't expire; as Dr. King said, "The time is always right to do what is right."

P.P.P.S. I also favor reparations for the American Indians- I just focus less on their plight mostly because we killed pretty much all of them and so there are fewer of them left currently suffering. So, while I don't have many specific thoughts on the subject, I definitely do favor reparations for American Indians in some form or fashion.

P.P.P.P.S. I must say that one of the aspects of writing this book that has made me feel the saddest and least hopeful is seeing how little the rhetoric of racist white people has changed. If you again check out the details of the poster in opposition to "reparations" from 1866, you will notice that it almost precisely mirrors the GOP position on "welfare" in 2017, but a lot of white people nevertheless express frustration that as a nation aren't more focused on "all the progress we've made".

End Affirmative Action

Discrimination can't fix discrimination, and ignoring the 14th Amendment can't strengthen it. Equal = Equal. This should not be a complicated concept to grasp.

On the rather long list of additional reasons why I do not like and do not support Affirmative Action is that it almost never helps deeply impoverished direct descendants of American slaves, aka the folks it was supposed to help. Rather, Affirmative Action looks at skin color alone, not poverty and not family history and not even nationality. As such, Affirmative Action tends to help black children of upper class parents and/or black children of immigrants and/or black children of prominent foreigners much more than it tends to help impoverished children who are direct descendants of American slaves.

As it stands right now, impoverished valedictorians from awful public schools whose grandparents lived through Jim Crow and who did not have a parent or counselor force them to take the SAT or ACT several times with ever-increasing levels of professional test-prep assistance get shut out COMPLETELY. So, kids who grew up in historically black neighborhoods facing historical and ongoing prejudice as well as low expectations from society at large but who do EVERYTHING right- straight A's and the whole nine yards- see their opportunity to attend an elite school instead go to a first or second generation American who happens to be black. Again, Affirmative Action was designed to correct historical injustices perpetuated by the US government on its own citizens- what historical and ongoing multi-generational injustice has any immigrant suffered in THIS COUNTRY? None. And that's my main problem. Affirmative Action tends to help kids who A) don't need help and B) aren't even the people the program was designed to help.

I know many of my more liberal friends disagree with me on this topic, but I am a very literal believer in the 14th Amendment's Equal Protection Clause, which Affirmative Action clearly violates. However, in this case, we justified violating The Constitution based on a particular historical injustice enforced by many other obvious 14th Amendment violations over the years that were designed specifically to target and oppress one group of people, but if your family doesn't descend from American slaves, you are not a member of that group. So, I think it's especially egregious to have a clearly unconstitutional policy in place that does not even remotely adhere to the justification for implementing said policy.

So, Affirmative Action is unconstitutional, largely ineffective at accomplishing it's intended purpose, and it has become a lightning rod to justify the absurd trend of white victimhood mentality, and it tends to diminish or dismiss the accomplishments of talented black people due to the presumption that their selection was non-meritorious (this same presumption also damages black people's careers, as a new hire in the private sector that is viewed as "window dressing" gets shafted come promotion time, especially to the top positions). For these reasons, it is well past time to end Affirmative Action as we know it.

Decriminalize Common Victimless Behavior

Unless there is an actual complaint from a citizen, the police should not concern themselves with:

Loitering

Drinking or Smoking Weed "in public"

Trespassing (unless a break in has occurred or a call has been made)

Spitting

Jaywalking

Riding a Bicycle or Skateboard on the Sidewalk

These so-called "crimes" tend to lead to selective enforcement, with black people bearing the brunt of police officers' ire on these topics. However, even if black people weren't disproportionally affected by the over-policing of minor victimless crimes, we still should not be over-policing minor victimless crimes in the Land of the Free.

For-Profit Prisons and Policing

This system must end, and should have never been implemented in the first place. Obviously, the owners of the private prisons need inmates to make money, which means they lobby politicians for longer sentences, etc. Remember, it was the police officers' unions in California that poured the most money into the failed attempt to beat back the legalization of marijuana. In the Land of the Free? Fuck that!! Every time anyone looks into this, they find that it hurts poor people, especially poor black people.

Municipalities should have a hard cap on the percent of the overall budget that can be derived from issuing tickets and other fines.

We must end the quotas for tickets a police officer must issue or arrests a police officer must make.

Apply the 2nd Amendment Equally

Liberals taking away gun rights from black people leads to more imprisoned black people for possessing "illegal" guns. Gun control should not be a higher priority than human freedom.

P.S. I want to again state that I do not understand how a person can bear arms without possessing them, and there is no reason other than racism that can explain the NRA's hypocritical and disgraceful silence on this topic.

Inmate Repatriation

Prisoner Wages

If prisoners contract out to private businesses, they must be paid minimum wage. And, yes, I'm fine with prisoners partially paying for their own expenses, but the main reasons why prisoners must be paid fair wages are A) the 14th Amendment's Equal Protection clause demands it and B) prisoners who are released need money to re-enter society without relapsing back into a life of crime.

Voting

Felons should be allowed to vote after they've served their time, because as far as I'm concerned, stripping a person of their right to vote is stripping them of their citizenship, which is absolutely cruel (albeit not unusual) punishment for crimes committed. To me, once our legal system has said you've paid your debt to society, your status as an American citizen should be fully restored.

Jobs

We need some sort of tax credit for companies that will hire felons and pay them a living wage, because desperately poor and jobless and hopeless ex-cons are substantially more likely to become recidivists.

P.S. Incarcerated Americans essentially lose most of their rights as citizens, almost like prison is a foreign country. As such, using the word "repatriation" to describe the re-introduction of felons into society makes sense, even though ex-cons are not the group of people to whom "repatriation" traditionally refers.

Jobs Baby Jobs

As we have mentioned in a previous chapter, Aristotle knew that poverty is the mother of crime, and we therefore desperately need businesses and jobs in impoverished black neighborhoods in our major cities. In the 1980's, Congressman Jack Kemp devised a strategy called "Enterprise Zones" to bring jobs to impoverished "inner-city" neighborhoods. England tried something similar, with mixed results, and America tried a bastardized version of Jack Kemp's proposal, but I continue to believe that tax incentives for businesses and individuals to invest in neighborhoods with unusually high employment are the best solution, with the keys being that the tax breaks only apply to new businesses or businesses already located in the "Enterprise Zones" in order to avoid the pitfalls of previous attempts to implement similar programs.

The Media Must Choose Better Examples to Make Our Point

Our entire criminal justice system is horribly and systematically unfair toward black people, but it seems that the examples of this the media chooses to over-focus on are never the right examples to move the needle. To my knowledge, every single black male friend of mine has been treated badly or harassed by the police for no apparent reason other than being a black male. This is a real and ongoing and very serious problem, and it gets almost no mention, at least not on a consistent basis; until we have occasional stories that get huge national attention, but they're never the kinds of cases that can move the needle

Choosing unimpeachable examples helps drive the discussion in a favorable direction, speaking broadly. For example, it frustrated me substantially that Michael Brown's death sucked all the oxygen out of Tamir Rice's death and John Crawford's death and sucked some of the oxygen out of Eric Garner's death. Michael Brown was not an unimpeachable example of the very real problem of the disproportional police violence toward black people, which makes people who are predisposed to deny this very real problem even more likely to dispute that the problem even exists.

On this same topic of media inaccuracy, please consider this editorial from Kareem Abdul Jabbar:

The Los Angeles Times referred to the New York City protests as "anti-police marches," which is grossly inaccurate and illustrates the problem of perception the protestors are battling. The marches are meant to raise awareness of double standards, lack of adequate police candidate screening, and insufficient training that have resulted in unnecessary killings. Police are not under attack, institutionalized racism is. Trying to remove sexually abusive priests is not an attack on Catholicism, nor is removing ineffective teachers an attack on education. Bad apples, bad training, and bad officials who blindly protect them are the enemy. And any institution worth saving should want to eliminate them, too.

In a nutshell, the media must move toward accuracy and away from sensationalism, because manufactured outrage based on an inaccurate premise does more harm than good, and the mischaracterizations of events causes nothing but harm.

Marketing

If we are ever going to fix our race-related problems, our race-related marketing efforts must focus on persuasion outside of our echo chamber not approval inside of our echo chamber. For example, Mic.com recently announced the "Black Monuments Project" with 50 suggestions for future black monuments. As a history nerd, I loved reading about a bunch of pretty damn amazing Americans with whom I was previously unfamiliar, and I support the notion that American monuments should be way more inclusive. That having been said, though, the cover page of the project's website is a likeness of Colin Kaepernick kneeling, which pretty much means that overtly racist white people will angrily close the page without even starting to scroll down. This is, of course, completely counter-productive.

Mic.com is not alone in this tactical marketing error, and moving forward, I hope we never prioritize flouting our moral superiority over making progress toward a more moral and more just nation and world. Pissing off people we disagree with might make us feel enlightened in the short term, but it doesn't do diddly shit in the long term, and reaching our long term goals should matter more than satisfying our short term egos.

Education

I'm so happy that some school systems in America are now stressing college OR career ready, rather than only college ready. We really let down a whole generation of poor children through the brainless naivety of liberal American politicians' insistence that everyone should go to college. High schools must be training grounds for life after high school, with the needs of each individual student at the center of a specific plan to prepare each child for successful entry into adulthood.

Also, as another note on education, it feels like we're always teaching black children what not to do, instead of what to do. For example, when I worked at Skyline High School in Dallas, we brought in a group of convicts to speak to the entire student body in an attempt to "scare the kids straight" or whatever, but we didn't bring in any of Dallas's highly successful black politicians, lawyers, doctors, entrepreneurs, etc. To me, schools (and society at large) should not try to scare black children into "behaving", they should try to inspire black children to reach their full potential as human beings.

EPILOGUE

It's true that we've come a long way, but my goodness do we ever have such a long way left to go.

In 1968 at the Mexico City Olympics, Tommie Smith and John Carlos decided to raise gloved fists on the podium during the playing of the Star Spangled Banner as a way to protest against racism. Collectively, white America was none too pleased with this action. Criticisms ranged from "they're disrespecting the flag" to "they're disrespecting our country" to "they have no right to use this platform for political purposes" and it wasn't too long thereafter that the United States Olympic Committee banned both men for life.

In 2016, Colin Kaepernick (and later others) decided to sit then kneel during the national anthem before NFL games as a way to protest against racism, specifically issues within our criminal justice system. Collectively, white America was none too pleased with this action. Criticisms ranged from "he's disrespecting the flag" to "he's disrespecting our country" to "he has no right to use this platform for political purposes" and it wasn't too long thereafter that he found himself unable to find an NFL team willing to sign him.

Perhaps more than any other event in my adult lifetime, white reactions to the NFL kneelers have highlighted how far we haven't come, and it's frustrating.

In this book, we have quoted Dr. King semi-frequently, but as we reach the book's end, I now want to quote another King:

Can't we all just get along?

Of course we can!!

But first we must forgive.

As white people, we must forgive ourselves. None of us chose to be a racist. It isn't our fault, but it is our problem, and we need to step up to the plate together, own it, and work to make it right.

Also, as white people, as crazy as this sounds, we must forgive black people. As James Baldwin profoundly noted:

The hardest thing for a person to do is to forgive someone they know they've wronged. White people live with the nightmare of the nigger they've invented. They have to have a nigger to justify the crime, so they don't see the person
(https://www.youtube.com/watch?v=3Wht4NSf7E4).

We as white people must embrace the truth in Mr. Baldwin's words. Even though black people aren't actually the monsters we've portrayed them as, this portrayal is so deeply ingrained into us that we must forgive them for being the monsters they aren't, or we will never be able to recognize their full humanity.

Black people must forgive white people and forgive America. I know this is a lot to ask, almost to the point of being unaskable, yet forgiveness is in my opinion the only path toward healing. We as white people caused the wounds that led to the scars, and therefore are and should be seen as culpable for both, yet that doesn't alter the reality that they're not our wounds, or our scars. Plus, even if we as white people could completely heal the wounds, we definitely can't heal the scars. There is no question that black people have open wounds, still, in 2018, that white people keep causing, and white people bear responsibility for the open wounds, and we as white people must have the ethical foundation to recognize this ONGOING national flaw and do our level best to tend to the open wounds that we continue to create. But I don't believe that white people can heal the scars. And black people have lots of scars. Truly, the total tonnage of scar tissue accumulated inside the broken hearts of black people can not be overstated, and even though I know that we as white people caused the wounds that led to the scars, I still feel earnestly that only forgiveness can heal the scars.

I'm not going to say black people must forgive each other necessarily, but I do think that black people need to be way less hard on each other, which may be at least partially related to the concept of "forgiveness".

The other huge key besides forgiveness is recognition, as we just can't possibly fix a problem by diminishing the scope of the problem or by denying that the problem exists. There is no doubt in my mind that admitting my racism to myself is the only reason I've been able to grow as a person and become less racist over time.

That having been said, it's also very important to understand that admitting my personal (and unfortunate) race-related reality shouldn't be confused with accepting it. I know that I am a racist, but I am not proud of it, and I do try to keep improving myself by checking myself, engaging in uncomfortable conversations about race and deliberately listening when I'm at my most uncomfortable, reading extensively about race relations (often from different perspectives), and writing quite a bit on this topic as well (obviously).

Putting these thoughts on paper has helped me in my ongoing efforts to de-racist myself, and I hope it helps others as well, as it is way past time that we finally bridge our racial divide and fully become the nation we were always destined to be.

We say we value freedom, yet we lead the developed world in incarcerating our own citizens, with shocking race-based disparities continually proven and re-proven.

We say we value equality, yet we continue to see massive, race-based, unequal treatment in criminal justice, housing, banking, employment, and truly just about every key pillar any American would need to support their American dream.

America is the greatest country in the entire recorded history of humankind. While confessing my bias, I nevertheless feel that this sentiment is at least as much of a demonstrated fact as it is a non-objective opinion. No other country before us ever risked the lives of its own citizens for humanitarian or moral purposes. No other country has been a greater deliberate force for good. No other country has been a beacon of light and hope that shined as brightly as America. All I'm saying is that we can and should and must strive to shine ever brighter, year by year, as long as our Republic continues to exist.